Anarchism in France:
the case of Octave Mirbeau

This book is dedicated to:

My wife Elizabeth
My mother and father, Ida and Philip Carr
And to the memory of Professor Stephen Ullmann (1914–76), a great scholar and teacher

Anarchism in France:
the case of Octave Mirbeau

Reg Carr

McGill–Queen's University Press
Montreal   1977

© Reginald P. Carr 1977

All rights reserved

Published 1977 by
Manchester University Press
Oxford Road, Manchester M13 9PL

Published in North America 1977 by
McGill–Queen's University Press
1020 Pine Ave. W., Montreal H3A 1A2

ISBN 0 7735 0301 3

Legal deposit 2nd quarter 1977
Bibliothèque nationale du Québec

Printed in Great Britain by
Elliott Brothers & Yeoman Ltd.,
Woodend Avenue, Speke, Liverpool L24 9JL.

Contents

Acknowledgements	*page* vii
Abbreviations	viii
Prologue	ix
Introduction	xiii
I The popular cause (1885)	1
II The novels of revenge (1886–90)	14
III From the 'social question' to the defence of anarchism (1891–3)	38
IV The extreme limits (1892–4)	56
V The journalist of revolt (1894–8)	83
VI The Dreyfus passion (1898–9)	99
VII The theatre of ideas (1897–1908)	111
VIII The social conscience of the *Belle Epoque* (1900–7)	134
IX *Dingo*, or 'There's life in the old dog yet!' (1908–13)	146
X The pity of war (1914–17)	156
Appendix of Mirbeau's principal anarchist texts	166
Select bibliography	178
Index	187

Qu'on nous donne des monographies sérieuses et des études de détails! Voilà le moyen de nous restituer, hors de ses mythes, cette Belle Epoque, qui fascine.

(Hubert Juin, *Ecrivains de l'avant-siècle*)

The writer comes to consciousness amidst particular conditions that include the things that the people of his age tend to do, the most powerful forces then felt to be acting in and on humanity, and the sorts of function his art has at that time. Living amongst all this, how could the writer, except by the most willed and improbable jump, shrug off his age and fail to make its particular scenes and concerns the dominant ones in his art?

(David Craig, *The Real Foundations: Literature and Social Change*)

Acknowledgements

This book was made possible by the help and encouragement of the following teachers, colleagues and friends:
  The late André Billy, of the Académie Goncourt
  Professor G. F. A. Gadoffre, of Manchester University
  M Pierre Michel, of Angers
  Dr P. M. Wetherill, of Manchester University
  The late Professor Stephen Ullmann

For access to their collections, and for permission to quote from or refer to manuscript material in their possession or under their control, I should like to thank the following individuals and institutions:
  M Hervé Bazin, President of the Académie Goncourt
  M Robert Borel-Rosny, of Saint-Germain-des Prés, Paris
  Bibliothèque de l'Arsenal, Paris
  Bibliothèque Nationale, Paris
  Bibliothèque Publique et Universitaire de Genève
  Bureau des Archives et du Musée, Préfecture de Police, Paris
  Institut Français d'Histoire Sociale, Paris
  John Rylands University Library of Manchester

I should also like to express my thanks to the staff of the Manchester University Press, and especially to Mr John Banks, for help and advice during the preparation of this book for publication.

But most of all: to my wife I owe the deepest debt—and not just for her typing of the various drafts of the manuscript. She alone knows the real cost of this book.

Abbreviations

B.A.M.P.P.	Bureau des Archives et du Musée, Préfecture de Police, Paris
B.P.U.G.	Bibliothèque Publique et Universitaire de Genève
F.G.B.A.	Fonds Goncourt, Bibliothèque de l'Arsenal, Paris
I.F.H.S.	Institut Français d'Histoire Sociale, Paris (Fonds Grave)
J.R.U.L.M.	John Rylands University Library of Manchester
La Révolte (S.L.)	*La Révolte, Supplément Littéraire*
T.N.	*Les Temps Nouveaux*
T.N. (S.L.)	*Les Temps Nouveaux, Supplément Littéraire*

Prologue

This book is a study of the links between the anarchist movement in France and the French writer Octave Mirbeau (1848-1917). The study begins in the year 1885 and ends in 1917, the year of Mirbeau's death. This was the period of anarchism's greatest influence in France, and these were the years between which Mirbeau wrote all his literary works.

1885 was the year when Mirbeau began to change his political outlook from extreme Right to extreme Left; it was the year in which he broke away from the reactionary influence of his conservative family background and began to find in the theories of anarchism a more appropriate philosophical basis for his life; and, above all, it was the year in which he began to consolidate his talent and experience in the creation of a remarkable literary *oeuvre*.

1885 was also the year when the anarchist movement—until then almost entirely based in Switzerland—began to make a real impact on the public consciousness of France; it was in 1885 that *Le Révolté*, the anarchists' leading propaganda journal, was transferred to Paris from Geneva by its editor, Jean Grave; it was in the same year that a major and influential anarchist work, Kropotkin's *Paroles d'un révolté*, was published, in Paris; and for the next twenty years or so, the anarchist movement was to exert a not inconsiderable influence on the political, social and intellectual life of France, and particularly during the years 1892-4, a period of unprecedented acts of terrorism which culminated in the assassination of the President of the Republic himself.

The study of the life and works of Mirbeau, an influential literary figure of the *Belle Epoque*, and one who 'sympathised' with many aspects of anarchist philosophy, casts much interesting light on the vogue which anarchism enjoyed amongst many French intellectuals of the period. Equally, the study of anarchism has an important contribution to make towards a more accurate assessment of the personality and writings of a now largely neglected author.

The following table gives a brief, selective chronology of the anarchist movement up to the year 1885 when this study begins:

1864   Inauguration of the First International Working Mens' Association, in London

1865 Death of Proudhon, 'Le Père de l'Anarchie' (author of *Qu'est-ce que la propriété?* (1840), *Les Confessions d'un révolutionnaire* (1849), and *De la justice dans la révolution et dans l'église* (1858))
1866 First Congress of the First International, Geneva ⎱ Predominance of
1867 Second Congress, Lausanne ⎰ anarchist
1868 Third Congress, Brussels ⎱ anti-authoritarian
1869 Fourth Congress, Basel ⎰ influence
1870 Abortive Lyons Rising (led by anarchist revolutionary, Bakunin)
1871 Paris Commune (giving rise to savage repression and deportation of most left-wing militants; exile of anarchists: Elisée Reclus, Louise Michel, etc.)
1872 Formation of the Fédération Jurassienne (Swiss-based anarchist splinter-group from First International)
1876 Death of Bakunin
1877 Arrival in Switzerland of anarchist prince Peter Kropotkin (after escape from Russian prison)
Benevento Rising (abortive Italian anarchist coup led by Cafiero—one of the earliest cases of 'propaganda by the deed')
1879 First number of Kropotkin's Geneva newspaper *Le Révolté*
Political amnesty from French parliament for exiled communards
1882 Anarchist-inspired riots in French mining towns of Roanne and Montceau-les-Mines
1883 *Procès des 66* at Lyons; Kropotkin jailed for four years
Louise Michel jailed for six years for leading open-air demonstration in Paris
Jean Grave made editor of *Le Révolté* in Geneva
1885 *Le Révolté* transferred to Paris
Publication of Kropotkin's *Paroles d'un révolté*

In 1885 Octave Mirbeau was thirty-seven years old. Prior to this time he had been a civil servant and political campaigner of the Right (legitimist and bonapartist), a journalist and critic in the royalist, conservative or reactionary press (*Le Gaulois*, *Le Figaro*, and his own *Grimaces*), and a not unsuccessful employee of the Paris Stock Exchange. He had made a few friends in the literary world (Maupassant and the young writers of the naturalist school, Barbey d'Aurevilly, Paul Bourget) and in the world of art (Monet, Rodin, Félicien

Rops), and had gained for himself something of a reputation as lover, man-about-Paris, and polemicist.

Born into the rural middle class, and educated by the Jesuits, Mirbeau's life and thinking were initially set in conservative, right-wing traditions. When Mirbeau was a young man the political Left in France was still very much a clandestine affair—the Empire still held sway. And though when the Empire fell the Left had its moment of power in the Paris Commune of 1871, there was then nothing to link the young Mirbeau with the radical theories of social reform which were later to attract his sympathy and support. In practical terms, the defeat of the Commune was a setback in the unsteady progress of the century towards the Left; in the 1870s chauvinism and reaction remained the order of the day, and the future of the country still seemed to lie with the parties of the Right. It was only during the 1880s, when the ideologies of the Left began to revive and to assert themselves, that Mirbeau's attention was drawn seriously to the possible solutions they offered to the moral, social and political problems which faced the 'generation of defeat' of which he was a part.

Mirbeau's years on the political Right lie outside the scope of the present study. It is nevertheless possible to see the individualism and the extremism of that period of his life as pointers to his later anarchist sympathies (see the author's M.A. thesis: 'Octave Mirbeau and anarchism' (University of Manchester, 1971), pp. 7–43). The following chronological table of Mirbeau's life is intended as a preface to the more detailed analysis of Mirbeau's anarchism: it ends approximately where the book begins.

1848	(16 February) Birth of Octave Mirbeau at Trévières (Calvados)
1859–63	Educated by the Jesuits in Vannes
1866–8	Unsuccessful studies for law degree in Paris
1870–1	Franco-Prussian War: lieutenant in the *Garde Mobile de l'Orne* (Army of the Loire)—wounded December 1870
1872–7	Art then theatre critic on bonapartist paper *L'Ordre* (owned by the family friend, the *député* Dugué de la Fauconnerie)
	Early literary friendships in Paris (Maupassant, Zola)
	Political articles on the bonapartist paper *L'Ariégeois* (1876–7)
	Chef de cabinet to the Prefect of l'Ariège (May–December 1877)
1879–82	Journalist on the monarchist paper *Le Gaulois* (dismissed

	1881), on the conservative *Le Figaro* (dismissed 1882), and *Paris-Journal*
	Boursier on the Paris Stock Exchange
1883	Editor of *Paris-Midi, Paris- Minuit* (January–April)
	Founder/editor of *Les Grimaces* (July 1883–January 1884)
1884–5	Contributor on *Le Gaulois* again (resigned May 1885)
	Contributor on the more radical *La France*
	Publication of *Lettres de ma chaumière* (January 1886)

Introduction

> Je ne conçois pas qu'un artiste, c'est-à-dire l'homme libre par excellence, puisse chercher un autre idéal social que celui de l'anarchie.
> (Octave Mirbeau, in *L'Ermitage*, 1893)

The life of Octave Mirbeau spanned some of the most colourful and eventful years of French history. The July monarchy was drawing its dying breath as Mirbeau entered the world on 16 February 1848, and when he died in February 1917—sixty-nine years later to the very day—France and the Third Republic were engaged in that 'war to end all wars' which was to be but the beginning of sorrows for the modern world.

It was during Mirbeau's lifetime that monarchism in France finally faded out and republicanism took hold of the reins of government, to be opposed in its turn by the increasingly popular ideologies of the Left. In literature, Romanticism took its final bow with the anachronistic flourish of the state funeral of Victor Hugo in 1885, and the battle for literary supremacy continued in earnest between the myriads of '-isms' which flitted across the literary scene, and among which only naturalism, symbolism and neo-catholicism had any staying power or permanent value. In the arts, great revolutions were taking place as each rising generation fought for recognition and sought to break the stranglehold of the academic conventions which stifled French art. The rhythm of social life became so intense during the middle of this period, that one writer styles it 'a generation of materialism',[1] while the years around the turn of the century are nostalgically spoken of as the *Belle Epoque*.

The period was *belle*, at least on the surface; yet not everybody enjoyed his right to a place in the sun, and the increasing outward prosperity of the upper échelons of society only served to highlight the misery of the working classes, and to provide grist for the mills of those who, in one way or another, opposed the injustices of capitalist republicanism. A gradual awareness of 'the social question', as it came to be familiarly, and often disparagingly, known,[2] reached the intellectuals and ultimately the politicians, and the demand for social reform came to characterise particularly the declining years of the century. Socialism, communism and anarchism fraternised in varying degrees with the intellectual *avant-garde* in an attempt to mitigate the oppression of an all-pervading capitalist republic which was manifestly corrupt, and in which everything belonged to a few.[3]

In all these phenomena—political, literary, artistic and social—Octave Mirbeau participated to the full. He was a child of the age in the most literal sense. After his death, his friend and collaborator Thadée Natanson wrote of him:

> C'était encore le polémiste de toutes les modes et de toutes les luttes d'idées qui vont de la fin du XIXe siècle au début de ce siècle-ci, du naturalisme au symbolisme et de l'Impressionisme à l'anarchie, en passant d'Emile Zola à Stéphane Mallarmé, et de Rodin et de Cézanne à Pierre Bonnard par Ibsen, Nietsche [sic], Wagner, Dostoiewsky et Debussy.[4]

Mirbeau's willingness to embrace any cause in which he had faith gained him a reputation for intellectual honesty such as few of his contemporaries could boast, and since his death there have been countless vindications of the sureness of his critical intuition.[5] Mirbeau made many enemies, of course, because of his frankness, but he was respected and loved by the great men of his time. Barbey d'Aurevilly, Goncourt, Heredia, Zola, Clemenceau and Jaurès, to name but a few, were all proud to call him their friend, and admired his intellectual probity as well as his artistic taste and talent. A catalogue of those writers and artists discovered, helped, encouraged or defended by Mirbeau makes breath-taking reading;[6] from the now legendary 'launching' of Maeterlinck in a *Figaro* article (24 August 1890), through the many campaigns to gain recognition for writers like Charles-Louis Philippe, Marguerite Audoux and Valéry Larbaud, artists like Monet, Pissarro and Gauguin, sculptors like Rodin, Meunier and Maillol, and many other now universally accepted artists, to words of encouragement and praise for such dissimilar writers as Léon Bloy, Paul Claudel and Marcel Schwob, not to mention his courageous defences of Goncourt, Gourmont and Zola—in all this, Mirbeau showed himself the child of his age, free from prejudice, directly in contact with all that was new and vibrant in those eventful years, alive to the impulses of his surroundings, and not ashamed to commit himself to what he believed in with all the strength of his ardent soul.

Coming to maturity as he did in the aftermath of the Franco-Prussian war, he was part of that generation of intellectuals for whom social questions became increasingly important as the century wore on—artists who abandoned the 'ivory tower' of many of their predecessors, to come down into the street; whose artistic creations are often only very faintly disguised transpositions of the social and political problems of the Third Republic under which they lived. René Dumesnil says of this period: 'A aucune époque la littérature n'a suivi de si près l'actualité et ne s'en est inspirée.'[7] This means, of course, that many of the artistic productions of the time, so popular and worthwhile when they appeared in their contemporary context, have failed the test of time, and must depend largely upon the efforts of historians of literature and art to restore their pristine reputations by an evocation of the circumstances which first inspired them.

In Micheline Tison-Braun's *La Crise de l'humanisme*, in Roger Shattuck's *The Banquet Years*, in George Woodcock's *Anarchism*, in Jean Maitron's *Histoire du mouvement anarchiste en France*, and in a host of other works, Octave Mirbeau is mentioned briefly, often in passing, as a 'literary anarchist', an 'anarchist sympathiser', or a 'champion of the anarchist cause'. Such fleeting references to a writer who was as widely known and read during his lifetime as he has been ignored and passed over in silence since his death are made principally within the context of the literary and artistic repercussions of the anarchist movement in late nineteenth-century France; few, if any, details are given of the nature and extent of the 'sympathy' which Mirbeau, or any other contemporary writer thus briefly referred to, may or may not have had for these volatile and extremist revolutionaries whose ideas and whose deeds are so much a part of the fabric of the history of the closing years of the nineteenth century.

Reference is sometimes made, usually at second hand and consequently often inaccurately, to one or two of the articles which Mirbeau wrote about the anarchists during the height of the era of terrorism in France between 1892 and 1894. These popular and recurrent extracts, handed down from one commentator to another, and more often than not quoted out of context, constitute the only evidence which is brought forward that Mirbeau was seriously interested in the anarchist cause. The mass of documents, letters, newspaper articles, police reports, and the numerous facets of Mirbeau's literary works which tie him in closely with the anarchist movement are left untouched and neglected at the expense of factual and historical accuracy.

In fairness to such commentators it must be said that it was never their intention, within the scope of their wider and more general studies, to analyse in depth the relationship between Octave Mirbeau and the anarchists—that was obviously the province of the biographer or critic who might dedicate his time and effort to the study of Mirbeau himself. Yet in spite of four critical biographies of Mirbeau, vastly different in scope and content,[8] Mirbeau's relationship with nineteenth-century anarchism—one of the few things for which he is at all remembered—remains as hazy and as undocumented as ever it was.

It is the aim of this book to bring to light many of the documents and facts which enable us to assess Mirbeau's anarchist sympathy in its historical perspective, and to propose this evaluation of his anarchist tendencies as an essential element in the understanding and interpretation of Mirbeau's literary works.

Mirbeau's association with the French anarchist movement was more than a mere symptom of his own systematic rejection of traditional ideas and of his consistent criticism of fossilised social and political institutions; it was a logical step in the direction of his own life, an integral part of his intellectual evolution, and an enduring and indelible influence on his writings. Coming to anarchism in maturity, unlike so many younger writers who flirted with anarchism out of bravado, escapism or merely out of youthful dilettantism, Mirbeau recognised in its theories many of the guide-lines of his own struggle for self-discovery, and joined forces almost naturally with the genuine exponents of anarchism, whose ideas gave a measure of stability to his own fitful idealism.

In his novels, his plays, his short stories and his newspaper articles on politics, art and social life in general, Mirbeau expressed a brand of anarchism which was so much in tune with the anarchism of men like Jean Grave and Sébastien Faure, that these leading libertarian propagandists were able to approach Mirbeau with confidence, and were glad to exploit and to acknowledge Mirbeau's willingness to put his celebrity at their disposal. The polemical aspect of Mirbeau's works can almost invariably be linked with some part of anarchist theory; yet these were Mirbeau's own views, and not the views of a sectarian fanatic who had no original thoughts of his own. The parallelism between Mirbeau's ideas and those of the anarchists is all the more remarkable because Mirbeau's precious individualism remained intact. Many of the documents brought forward in this book show how skilfully Mirbeau could defend anarchist positions whilst putting forward his own modifications, or even occasionally criticisms of them.

Anarchism was for Mirbeau a means and not an end. He was not an anarchist in the strictest political sense, but he was glad to use anarchism as the most convenient philosophy whose terms he could borrow in the common idealistic struggle towards a better world. If Mirbeau, like the anarchists, devoted too much attention to the more unpleasant, sordid side of life, it was because he believed, like Thomas Hardy, that a 'way to the better . . . exacts a full look at the worst'. It is in a sense unfortunate that both Mirbeau and the anarchists he supported are remembered for their violence and their apparent nihilism and not for the sincerity and the idealism which caused them to criticise the *status quo* as they did. An appreciation of Mirbeau's anarchism, rooted in his rather simplistic desire for a more harmonious and a freer society, adds an important critical dimension to the significance of his life in the context of the age in which he lived, and can perhaps help to redress the balance of the unfavourable and largely misguided criticism of his works which has prevailed since his death.

Notes

1 C. J. H. Hayes, *A Generation of Materialism, 1871–1900* (New York: Harper Torchbooks, 1963).
2 *Cf.* Gambetta's famous remark: 'Il n'y a pas de question sociale!'
3 'Tout appartient à quelques-uns!' is a much-quoted line from a widely-read anarchist publication: Sébastien Faure, *La Douleur universelle* (Paris: Savine, 1895), p. 180.
4 Thadée Natanson, 'Sur des traits d'Octave Mirbeau', *Les Cahiers d'Aujourd'hui*, No. 9 (1922), pp. 115–16.
5 Remy de Gourmont has nothing but praise for Mirbeau as a critic: *Promenades littéraires*, 1ère série (Paris: Mercure de France, 1919), pp. 69–78.
6 The five volumes of *Des Artistes*, *Gens de théâtre* and *Les Ecrivains*, all published after Mirbeau's death by Flammarion (1922–6), contain many of Mirbeau's best critical articles; but even they do not give a complete picture of Mirbeau's acumen in almost every branch of the arts.
7 René Dumesnil, *L'Epoque réaliste et naturaliste* (Paris: Tallandier, 1946), p. 374.
8 Edmond Pilon, *Octave Mirbeau* (Paris: Bibliothèque Internationale d'Edition, 1903); Maxime Revon, *Octave Mirbeau—son oeuvre* (Paris: Editions de la Nouvelle Revue Critique, 1924); John A. Walker, 'L'Ironie de la douleur—la vie et la vision d'Octave Mirbeau' (unpublished Ph.D. thesis, University of Toronto, 1954); Martin Schwarz, *Octave Mirbeau, vie et oeuvre* (The Hague: Mouton, 1966).

Chapter I
The popular cause (1885)

Quinze ans après l'avènement de la République, et les incendies de la Commune une fois éteints, il semblait convenable et même utile de s'intéresser au sort des ouvriers, les nouveaux parias.

(Léon Daudet)

Prenez garde, regardez sous terre, voyez ces misérables qui travaillent et qui souffrent. Il est peut-être temps encore d'éviter les catastrophes finales.

(Emile Zola in 1885)

By any standards, the year 1885 was a remarkable year. Politically, socially and artistically, France was shaken out of its torpor as it experienced a series of new stimuli which were to set the tone for its entry into the twentieth century.[1] No single year seems to have been more full of endings and of new beginnings in almost every field of activity. In politics, the year 1885 saw the final end of the period of post-1870 reaction which had held down the growth of socialism since the repression of the Paris Commune. The trades unions had been legalised in 1884, and in 1885 Jules Guesde's newly-formed 'Labour party' polled no fewer than 30,000 votes in the parliamentary elections, while the parliamentary socialists, in the person of Georges Clemenceau, scored a remarkable victory over the imperialistic policy of the republican government of Jules Ferry. Meanwhile, on the extreme Left, the anarchists chose 1885 as the moment for their permanent installation in Paris,[2] and in October of the same year they published their first really widely-read socio-political volume, the *Paroles d'un révolté* of the prison-bound Prince Peter Kropotkin. The republican government, threatened from both Left and Right, was trying to effect a compromise, but leaned increasingly towards the Left, inexorably affected by the wind of change which was blowing in that direction. Anti-clerical measures had accompanied a more humanitarian attitude towards the problems of education, health and public assistance, and the year 1885 was to give increased impetus to this movement of social awareness and reform. Even Pope Leo XIII, in his encyclical of 1885 (*Immortale Dei*), showed he was prepared to come to terms with the democratic French republic, while the new troubles in the mining communities of Anzin (1884) and Decazeville (1885-6) highlighted the economic difficulties of the country and showed the need for an improvement of the worker's lot at both local and national levels.

In literature too, the year 1885 brought a new and exciting burst of activity, with first the symbolists, and then the naturalists reacting in their differing ways to the challenge of the new era that was dawning. Mallarmé's Mardis had begun in 1884, while Goncourt's Grenier opened in February of the following year; and these two literary salons represent very clearly the two main intellectual responses to the social problems of France in 1885, with the symbolists instinctively retreating into esoteric aestheticism, and the naturalists releasing a flood of sociological realism. *Le Petit Bottin des lettres et des arts* (1884), *A Rebours* (1884), *Jadis et Naguère* (1885), 'Prose pour des Esseintes' (1885) and *Les Cantilènes* (1886) alternated at regular intervals with *Sapho* (1884), *Bel-Ami* (1885), *Nell Horn* (1885), *Germinal* (1885) and *L'Insurgé* (1886).

Though naturalism itself later fell into bankruptcy and was unable to survive outside the novels of Zola, its effect upon the direction of late nineteenth-century literature was considerable, and particularly in the question of sociological subject-matter.[3] One unlikely ally for the naturalists in this respect was the stream of Russian novels which began to reach France around 1885. Vogüé, with *Le Roman russe* (June 1886)—a collection of articles which first appeared in *La Revue des Deux Mondes*—started a craze which he hoped would be detrimental to naturalism; and yet the naturalists themselves either welcomed the Russian writers as reinforcements for their own realist aesthetic or looked on them, with enthusiasm or indifference according to taste, as participators in the same movement of sociological and psychological realism.[4]

Though the *fin-de-siècle* did not belong to the naturalists or the realists as a concerted movement, the aesthetic and personal interest which they took in the everyday life and problems of the social organism lived on as one of the dominant influences on the literature of the waning century. It is ironic therefore that just at the time when sociological problems were increasingly occupying the minds of literary and political intellectuals, two of the very men who had brought politics and sociology into literature should pass off the scene, when first Jules Vallès then Victor Hugo died within a few months of each other in 1885. Both men had become living symbols of the triumph of libertarian ideals;[5] Hugo perhaps in the anachronistic style of one of his own Romantic heroes, with Vallès much more the real-life revolutionary like his own Jacques Vingtras. Both men were given funerals they would surely have been proud to see; for Hugo there was the homage of an entire nation, while for Vallès there was the respect of an entire class. Both men had done much to humanise French literature by bringing everyday realities up to the level of art—Hugo on a grander, more epic scale, Vallès at a more work-a-day level. Hugo's was the better, more enduring part; but Vallès could at least claim to have done much in sensing and directing the movement of the century. In the closing years of his life, after his return from exile in 1880, Vallès conducted a series of humanitarian campaigns which would do credit to any modern social reformer, and in the domain of literature he was directly responsible for the reorientation of naturalism towards sociological and political commitment.[6]

From a rather objective, though sympathetic portrayal of misery in early novels such as Goncourt's *La Fille Elisa* (1877), Zola's *L'Assommoir* (1877), and Huysmans' *Les Soeurs Vatard* (1879), naturalism moved steadily towards sociological commitment, in novels like Rosny's *Nell Horn* (1885) and Zola's *Germinal* (1885), and finally became totally committed to the movement for social reform in Zola's *Trois Villes* (1894–8) and his *Quatre Evangiles* (1899–1903). This progression clearly mirrors one important aspect of the progression of the age, and it was a movement in which Octave Mirbeau participated in his own individualistic way.

Mirbeau's early association with the naturalist school in its infancy had not been long or deep enough to draw him away from his rightwing environment during the 1870s; yet its influence on him was nonetheless quite marked.[7] The naturalists had at least taught him 'how the other half lived'; and if they had made him look on the black side, they had by no means destroyed his ingenuous idealism. Mirbeau had hoped initially that he could realise his ideals within the context of the social and political position into which he had been born; but as the years passed, his idealism was increasingly exasperated and he found disillusionment at every turn. The year 1885 found him in the kind of uncertainty to which he had often fallen prey; but before the year was out, he had found another cause to believe in, and it was a cause which proved to be closer to his own inclinations, and one to which he was to cling as fervently as he was to reject his unwanted birthright.

Mirbeau's first step towards a new allegiance was taken when he began to write for the radical *La France* in October 1884, while continuing to collaborate on the monarchist *Le Gaulois*. Mirbeau clearly preferred writing for *La France*, for he was able to write more freely and more openly there about subjects which aroused his anger or his enthusiasm.[8] Increasingly, he tried to imbue his chronicles on *Le*

Gaulois with the same rather anti-establishment flavour of his articles in *La France*. One example of this was the article 'Auteurs et critiques' (*Le Gaulois*, 9 February 1885), in which Mirbeau not only defended Becque's much-maligned play *La Parisienne* but also praised Becque himself, and sharply criticised established and reputable theatre critics like Sarcey and Bigot for their rejection of Becque's naturalistic aesthetic. The editor of *Le Gaulois*, Arthur Meyer, was now finding Mirbeau difficult to contain; and after suppressing several articles, Meyer resorted to altering what Mirbeau had written, in an attempt to attenuate the virulence of Mirbeau's pen. For Mirbeau this was too much, and in spite of the financial loss involved he terminated his regular contributions to *Le Gaulois* and concentrated his journalistic verve in the freer forum which he enjoyed in the columns of *La France*.

As if to start off this new phase on the right footing and to make his intentions clear from the outset, Mirbeau republished in *La France* the same outspoken article he had given to *Le Gaulois* on his return from Brittany the previous year ('Le Journalisme'); and when Victor Hugo died shortly afterwards, Mirbeau gave further proof of his new allegiance by writing an article which was full of admiration and respect for Hugo's genius, and for his sympathy with the underprivileged.[9] Mirbeau was now clearly standing at the crossroads of his intellectual evolution, and as he turned left, he began to look about for new causes to support. He started cautiously at first—no doubt he suffered from his reputation—occasionally displaying some vestige of the influence of his origins;[10] but by the end of the year, he was firmly committed to the Left.

One article from *La France* is sufficient to illustrate the colour of Mirbeau's sympathies in the summer of 1885; and significantly enough, it was an article which found its way into the press cuttings of the police archives. 'Vermine judiciaire' (*La France*, 17 June 1885) was an all-out attack on the penal code, on law-court reporters and on the jury system. It had been sparked off by the death sentence passed on a clockmaker called Pel, convicted of murder on purely circumstantial evidence. The affair is noteworthy because of Mirbeau's wholehearted support for what was always a favourite left-wing hobby-horse: the need for reform of the penal code. As Mirbeau said in his article, the argument concerned principles rather than Pel himself; the unsatisfactory conclusion of the court-case, and the undesirable part played by the press in preconditioning the minds of the jury, had opened Mirbeau's eyes to the terrible anomalies in the legal system, and caused him to write: 'Cela est triste à dire; mais, aujourd'hui, il en est de la justice comme des magasins de nouveauté.' The Pel affair fired Mirbeau with a desire to see a radical reform of the penal code, and this desire became a cornerstone of his humanitarian philosophy. It was to be an important factor in his ultimate sympathy for the anarchists, who criticised the French legal system for similar reasons and in much the same way as Mirbeau did, not only in this one article, but also throughout his subsequent writings.[11]

The great turning-point in Mirbeau's life was also marked by his adoption of a literary genre in which he was to excel: the short story with a moral or sociological twist. The *Lettres de ma chaumière* were Mirbeau's first tentative productions of this form of pithy tale. Hitherto, his literary production had been divided clearly into two categories: first, there had been the conventional short stories in the style of Maupassant or, particularly, of Barbey d'Aurevilly and Poe, and secondly, the vigorous polemical articles, which undoubtedly deserved more than the fate generally reserved for such ephemera, but which were untenable as literature. But now, in 1885, perhaps because Mirbeau felt that he had something new to say and wanted to reach as wide an audience as possible, he began to combine his polemical verve with his talents as a story-teller, by producing short stories which had more of a social and moral significance than anything he had written before. From the *Lettres de ma chaumière* onwards there was to be a noticeable increase in the sociological content of all Mirbeau's writings as he strove to find, and to preserve, the successful balance between the polemical and the aesthetic aspects of his pen.

It is difficult to tell whether, in July 1885, Mirbeau was already thinking ahead to the possible publication in book form of the best of his new short stories, but it is clear from the collective title *(Lettres de ma chaumière)* which he gave them from the outset as they were published at regular intervals in *La France,* that they were conceived in the same spirit and with the same end in view; to express Mirbeau's comments on as many aspects as possible of the life of late nineteenth-century rural communities in an amusing and worthwhile art-form. In the summer and autumn of 1885 Mirbeau was living in a small cottage only a few miles from his home town of Rémalard, and it is clear from the first 'letter' he sent to *La France* that Mirbeau valued the opportunity to put the busy life of the parisian journalist behind him for a while and to savour the peace of his rural retreat:

> Ah! comme je vais être bien là, en ce petit coin perdu, tout embaumé des odeurs de la terre reverdissante! Plus de luttes avec les hommes, plus de haine, la haine qui broie les coeurs; rien que l'amour, ce grand amour qui tombe des nuits pacifiées et que berce, comme une maternelle chanson, la chanson du vent dans les arbres.[12]

From his quiet vantage-point, Mirbeau surveyed the life which was going on around him, and set down his impressions in his own semi-autobiographical, semi-imaginative style, making his characters, particularly his peasants, larger than life, preferring humour to satire, and always spicing the whole with a touch of sociological comment, either by open statement or, more often, by subtle and delightful inference. Such, for example, is the story 'La Justice de paix' (*La France*, 24 July 1885), which was dedicated in the published version to Maupassant. This pithy, humorous tale of the earthy immorality of the Norman peasantry, and of the ridiculous role of the law as arbitrator in deciding the 'price' of another man's wife, has all the elements of Maupassant at his best, as well as the polemical overtones of Mirbeau the sympathetic critic of society.

When the *Lettres de ma chaumière* finally appeared in book form in January 1886, the stories numbered twenty-one. Into those few short tales, Mirbeau compressed not only a panoramic view of the Norman peasantry but also a microcosmic view of the human condition in general. Less objective and more socially conscious than Maupassant, Mirbeau set himself up both as sympathiser and as critic of human nature. He believed that social evils stem from the individual; but his own intense humanity would not allow his criticisms to be entirely ruthless, and his *Lettres de ma chaumière* are a poignant mixture of pity and irony, in which his tragico-comic peasants typify the tragedy and comedy of the social organism as a whole. Indeed the observation and criticism of social evils came to constitute the very *raison d'être* of almost all of Mirbeau's published work, and this tendency is discernible already in his *Lettres de ma chaumière*. In a tale called 'La Mort du chien', which foreshadowed his last completed novel *Dingo* (1913), Mirbeau spotlighted the brutality of man and contrasted it with the dignity of an unfortunate and persecuted animal. Human cruelty, an ever-recurring theme in Mirbeau's writings, was also exposed in 'La Bonne', the tale of the rape of a young peasant girl who goes into service in the city. The inbred miserliness and the insensitivity of the poverty-stricken peasantry were illustrated in 'Le Père Nicolas' and in 'La Mort du Père Dugué'. Yet in spite of such attacks on human nature as the source of social ills, Mirbeau's generous humanity, and his sympathy for the adverse circumstances of his Norman peasants, pervaded, in varying intensity, the whole series of the *Lettres de ma chaumière*, the tales 'Le Petit Mendiant' and 'L'Enfant' being particularly outstanding in this respect.

For those who exploited the peasants and who devastated the countryside for their own ends Mirbeau had nothing but condemnation, as in the tales 'La Chasse', 'Agronomie' and 'Paysages d'automne'.

'Agronomie', with its unforgettable monster Théodule-Henri-Joseph Lechat, shows how already Mirbeau had created the central character of what was to be his greatest social satire, the notorious Isidore Lechat of *Les Affaires sont les affaires* (1903). 'Paysages d'automne', dedicated to Goncourt, contained one scene in which a hungry workman was close to murdering someone simply to obtain food, and another in which the electoral promises of a local candidate were shown to be all things to all men and faithful to none. And if, in addition to all this social awareness, Mirbeau betrayed his reactionary origins in his violent opposition to republicanism, as in the tale 'Le Tripot aux champs',[13] he immediately reaffirmed himself as a man of the Left in his new pacifist attitude to war, illustrated in 'La Guerre et l'Homme', a story which the anarchists found suitable for their own propaganda purposes several years later,[14] and which in itself was highly indicative of Mirbeau's new outlook.

It was thus the French countryside which provided Mirbeau with his first social canvas; and throughout his career as a writer he was to fall back constantly upon his personal knowledge of the idiosyncrasies of the agrarian classes, to illustrate basic human foibles, or to evoke sympathy for the conditions under which humanity suffered and struggled to preserve its independence and its dignity. One of Mirbeau's articles, published by the anarchists in 1893, contains the following passage:

> A la campagne, dans les petits villages silencieux, où l'homme est moins dense et moins caché que dans les grandes villes impersonnelles et hurlantes, on voit mieux tout ce qui pèse sur lui, tout ce qui l'écrase; on se rend compte davantage de la servitude effroyable à laquelle il est condamné, éternel forçat . . .[15]

—and this was undoubtedly one of the main reasons why, in 1885, Mirbeau wrote his *Lettres de ma chaumière* and chose to set them in a social context which he knew so well.

Mirbeau was preparing his short stories for publication in October 1885 when a great controversy broke out in Paris over the republican government's censorship of the stage version of Zola's novel *Germinal*, which had appeared earlier in the year. The play had been written by Zola in collaboration with Busnach, and on 27 October it was formally banned by the cabinet for 'la tendance socialiste de l'oeuvre, et particulièrement le septième tableau, la grève des mineurs, où les gendarmes sont amenés à tirer sur les ouvriers en révolte'.[16] Zola, who had witnessed some of the terrible events of the Anzin miners' strike in 1884, claimed that *Germinal* was 'une oeuvre de pitié, et non de révolution';[17] but the play was judged revolutionary just the same. The authorities no doubt disapproved of the role assigned in the drama to the representatives of law and order; but they were, surely, more concerned about the airing which Zola had given in his play to views of a very extreme and subversive nature. The character of Souvarine the Russian anarchist, for example, figured prominently in the stage version of *Germinal*, just as it had done in the book. The government was very well aware that the appearance of *Germinal* and the creation of the character of Souvarine coincided with the installation of the anarchist movement in Paris, and though there was no suspicion of complicity between Zola and the anarchists, the government thought it wise not to encourage the spread of subversive ideas.[18]

Mirbeau, from his distant cottage, joined in the journalistic polemics which ensued as a result of the banning of the stage version of *Germinal*; and in doing so, he clearly stated once and for all where his allegiance now lay. In an important article, Mirbeau attacked the French government, criticised governments in general, insisted that the social question should be discussed on stage, vigorously defended Zola and *Germinal*, regretted that the working classes were not more aware of the depths of their own misery, tiraded against the politics of repression, and finally expressed his relief that there were men like Kropotkin, Reclus and Tolstoy 'qui ont poussé le cri de pitié et opposé à la politique usurpatrice des méchants la doctrine méconnue de Jésus'. And Mirbeau concluded on a note of defiant optimism:

> On aura beau vouloir étouffer ce cri, on ne parviendra pas à l'empêcher de retentir sur les siècles à venir, car il faut des siècles et des siècles pour féconder une idée.[19]

It was evident from this article that a great change had come over Mirbeau. Gone was every trace of the fierce young reactionary, of the *chef de cabinet* of the time of the Ordre Moral, of the zealous monarchist of the Meyer circle, and of the exasperated bonapartist of *Les Grimaces*. Here was a new Mirbeau, condemning the principle of all government authority, demanding the right of public discussion of sociological problems, and openly expressing his sympathy for the working classes and his admiration for the leading philosophers of the extreme Left.

Mirbeau's confession of his new-found faith was too sincere, too eloquent, to pass unnoticed. After appearing in *La France*, it was reproduced the following day in the left-wing paper *Le Cri du Peuple*, which had been founded by Vallès and had been handed on at his death to his protégée, Mme Séverine. Under the heading 'La Parole à l'ennemi', Mme Séverine introduced Mirbeau and his article in these cautious but approving terms:

> ... cet adversaire est un homme de talent, et il a écrit hier, dans *La France*, un admirable article, dont les conclusions concordent trop avec nos doctrines, pour que nous hésitions une minute à le mettre sous les yeux de notre public.
> *Le Cri du Peuple* ... ne cherche qu'une chose et ne poursuit qu'un but: le vrai, le bien.
> C'est du camp voisin, qu'a jailli cette fois la note la plus humaine, le cri le plus émouvant—nous l'enregistrons.
> La parole est à l'ennemi.[20]

It was not to be long before Mirbeau had given proof enough of his sincerity as a new recruit to the Left for him to be applauded, no longer as an enemy but as a friend and ally.

The publication in March 1885 of the novel *Germinal* had given added impetus to Mirbeau's growing awareness of the social inequalities of his day, opening up to him as it did the nightmare world of the nineteenth-century mine-worker. He described his feelings after reading *Germinal* in these terms:

> Il nous en reste un sentiment de terreur profonde, et aussi une pitié douloureuse, pour ces déshérités des joies terrestres, pour ces condamnés aux ténèbres, qui peinent, halètent, succombent dans ces nuits sépulchrales, et qui jamais ne voient le soleil se coucher aux horizons lointains, ne respirent jamais l'air qui se vivifie aux sources de la vie et de la fécondation universelles.[21]

By October of the same year, when the stage version of *Germinal* was banned, Mirbeau had graduated from sympathiser to convinced supporter of the popular cause. The banning of the play now seemed more to him than a mere artistic injustice; he saw it clearly as a political move against the interests of the working class:

> Politique éternellement inhumaine qui ne pense qu'à protéger les puissants, gaver les riches, sourire aux heureux, et qui ne songeait pas à glisser un regard ému dans les taudis des misérables, ou à porter une parole consolante au fond de ces géhennes, où des êtres comme nous, naissent, vivent et meurent, sans avoir vu, jamais, tristes fleurs d'humanité, le soleil d'amour qui réchauffe.[22]

The circumstances which had brought Mirbeau to an endorsement of the principles of the extreme Left are manifold and complex. From the natural bent of his independent spirit, through his experiences of Jesuit college life and of wartime horror and injustice, from his disappointment with the answers which his family ties forced upon him, to his taste of freedom in the world of literature and the arts, Mirbeau had been moving always in that direction. Yet the scales were finally tipped, as the conclusion to the article on *Germinal* implies, by Mirbeau's contact with the writings of Kropotkin, Reclus and Tolstoy. Anarchists all three, though of varying types—Tolstoy had his own very personal brand of Christian anarchism—they represent the key to the change which took place in Mirbeau during the latter half of 1885. They were the compound catalyst which caused Mirbeau's own ideas to crystallise, and they constituted a trilogy of enduring influences.

Tolstoy's *My Religion*, first published in 1884, appeared in translation in France under the title *Ma Religion* the following year, and Mirbeau acquired his own copy of the first edition.[23] Tolstoy, with his newly found religious faith, showed himself to be intensely concerned with poverty and social evils in general; yet his work was regarded by the authorities, both Russian and French, as potentially dangerous, because of the way it undermined the governmental and religious institutions of the time. Mirbeau found himself in agreement on so many points with Tolstoy that he began to see more clearly than ever before the need for the kind of radical and wholesale changes which Tolstoy implied were necessary, and which Mirbeau himself had looked for on the opposite side of the political fence. Mirbeau's deep aesthetic admiration for Tolstoy's novels and stories no doubt also facilitated his sympathy for Tolstoy's Christian anarchism, though Mirbeau himself remained a confirmed atheist.[24]

1885 also saw the publication of Kropotkin's important *Paroles d'un révolté*. Kropotkin, from his prison cell at Clairvaux, had entrusted the publication of this collection of articles to his friend and colleague Elisée Reclus, and the book appeared with an eloquent and appealing preface by the great anarchist-geographer. We know from a later letter that Mirbeau was familiar with this work;[25] and since he mentions Kropotkin and Reclus together in the article on *Germinal*, we can assume that Mirbeau had read the *Paroles d'un révolté* by October of that year. This book, which remains the textbook of nineteenth-century anarchism, could not fail to captivate Mirbeau by its sanity, its generosity and its sincerity. The very preface expressed in Reclus' own words the selfsame ideas on the decadence of society which Mirbeau had been wasting for so long on a smug and indifferent public.[26] The need for sweeping changes, the abuses of universal suffrage, the inconsistencies of the legal system, the mediocrity of established art, the dangers of religious education, the stupidity of war, the exploitation of the urban and rural working classes—all these were topics which Kropotkin dealt with at length and on which Mirbeau found himself in complete agreement. Now at last he could begin to identify himself with an ideology in which he could have lasting faith. It is not too much to say that Mirbeau's contact with the *Paroles d'un révolté* in

1885 was the last nail in the coffin of his former reactionary self.

Again, Mirbeau's very personal response to the problems of the age and to the ideas which were in the air at the time was typical of at least a section of the generation which had experienced the 1870 defeat. The ground had been prepared for Tolstoy and the anarchist theoreticians by the manifest failure of the Republic to establish the kind of equitable society which was consistent with its principles. Close cultural ties with the autocratic Russian Empire led to the influx of refugees and the infiltration of revolutionary ideas. The pessimistic nihilism of the 60s and 70s, of which Russians like Turgenev had been the carriers to France, was replaced by the more sinister forms of open revolt; and in Russia, assassination became an occupational hazard for the nobility. Bakunin and Kropotkin, exiled from Russia, centred their attention largely upon the comparatively liberal French capital, and regarded it as the ideological centre of the western world. Count Melchior de Vogüé thought to do harm to the 'unhealthy' literature of the naturalists with his introduction into France of the more spiritually-minded and less sordid Russian novel; yet instead he inadvertently increased the volume of subversive ideas in circulation, for the Russian writers only added their contribution to the anti-establishment literature of their realist counterparts in France.[27]

The financial crash of the Union Générale in 1883, the recurring economic crises, the strikes and the riots indicated that all was not well in France, and the intellectuals at least began to search more deeply for possible remedies—of which the extreme Left's 'solution' was but one out of many. The effect of Russian literature and anarchist doctrines, in conjunction with the influence of Vallès upon the naturalist and neo-realist writers was quite marked. From *Germinal* onwards, Russians, anarchists and socialists of every shade became stock characters in fiction;[28] and this fact, coupled with a steadily increasing tide of sociological treatises and textbooks in circulation in France, served to draw the attention of more and more Frenchmen to the controversies surrounding the popular cause.

As for Mirbeau, he had languished for long enough in the arid deserts of the Right; and though many of his ideas were still embryonic, he had seen enough light to know where his future path now lay. The mark of his sincerity in his new outlook on society—his ideas were basically the same, only the viewpoint had altered drastically—is the cleanness of the break he made with his past and the enthusiasm with which he began to set his ideas down in literary form. The fruit of his new beginning was a *crise de fécondité* of novels. In these, Mirbeau unburdened himself of the frustration and disappointment he had carried with him for so long.

Notes

1 Roger Shattuck comments on the significance of 1885 as a turning point in the following terms: 'The twentieth century could not wait fifteen years for a round number; it was born, yelling, in 1885.' *The Banquet Years* (London: Faber, 1958), p. 4.
2 The first Paris number of *Le Révolté* is dated 12 April 1885.
3 On the social awareness of naturalists and symbolists, see especially Jean Ajalbert, 'Le Flirt rouge', *Le Gil Blas*, 6 June 1893, and E. W. Herbert, *The Artist and Social Reform. France and Belgium, 1885–1898* (New Haven: Yale University Press, 1961), pp. 146–7.
4 See F. W. J. Hemmings, *The Russian Novel in France, 1884–1914* (Oxford: Oxford University Press, 1950).
5 *La Plume* devoted two special numbers to Hugo, in July 1893 and March 1902, and these laid emphasis on the sociological content of his life and work.
6 See Gaston Gille, *Jules Vallès*, vol. 1 (Paris: Flammarion, 1941), pp. 353–60 and 394–422.
7 Details of Mirbeau's contacts with the naturalist school (1875–7) are to be found in the author's M.A. thesis, pp. 32–6.
8 It was at this point that Mirbeau caught the attention of left-wing journalists like Gustave Geffroy, as shown by the press cuttings in the Fonds Goncourt of the Bibliothèque de l'Arsenal (F.G.B.A.).
9 'Le Journalisme' appeared in *La France* on 14 May, a few days before the final break with *Le Gaulois*; but the article's timely reappearance was clearly symbolic of Mirbeau's condemnation of Meyer and the reactionary press. 'Victor Hugo' appeared in *La France* on 24 May.
10 As for example in the anti-semitism of 'La Chasse', and the reactionary anti-republicanism of 'Le Tripot aux champs', both short stories published in *Lettres de ma chaumière*.
11 'Le Petit Gardeur de vaches' (*Le Journal*, 30 September 1895), 'La Vache tachetée' (*Le Journal*, 20 November 1898), and the one-act play *Le Portefeuille* (1902), were perhaps Mirbeau's most significant contributions to the attack on the French legal system made by left-wing intellectuals during this period. Mirbeau's attitude was almost identical to that of the anarchist Jean Grave, as expressed in *La Société mourante et l'anarchie* (Paris: Tresse et Stock, 1893), pp. 96–9.
12 'Ma chaumière', quoted from *Contes de la chaumière* (Paris: Flammarion, 1923 edition), pp. 8–9. First published in *La France*, July 1885, this story formed the opening to the published volume of the *Lettres de ma chaumière*.
13 *Significantly, Mirbeau excluded this tale from the 1894 edition of his short stories.*
14 *The anarchists reproduced this short vignette in La Révolte (S.L.), No. 15 (24 December 1892).*
15 'Le Rôle de l'Etat', *La Révolte* (S.L.), No. 28 (25 March 1893).
16 'Spectacles et concerts', *Le Temps*, 28 October 1885; quoted from Lawson A. Carter, *Zola and the Theater* (Paris: P.U.F., 1963), p. 137.
17 *Ibid.*, p. 140.
18 *Cf.* Francis Magnard: 'Les coups de fusil de *Germinal* eussent été comme un commentaire vivant des discours enflammés, des déclamations des clubs, des provocations haineuses de la presse anarchiste. Il fallait les supprimer . . .' (*Le Figaro*, 27 October 1885); quoted from Carter, *op. cit.*, p. 139.
19 *Germinal*, *La France*, 28 October 1885.
20 'La Parole à l'ennemi', *Le Cri du Peuple*, 29 October 1885.
21 'Emile Zola et le naturalisme', *La France*, 11 March 1885.
22 *Germinal*, *op. cit.*

23 Cf. *Catalogue de la vente de la bibliothèque d'Octave Mirbeau* (Paris: Leclerc, 1919).
24 On Mirbeau's admiration for Tolstoy as a novelist, see his article 'Un Fou', *Le Gaulois*, 2 July 1886.
25 Letter to Jean Grave, undated but *c*. 1893 (Grave Archives, Institut Français d'Histoire Sociale—I.F.H.S.).
26 In his preface Reclus speaks of 'les phénomènes de décrépitude que présentent les Etats et . . . les lézardes qui s'ouvrent, les ruines qui s'accumulent'. P. Kropotkin, *Paroles d'un révolté* (Paris: Marpon et Flammarion, 1885), p. vi. Compare this with Mirbeau's article 'La Fin', *Les Grimaces*, 6 October 1883.
27 Vogüé hoped the Russian novel would encourage a patriotic and religious revival, but other conservative writers were quick to spot the dangers the Russian writers presented; *cf.* A. Leroy-Beaulieu, 'La Religion en Russie', *La Revue des Deux Mondes*, 15 September 1888, pp. 414–43.
28 *Cf.* for example Zola's *Germinal* and *Paris*, Rosny's *Le Bilatéral*, Mauclair's *Le Soleil des morts* and Mirbeau's own *Sébastien Roch*.

Chapter II
The novels of revenge (1886–90)

> ... des livres simples et puissants comme des cris.
>
> (Achille Segard)

Political campaigner, administrator, financial speculator, journalist, editor, critic and short-story writer—Mirbeau had tried his hand at all of these, and still he had not found his niche; no area of activity had satisfied him for long, and nothing that he had so far written was of any lasting literary worth. His old friend Maupassant had often expressed his regret, as he did in a letter written early in 1886, that Mirbeau had not yet put his 'talent très ardent et très réel' to more worthwhile use.[1] Mirbeau's mistress, whom he was soon to marry, had literary pretensions of her own and was very keen that Mirbeau should make a success of writing as a career.[2] The *Lettres de ma chaumière* had passed unnoticed by critics and public alike, and Mirbeau was faced with the hard fact that if he did not attempt some new form of expression he would pass into middle age as a competent journalist and nothing more.

The advice of his friends, the promptings of his mistress, and his own awareness of the need to branch out into something new, were not however sufficient in themselves to transform Mirbeau into the hotly-discussed, best-selling novelist he became with the publication of *Le Calvaire* in December 1886. The all-important stimulus was provided by his contact with the radical ideas of the political, artistic and social Left, which had enabled him at last to throw off the shackles of his origins. At once Mirbeau felt free to express the feelings he had been obliged to conceal, or of which he had only vaguely sensed the existence, and *Le Calvaire* was to be the first of many books into which Mirbeau emptied the rancour of his liberated soul. In his short stories Mirbeau had observed the life of society and had described it with a satirist's pen; in his articles he had defended or attacked those with whom he came into daily contact. But now, in his novels, he was to turn to his own very personal experiences, choosing to lay bare his own existence, and with such intensity that it is difficult to disentangle the purely fictional from the strictly autobiographical.

Le Calvaire, if it is remembered at all, is now remembered as a love-story in the tradition of *Manon Lescaut*; and there is no doubt that Mirbeau used his first novel to ease the painful memory of his ill-treatment at the hands of an unfaithful mistress. The echoes of Mirbeau's unfortunate experience still reach us through the pages of Goncourt's diary, where we read in the entry of 20 January 1886:

> Le seul amoureux sincère, le seul amoureux vrai de ce temps serait le nommé Mirbeau,—une sorte de réduction d'Othello! Un soir qu'il était venu passer la nuit avec la femme pour l'amour de laquelle il s'était fait coulissier et qu'il la suprenait découchée, il entrait dans son cabinet de toilette et déchirait et mettait en lambeaux, de ses mains homicides, le charmant petit chien de sa maîtresse, le seul être qu'elle aimât sur la terre.[3]

This incident from Mirbeau's life figured prominently in *Le Calvaire* when it was written later in 1886, and it illustrates not only the depths of Mirbeau's emotions but also the extent to which his novels are a reflection of his private life and a guide to his intimate thoughts.

The letters of Paul Bourget, with whom Mirbeau was friendly at this time, also make reference to Mirbeau's unhappy love-affair.[4] Mirbeau had known Bourget for some time prior to 1886; they had sat together at the *Boeuf Nature* dinners organised by Zola in the 1870s, and they had met again at Barbey d'Aurevilly's, and shared the favour of the 'Connétable des lettres'. Mirbeau had praised Bourget's *Essais de psychologie contemporaine* in *Les Grimaces* (November 1883), and Bourget in his turn gave Mirbeau's first novel an enthusiastic write-up in January 1887.[5] In 1886, at the time *Le Calvaire* was written, Bourget and Mirbeau met on common ground: their literary aspirations were sufficient to make them companions. But Bourget, who had fraternised in his youth with the revolutionaries of the Paris Commune, was now beginning to adopt right-wing ideals, and was already frequenting the opulent circles of the upper middle class. Mirbeau was plainly heading in the opposite direction, as this later reminiscence by him illustrates:

> J'ai connu Bourget autrefois . . . Je l'ai beaucoup connu . . . Nous étions fort amis. Cela me gêne un peu, pour en parler . . . Et puis, il a pris par un chemin . . . moi, par un autre . . . Etant plus jeune que moi, il me protégeait, m'éduquait, me tenait en garde contre ce qu'il appelait les emballements un peu trop naïfs, un peu trop grossiers aussi de ma nature . . . Un jour que nous remontions les Champs-Elysées, il me dit: «Laissez donc les pauvres . . . ils sont inesthétiques . . . ils ne mènent à rien.» Et, me montrant les beaux hôtels qui, de chaque côté, bordent l'avenue: «Voilà, cher ami . . . c'est là! . . .»[6]

Mirbeau's increasing social awareness and Bourget's growing social ambition finally drove the friends apart, and the Dreyfus Affair only confirmed the wedge which had been driven between them. Bourget in fact became one of Mirbeau's favourite whipping boys during the Affair, and later novels like *Le Journal d'une femme de chambre* and *La 628–E8* are full of satirical references to Mirbeau's former friend whom he repudiated out of social conscience.

Yet in 1886 it was Bourget who was indirectly responsible for the publication of *Le Calvaire*. It was he who introduced Mirbeau to the milieu of *La Nouvelle Revue,* presided over by the celebrated Juliette Adam. It was in this periodical that Mirbeau's first novel was published, in serial form, from September to November 1886. Mirbeau enjoyed the intellectual stimulation this new milieu afforded him, yet even here he was unable to secure the complete expression of his views, even within the compass of a work of art, for the second chapter of *Le Calvaire* was politely 'withheld' from publication because of its antipatriotic sentiment. Mirbeau nevertheless succeeded in having this important chapter reintegrated when the novel was published by Ollendorff in December 1886, and once again he found himself the centre of a scandal.

This second chapter of *Le Calvaire* contains a detailed description of the narrator Jean Mintié's experience in the French army during the disastrous campaign of 1870–1. The selfishness, the brutality and the stupidity of men at war are depicted in minute detail; and as Mintié's regiment prepares to meet the Prussians, the iniquity of it all dawns on him in a way which clearly mirrors Mirbeau's own spiritual awakening. There are two or three pages here redolent of the influence of Tolstoy's Christian anarchism, with which Mirbeau had so recently been in contact. And not only the philosophy, but also the style and even the situations of this section of *Le Calvaire* reveal the debt which Mirbeau owed to the author of *War and Peace*. The chapter reaches its climax with the involuntary killing of a Prussian cavalryman, and Mirbeau takes the opportunity, through the mouth of Mintié, to express his antipathy to war, and, like Tolstoy, to appeal to the feelings of humanity and universal brotherhood which lie dormant in the human soul.

The similarities to Tolstoy were so marked that even the editors of *La Nouvelle Revue* found space to comment on them in the same breath as their refusal to print this chapter:

> A notre grand regret, il nous est impossible d'insérer, dans la *Revue,* le deuxième chapitre du roman de M. Mirbeau . . . Les tableaux, traités à la manière de Léon Tolstoï, sont si cruels, que nous n'avons pu les lire sans être pris d'un véritable désespoir patriotique.[7]

Mirbeau replied in unusually restrained terms, insisting that as an artist he had the right to see things in his own way, and that he had the obligation to describe truthfully what he had seen:

> Je m'efforce d'exprimer les chose telles que je les vois et comme je les vois et comme je les sens. J'ai la passion de la vérité, si douloureuse soit-elle, et je n'entends rien aux précautions oratoires, aux réticences académiques, qui me semblent inutiles chez un écrivain sincère.[8]

The incriminated chapter was evidently good publicity, and it dominated the rest of the book, ensuring that Mirbeau's first novel became a best-seller. There were twenty editions of the novel in 1887 alone, and for the ninth edition Mirbeau saw fit to write a preface in which he answered the criticisms which had arisen as a result of his reflections on the Franco-Prussian war. It is a measure of the sensitivity of the French about the 1870 defeat that a single chapter of what was to all intents and purposes a love-story could excite such passions and provoke such anger as it did.[9] The extremist patriots took great exception to Mirbeau's view of the French defeat, and were particularly angered by Mintié's symbolic gesture of embracing the dead Prussian soldier. In his preface to the ninth edition, Mirbeau lightly mocked those who had called him sacrilegious, iconoclastic and refractory, and who had even accused him of being a German spy; and insisting that he himself was patriotic, he penned some words which contain the key to many of his subsequent attitudes, revealing as they do a significant point of contact with the kind of patriotism which Reclus and the anarchists preached—in strict contradistinction to the noisy and sensation-seekinl chauvinism of the post-1870 germanophobes who had taken such exception to *Le Calvaire*:

> Le patriotisme tel que je le comprends, ne s'affuble point de costumes ridicules, ne va point hurler aux enterrements, ne compromet point, par des manifestations inopportunes et des excitations coupables, la sécurité des passants et l'honneur même d'un pays . . .
> Le patriotisme, tel que je l'aime, travaille dans le recueillement. Il s'efforce de faire la patrie grande avec ses poètes, ses artistes, ses savants honorés, ses travailleurs, ses ouvriers et ses paysans protégés. S'il pique un peu moins de panaches au chapeau des généraux, il met un peu plus de laine sur le dos des pauvres gens.[10]

Le Calvaire was based almost entirely upon Mirbeau's own experiences. In the chapter about Mintié's part in the war, Mirbeau was drawing upon his bitter memories of the disasters he had witnessed himself. Though his experiences were perhaps distorted by the suffering involved, Mirbeau's picture of the horrors of war was nevertheless far more authentic than that which could be read in the history books or that which was being taught in the history classes. Yet many critics denied the truthfulness of Mirbeau's portrayal of war, while others accused him of treason—as Jules Huret wrote several years later:

> L'hypocrisie de la critique a fait naturellement un crime à l'auteur de la sincérité de sa lamentable peinture. Combien de siècles d'éducation faudra-t-il encore à l'esprit français pour l'amener à l'amour de la vérité pour elle-même?[11]

Le Calvaire, at the time it was written, was treated as much as a political and social touchstone as it was discussed as a realist novel. Its readers were either for or against Mirbeau's attitudes; not for the last time did one of his works divide his readers sharply into two classes in this way. *Le Calvaire*, and indeed all of Mirbeau's works, were never wholeheartedly accepted by the established critics, not because his works were necessarily inferior as works of art, but because few critics could safely or willingly endorse the radical ideas which permeated Mirbeau's writings, reflecting the change of 1885.

The story of *Le Calvaire*, written entirely in the first person, begins with the childhood of the narrator Jean Mintié at Saint-Michel-les-Hêtres in l'Orne. Mintié's father, the village notary, whom Mintié despised for his hypocrisy, and his mother, whom he admired for her sensitivity, both contain elements borrowed from Mirbeau's own parents. Mintié's childhood, like Mirbeau's, is not a particularly happy one. After recounting his mother's strange illness and premature death, Mintié tells of his boredom under a pedantic and incompetent private tutor, and here Mirbeau avails himself of the opportunity to avenge himself of the things he suffered at the hands of those who in his childhood were given charge over him, but who made no attempt to adapt their approach to his sensitive nature.

Mirbeau's criticism of his own upbringing and education is not however confined in *Le Calvaire* to remarks put directly into the mouth of the narrator: it is part of the very fabric of the story. The tragic figure of Mintié, his unhappy fate, and even the insufficiencies of his character, with which the reader becomes impatient, are clearly shown to be engendered by his inimical background, by his indifferent parents, and by his unsettling contact with war and with the corruptness of parisian society. Mirbeau, who was thirty-eight when he wrote *Le Calvaire*, had reached an age when he could look back at his life and see more clearly the motivating forces which had been operating in it; and the fact that he made the hero of his first novel the victim of so many hostile forces betrays to the reader the grudge which Mirbeau bore against the world in which he had grown up, or at least against that section of it with which he had been forced to keep in contact against his will.

From a Freudian point of view, Mirbeau's misfortunes with an untrustworthy mistress were responsible not only for the creation in *Le Calvaire* of the painful relationship between the fictional Jean Mintié and Juliette Roux but also for the evolution in Mirbeau himself of an enduring and deep-seated misogyny. In a man who prided himself in later years on having rid himself of all his former prejudices, this misogyny represented a flaw which was, however, too subconscious to mar the overall sincerity of Mirbeau's claim. From his suffering at the hands of a parisian flirt, Mirbeau developed a philosophy of the female species which was to colour much of his creative work with an erotic sadism which often borders on the obscene. In its literary expression this philosophy drew much inspiration from the literature of the *femme fatale*,[12] but it owed most to the satirical obscenities of the Belgian artist Félicien Rops, with whom Mirbeau was friendly at this time, and whom he greatly admired. For Mirbeau, Rops' portrayal of woman as the incarnation of evil tallied too closely with his own experiences for it not to impress him deeply, and Rops remained one of the most important of the formative influences on Mirbeau's literary style, as the savage eroticism of *Le Jardin des supplices* and certain parts of *Le Journal d'une femme de chambre* demonstrate. In *Le Calvaire*, Juliette Roux becomes a nightmarish figure, haunting Mintié like a demon of evil, corrupting and degrading him until he can sink no lower, and finally abandoning him when he has nothing left to offer. Only then, when he has suffered such systematic torture—whence the grim title of the novel— does Mintié turn his back on Juliette and on the kind of society she represents; and only then does he cease to be an aimless and spineless parasite, and staggers off, clad in the outfit of an honest workman, away to where his wounds can heal and to where he can start anew.

Le Calvaire is the meeting-place of the many themes of Mirbeau's chequered career. It is essentially a novel of revolt against the malevolent influences which had sought to bind his independent and generous nature. It was intentionally a novel of revenge against authority and despotism in their various forms, throwing the spotlight on them, revealing their nefarious influence on the individual, and accusing them of responsibility for the human weakness upon which the forces of evil could feed at will.

The painter Lirat in *Le Calvaire*—the friend who replaces Mintié in Juliette's arms—and the evident influence of Félicien Rops, bear witness to the personal interest which Mirbeau had begun to take in the visual arts. Mirbeau had long admired the Impressionist *avant-garde*, as the perspicacious art-critic Félix Fénéon noted in 1886,[13] and he had written many articles in demonstration of his progressive artistic taste. But now he had begun to frequent more systematically milieux in which he became acquainted with most of the leading artists of his day. By the time *Le Calvaire* was written Mirbeau had formed lasting friendships with such men as Monet, Rodin and Gustave Geffroy, the truest friend of all—'le bon Gef', the one Barbey d'Aurevilly nicknamed 'le juste de *La Justice*'.[14] There is little doubt that Mirbeau's friendship with Geffroy, journalist, art-critic, biographer of the revolutionary Auguste Blanqui, and himself a novelist of communard sympathies, cemented Mirbeau's allegiance to the Left and caused him to associate more clearly in his mind the revolutionary ideals of *avant-garde* art and of political agitation for social reform.

Mirbeau, who had almost lost his job on *L'Ordre* for his admiration for Monet, was delighted to receive a visit from the artist on Noirmoutier island in Brittany, where he had gone with Alice Regnault to prepare *Le Calvaire* for publication in 1886. This visit was the real beginning of a lifelong friendship, as the sustained correspondence between Mirbeau and Monet illustrates.[15] Mirbeau was clearly referring to Monet and to the artists to whom Monet later introduced him, like Bonnard, Vuillard and Vallotton, when he wrote:

> C'était une joie que leur amitié, et, en même temps qu'une joie, un profit. Pour moi, j'y ai beaucoup appris, même dans les choses de mon métier. Ils m'ont ouvert un monde spirituel qui, jusqu'à eux, m'était en quelque sorte fermé, ou obscur . . . Je ne le dis pas sans émotion, ils ont donné à ma conscience, qui, trop longtemps, avait erré dans les terres desséchées du journalisme, une autre conscience.[16]

The artists' debt to Mirbeau was no less considerable than the debt he owed to them—Monet, Rodin and Gauguin were not alone in benefiting from the enthusiasm which Mirbeau put at their disposal. It is for the historian of art to assess the importance of Mirbeau's role as the champion of the artistic *avant-garde* of his time;[17] but it is clear that from an intellectual point of view, Mirbeau's contact with the world of art was of capital importance to him. Mirbeau's growing appreciation of the freedom expressed in the works of the rising generation of artists was part and parcel of the same spiritual awakening that revitalised his whole outlook on life, giving him a new awareness, and inspiring him to creative activity of his own.

By the summer of 1887 Mirbeau was a successful novelist; and this fact was no doubt a contributory factor to his marriage in May of that year to his mistress Alice Regnault. His union with this ex-*Variétés* actress set the seal on his break with his family and his right-wing origins. The rural bourgeoisie from which he stemmed and the right-wing circles in which he had moved for so long had tolerated his occasional outbursts of criticism and had pardoned them as youthful peccadilloes. But with *Le Calvaire*, and with his marriage to an actress, Mirbeau had openly declared his hostility to his caste, and he was now at the point of no return. After the personal revenge which he exacted by means of his first novel, Mirbeau's attitude towards his background began to harden out of intellectual conviction. Not only his new friends but also the books he read caused him to recognise the need for radical changes in the political, economic and artistic life of French society. Spencer, Büchner, Darwin and Guyau were among the scientific philosophers Mirbeau was reading at this time,[18] and their ideas coloured Mirbeau's own philosophy with the atheistic and evolutionary rationalism which was calling into question the authority of ancient institutions and undermining the very fabric of society. These writers, along with Tolstoy, Kropotkin and Reclus, provided Mirbeau with the ammunition he needed to intensify his opposition to the kind of social organisation he saw around him and to the intellectual tyranny under which he had suffered for so long himself.

The vehemence of Mirbeau's criticisms increased in proportion to his awareness of the cause of the ills besetting society. In *L'Abbé Jules* and *Sébastien Roch* he was to show what harm could result from the repression of an individual's natural self-expression, while in *Le Jardin des supplices* his field of criticism was to widen to take in the whole of society. *L'Abbé Jules* and *Sébastien Roch* were based, like *Le Calvaire*, on Mirbeau's own life, and it was by applying his new ideas to his personal experiences, in the writing of these novels, that Mirbeau prepared himself to face the larger issue of a society in need of correction.

L'Abbé Jules was conceived as a novel of the revolt of an individual against the middle class values which had been forced upon him. The eponymous hero of the book was intended to be a sympathetic villain whose misdeeds were the direct result of the repression to which society had subjected him. Under the hyperbolic pen of Mirbeau, however, the Abbé Jules degenerated into a monster, terrorising all with whom he came into contact. Based on a character taken from real life, he transcends reality, and causes the reader to doubt the validity of Mirbeau's criticisms of the society of which he is meant to be the victim. The monumental monstrosity of Jules' character would undoubtedly undermine the moral thesis of the novel were it not for the stratagem employed by Mirbeau to reduce this effect—that of narrating the story through the eyes of a child, the young nephew of Jules, Albert Dervelle. This ploy certainly rescues *L'Abbé Jules* from the tendency which Mirbeau had to overexaggeration and which reached its crescendo with *Le Jardin des supplices*. There were those who still accused Mirbeau of creating a meaningless and vulgar monster, an exception which proved nothing, but the perspicacious reader missed none of Mirbeau's sympathy for the Abbé Jules' sufferings due to the repression of his natural instinct. Mallarmé, for example, with whom Mirbeau was becoming friendly at this time, wrote him a letter which compensated Mirbeau for all the adverse criticism which his novel had received, for Mallarmé had clearly understood Mirbeau's intention in creating the Abbé Jules, as Mirbeau's reply to Mallarmé's kind letter reveals:

> Il y a, dans votre lettre, une phrase qui m'a vivement ému, car elle résume parfaitement ce que j'ai tenté dans l'*Abbé Jules*, et ce qu'on ne veut pas y voir: «Or vous avez créé là un douloureux camarade.» Cette phrase me paie de tous mes doutes et de toutes mes angoisses.[19]

Flushed with the success of *Le Calvaire*, Mirbeau had begun working on *L'Abbé Jules* immediately on his return from England after his marriage. The Mirbeaus set up house in Kérisper, near Sainte-Anne-d'Auray in Brittany, not far from Vannes, where Mirbeau had gone to Jesuit college over twenty years before. It was there, in July 1887, that he began writing his new novel, keeping his friend Monet informed of his painful progress.[20] Surrounded by some of the loveliest countryside in France, Mirbeau saturated the character of the Abbé Jules with his own love of nature, and wove into his strange novel an impassioned appeal to humanity to learn the lessons of freedom and harmony which nature teaches to those who will stop to listen. The pantheistic philosophy which Jules tries to inculcate into his young nephew Albert is clearly a *reductio ad absurdum* of Mirbeau's own rousseauistic attitude to nature; and when Jules insists that he would not have been the degenerate rogue he was if he had been allowed to pursue his naturistic ideals, we feel that Mirbeau himself is speaking directly to us through the mouth of this fictional priest:

> ... si j'avais connu autrefois ces vérités, je n'en serais jamais où j'en suis aujourd'hui. Car je suis une canaille, un être malfaisant, l'abject esclave de sales passions ... Et sais-tu pourquoi? Parce que, dès que j'ai pu articuler un son, on m'a bourré le cerveau d'idées absurdes ... On a déformé les fonctions de mon intelligence, comme celle de mon corps, et, à la place de l'homme naturel, instinctif, gonflé

> de vie, on a substitué l'artificiel fantoche, la mécanique poupée de civilisation, soufflée d'idéal . . . l'idéal d'où sont nés les banquiers, les prêtres, les escrocs, les débauchés, les assassins et les malheureux . . .[21]

This vague and sentimental anarchism is the motivating force behind the revolt of the Abbé Jules who, like Mirbeau himself, takes vengeance on society by mystifying and terrifying those who have contributed to its nefarious influence.

The story of *L'Abbé Jules* begins, like *Le Calvaire*, with the narrator's childhood reminiscences; and here we are allowed to catch another glimpse of the boredom of Mirbeau's early years. Mirbeau again takes the opportunity to satirise the life of the provincial bourgeoisie, particularly in the relations between the Dervelle family and their neighbours the Robins. Mirbeau's enduring antipathy towards legal administrators is given full rein in his characterisation of Monsieur Robin, the local J.P. who makes the grand boast that he knows the Code by rote, but who is as venal and as corrupt as those on whom he is allowed to pass sentence:

> A la veille des audiences, on voyait entrer chez lui des paysans avec des paniers bondés de volaille et de gibier, qu'ils remportaient vides, à la suite de quelque discussion juridique, sans doute.[22]

The picture of the superstitious, money-grubbing villagers of Viantais is broken off by the narrator's account of the life and doings of the dreaded Abbé Jules. It had been a surprise to everyone when Jules Dervelle became a priest, but the narrator makes it quite clear that Jules did this to exact his revenge on the society which had stunted his natural development. Jules exploits his position for his own ends, and experiences an almost satanic joy in doing so; the catalogue of his crimes makes one wonder why his removal from office did not come sooner. His return to Viantais after six years' debauchery in Paris is the beginning of a closer association between the narrator and his uncle, and from this time on we begin to see more clearly that Jules has been the victim of society, and not the tormentor of it as he first appeared. Ironically, this contact between Jules and his young nephew was permitted by Albert's parents, who overcame their antipathy towards Jules in the hope of inheriting the fortune which he had somehow managed to accumulate. Jules is even entrusted with Albert's education; and in a chapter which is reminiscent of Rousseau's *Emile*, the renegade priest sets about disabusing the young narrator of all the false notions which his family had taught him and the values he had learned to respect:

Ecoute-moi donc . . . Tu réduiras tes connaissances du fonctionnement de l'humanité au strict nécessaire: 1o L'homme est une bête méchante et stupide; 2o La justice est une infamie; 3o L'amour est une cochonnerie; 4o Dieu est une chimère . . . Tu aimeras la nature; tu l'adoreras même . . .[23]

It is not difficult to see why the critics and the public did not appreciate such lessons as this, of which *L'Abbé Jules* is full. Mirbeau himself was, as usual, mildly displeased with his novel; though in later years he said it was perhaps 'le moins mauvais',[24] and he was heartened by its reception amongst his literary and artistic friends. Mallarmé in particular was unusually lavish with his praise, and the novel cemented the ties of friendship between him and Mirbeau, and led to a regular correspondence which ended only with Mallarmé's sudden death in 1898.

Mirbeau's friendship with Mallarmé brought him into contact with the rising generation of symbolists who frequented the Mardis of the rue de Rome; and though Mirbeau did not subscribe to the symbolist aesthetic—he was never a lover of poetry in any case—he learned to appreciate the originality of much symbolist talent, and found himself in agreement at least with the attitude of opposition to the bourgeois republic which prevailed in symbolist circles.[25] It was through Mallarmé too that Mirbeau came into contact again with the leading symbolist critic Félix Fénéon, who was soon to begin expressing his opposition to society by writing anonymous articles in underground anarchist journals like *La Revue Libertaire* and *Le Père Peinard*.[26] In 1888 Fénéon was co-editor with Jean Ajalbert of Dujardin's *La Revue Indépendante*, in which Mirbeau had published an article the previous year;[27] and Fénéon was to be another friend who cemented Mirbeau's allegiance to the extreme Left.[28]

L'Abbé Jules, then, was even more important in Mirbeau's personal life than it was in his career as a successful novelist. It gave him an entrance to a wider range of intellectual circles, and convinced any who still doubted that Mirbeau was now wholly committed to revolutionary ideals. It even brought Mirbeau's writings to the notice of the anarchists, with whom he had so far had no direct contact, but who immediately recognised in him a kindred spirit. *L'Abbé Jules* was published at a time when Jean Grave was busy publishing a literary supplement to his anarchist journal *La Révolte* and was casting about for suitable material to republish there. Grave could not fail to be struck by the revolutionary tone which Mirbeau adopted in *L'Abbé Jules*. The anarchism of the abbé is, as his young nephew says, 'un anarchisme vague et sentimental';[29] it does not progress far beyond the negative, and it is not based on any positive ideological formula other than that nature is good and can show humanity the way to beauty and truth. Yet this was undoubtedly true of much nineteenth-century anarchist thought. Though most anarchists, and Mirbeau as well, went on to build upon the ruins which their nihilistic theories left behind, the critical negation of society and its values was an essential first step, and *L'Abbé Jules* was very much in this tradition. Jules was a character dear to the hearts of all those who, like Mirbeau, objected to the repression of the individual, and sought to replace such repression with freedom from constraint. The abbé's final act, of leaving his fortune to the first priest to defrock himself, is the ultimate, ironical gesture of defiance against the society which had made him what he was, and against the cupidity of those who thought his fortune would be theirs. The anarchists especially appreciated the literary form which Mirbeau was able to give to ideas which they were trying, in their own way, to spread. Jules' lessons about naturism, free love and the non-existence of God were ready-made propaganda for those who preached these principles in a more doctrinal and less palatable form.

Owing to the copyright difficulties which Grave was likely to experience—and which he later experienced to his cost—he left republication of the relevant sections of *L'Abbé Jules* for a future occasion,[30] and turned to Mirbeau's newspaper articles and to his earlier works of fiction for possible material to include in his literary supplement. And Grave did not have far to look, for the approaching elections inspired Mirbeau to write a stinging attack on the French electoral system, in an article which was so virulent, in fact, that he was very fortunate to squeeze it past the editorial censorship of *Le Figaro*, where it first appeared on 28 November 1888. The article, 'La Grève des électeurs', was deemed by Grave to be of such importance that he republished it almost immediately, and not in his literary supplement, but on the front page of *La Révolte* itself (19 December 1888). It seems to have been Grave's practice to request permission from any author he wished to republish in this way; and as he later noted, only a few writers refused him such requests.[31] In view of this, and in view of the fact that Grave was 'en correspondance déjà' with Mirbeau when he wrote his first surviving letter to Mirbeau in 1890,[32] it seems probable that he also wrote asking Mirbeau's permission to reprint his article, so that Mirbeau's first direct contact with the anarchist movement would come in the form a letter which he received at the beginning of December 1888 requesting permission to republish 'La Grève des électeurs'. Though Mirbeau's reply to Grave has not survived,[33] it was evidently favourable to the anarchist's request, and thus began an epistolary acquaintance which was to bring Mirbeau still closer to the mainstream of nineteenth-century French anarchism.

Electoral abstention had long been a basic part of anarchist doctrine and practice. In 1885, Mirbeau himself had read these words in the *Paroles d'un révolté* concerning universal suffrage:

> . . . le suffrage universel, la liberté de la presse, etc. . . . ne sont qu'un instrument entre les mains des classes dominantes pour maintenir leur pouvoir sur le peuple.[34]

This was a view shared by all the anarchists,[35] and it was a view to which Mirbeau had come round through his own experience of the inadequacies of the electoral system. Mirbeau's article, though not intended as a means of anarchist propaganda, was nevertheless so close to the anarchist tradition, and it put the case against electoral participation in such a forceful and amusing way, that the anarchist readers of *La Révolte* clamoured for offprints of the article to be made, and not even 20,000 copies were able to silence the demand. 'La Grève des électeurs' was so popular in anarchist circles that years later it was still being printed as the standard anarchist abstentionist pamphlet, and Jean Grave wrote of it: 'Nous n'en connaissons pas de meilleur que l'article de Mirbeau: *La Grève des Electeurs*, paru il y a sept ou huit ans, mais toujours d'actualité.'[36] The French police naturally obtained their own copy of the article, and it went into the file which they had opened on Mirbeau, and which was soon to swell as his contacts with the extreme Left multiplied.[37]

Jean Grave's idea of reproducing extracts of sociological interest from literary authors as a means of anarchist propaganda was originally the brainchild of his friend Baillet, who had published two numbers of the ephemeral *Glaneur Anarchiste* in January 1885, containing extracts from Diderot, Blanqui and Boucher de Perthes. The first number of Grave's literary supplement to *La Révolte* (19 November 1887), reiterated the same intentions as Baillet's *Glaneur*:

> . . . démontrer aux travailleurs que les idées dont nous nous faisons les défenseurs ne sont point nées d'hier . . . rappeler aux heureux du jour,—peut-être leur apprendre—qu'ils sont les bénéficiaires des révolutions précédentes et qu'ils auraient mauvaise grâce à renier aujourd'hui ceux dont le seul crime consiste à vouloir mettre en pratique les théories de leurs devanciers eux-mêmes.

Though both Kropotkin and Reclus were initially cool about the efficacy of a literary supplement as a means of propaganda, Grave's persistence and his success made them and the anarchists as a whole admit that even such extracts from predominantly bourgeois literature could serve the anarchist cause.

Of all the writers who were co-opted into this kind of involuntary propaganda, Mirbeau was to be the one on whom Grave relied most heavily. In January 1889, the Boulanger affair caused Mirbeau to write a satirical article about the sad state of society, an article in which the key phrase—'le mécontentement général'— is lifted straight out of the *Paroles d'un révolté*;[38] for Kropotkin, this 'general discontent' was a sign of the near decomposition of the ancient forms and traditions of society, and this was a subject on which Mirbeau loved to expatiate. In this article ('Le Mécontentement'), Mirbeau took hold of Kropotkin's ideas and elaborated on them; and thinking no doubt of the anarchists, Mirbeau argued that plebeian revolutionaries were fully justified in their conflict with society, for 'dans leur oeuvre farouche [ils] se montrent plus logiques, sinon plus rassurantes que les pleurardes bourgeoises'; Mirbeau's condemnation of all governments, 'qui ont toujours joué dans l'Humanité un rôle d'obstruction et de destruction', and of the legal system, was tailor-made for use as anarchist propaganda, and shortly after it had appeared, surprisingly, in *Le Figaro* (9 January 1889), it was reprinted in the literary supplement of *La Révolte* (4 February).

During the winter of 1888–9, which he spent mostly in Menton in an attempt to overcome the neurasthenia and fever which was plaguing him, Mirbeau began work on his third novel, *Sébastien Roch*.[39] If *Le Calvaire* and *L'Abbé Jules* had contained elements of the anarchism which was now becoming Mirbeau's hallmark, *Sébastien Roch* was to be the novel most directly inspired by his extreme left-wing preoccupations and by his individualistic revolt against the pressures of a middle-class society. The most consciously anarchistic of his early novels, *Sébastien Roch* was also the one which gave him most trouble to write, for he wrestled with it for almost a year, and seemed ill-pleased with it at every stage of its composition.[40]

Mirbeau returned to Paris from Menton in May 1889 with only a hundred pages of his novel written. He and his wife set up house at 26 rue Rivay, in the noisy district of Levallois-Perret, where Mme Mirbeau owned some property. By a strange coincidence, Levallois-Perret was also the part of Paris in which the anarchists were most numerous and most active; it was the home of many of the anarchist militants, including Louise Michel; there were two anarchist groups there at the very time when Mirbeau arrived, and the larger of the two groups bore the name La Révolte, and met in the Salle Isselée of the rue de Courcelles, only a short distance from Mirbeau's home. It seems impossible that Mirbeau could have had no contact with these *compagnons* on his very doorstep, especially as another of his friends,

Jean Ajalbert, who also lived in Levallois-Perret, is known to have frequented the anarchist-inspired Club de l'Art social.[41]

It was while Mirbeau was in Levallois-Perret in July 1889 that Grave began to republish the second chapter of *Le Calvaire*—the chapter which had caused the scandal three years earlier. It appeared in the literary supplement of *La Révolte* in six parts, between July and September, and the anarchist readers must have found it to their taste, for *Le Calvaire* became a firm favourite in the anarchist library. Six years later, an anarchist wrote of *Le Calvaire*: 'Ce livre, où s'affirment déjà les tendances socialistes de l'auteur, mérite d'être lu surtout pour les pages admirables sur la guerre qui forment une partie du volume.'[42] It was Mirbeau's concentration on war in that remarkable chapter which gave Jean Grave the idea, some years later, of grouping together by subject the pick of the extracts from the literary supplements of *La Révolte* and its successor *Les Temps Nouveaux*. Mirbeau's chapter was the first of these special volumes to be published, and it appeared, as it had done when Grave first reprinted it in *La Révolte*, under the title 'La Guerre'.[43]

Mirbeau was still living in Levallois-Perret—he removed to Les Damps by Pont-de-l'Arche in August 1889—when the local elections came round again in Paris. Once more Mirbeau stepped into the fray with another article in the vein of 'La Grève des électeurs'; this new article was called 'Prélude', and it appeared in *Le Figaro* of 14 July. Mirbeau's cutting analysis of the electoral farce, of 'l'infinie sottise, l'infinie malpropreté de la politique', reveals him at his satirical best. His imaginative portrait of Boulanger, handing out promises of prosperity before the elections, and uniforms, knapsacks and rifles afterwards, is something which deserves a better fate than the one which seems reserved for such journalistic ephemera. The last paragraph in particular, in which Mirbeau expands his irony into direct address, deserves quoting, and it was for this no doubt that Jean Grave reprinted the whole article in *La Révolte* for, apostrophising the typical voter, Mirbeau wrote:

> Eh bien! mon brave électeur, normand ou gascon, picard ou cévenol, basque ou breton, si tu avais une lueur de raison dans ta cervelle, si tu n'étais pas l'immortel abruti que tu es, le jour où les mendiants, les estropiés, les monstres électoraux viendront sur ton passage coutumier étaler leurs plaies et tendre leurs sébiles, au bout de leurs moignons dartreux, si tu n'étais pas l'indécrottable Souverain, sans sceptre, sans couronne, sans royaume, que tu as toujours été, ce jour-là, tu t'en irais tranquillement pêcher à la ligne, ou dormir sous les saules, ou trouver les filles derrière les meules, ou jouer aux boules, dans une sente lointaine, et tu les laisserais, tes hideux sujets, se battre entre eux, se dévorer, se tuer. Ce jour-là, vois-tu, tu pourrais te vanter d'avoir accompli le seul acte politique et la première bonne action de ta vie.[44]

Not only the electoral campaigning, and all the noise and show that went with it, but also the disruption caused throughout Paris by the Universal Exhibition being held there that year, made Mirbeau irritated by city life, and he became anxious to leave the capital and find a place in the country.[45] And it was not simply the upset caused by the Universal Exhibition which annoyed Mirbeau; he saw it also as a further sign of the decadence of capitalist society, 'le dernier élan d'une société moribonde . . . le suprême cri d'une civilisation qui agonise'.[46] In an article which the anarchists found to their liking, he even drew an implied comparison between the Paris of 1889 and ancient Babylon just before its overthrow by the Medo-Persians:

> Ce qu'il y a de plus incroyable, c'est que les classes dirigeantes se réjouissent. Elles sont fières de cette oeuvre, qui est la leur, et où je vois le *Mané-Thécel-Pharès* de leur règne! Elles ne comprennent donc pas que les anarchistes, seuls, ont le droit de se réjouir, car où donc trouveraient-ils, autre part qu'ici, un meilleur recrutement de révolte! . . .[47]

It was with articles like this, in which Mirbeau made common cause with anarchist theoreticians like Reclus and Kropotkin, that he made his debut in the anarchist press. He began by expressing ideas similar to those advocated by the anarchists, and they were only too glad to give these ideas an airing in their leading journal. Increasingly, however, their own ideas were to have an effect on Mirbeau, and in his own individual way he became the leading literary interpreter of anarchist ideology. From July to December 1889 articles by Mirbeau appeared regularly, at least once a month and sometimes more, in the literary supplement of *La Révolte*. Almost every article which Mirbeau wrote, whether in *Le Figaro* or in *L'Echo de Paris*, on which he had begun to collaborate in January 1889, contained something which the anarchists could turn to their advantage; and while Mirbeau settled himself in his new country home in Normandy and occupied himself with the completion of *Sébastien Roch,* Jean Grave continued to select material from Mirbeau's regular newspaper columns for republication in his anarchist literary supplement.

Sébastien Roch, as Mirbeau had written to Mallarmé earlier in the year, was 'le roman d'un adolescent violé par un jésuite, la conséquence de ce viol, sur la formation de son esprit et la direction de ses idées'.[48] It was like his two previous novels in that it was basically autobiographical, that it was the story of an individual's failure, and that its thesis was that society was to blame. Yet *Sébastien Roch* turned out to be an altogether tidier and crisper novel; its characters are more well-defined, its plot is more feasible, its thesis is more successful, and its criticisms more pointed and meaningful. In choosing to make a

Jesuit responsible for the victimisation of his main character, Mirbeau was able to centralise both the action and the social criticism of his novel. In *Le Calvaire* and in *L'Abbé Jules* a diversity of influences had been responsible for the failure of Jean and Jules, and none of these influences had stood out sufficiently for Mirbeau to use as a focal point of his social criticism. In *Sébastien Roch* however, Mirbeau was able to focus the spotlight on one institution, the Jesuit college of Vannes, on one group of people, the Jesuits who ran it, and on one man, Father de Kern, the one who put the finishing touches to the systematic destruction of an innocent child. From this central theme proceeds all of Mirbeau's condemnation of the social organism as a whole; from Monsieur Roch's parental egotism in sending his son to the famous Jesuit college to the perpetuation of class-consciousness by the boarders there; and from the strictness of Jesuit teaching-methods to their reliance on fear and superstition in the maintenance of their religious authority—each of these had wider implications, but all are bound together by Sébastien's unfortunate experiences in Vannes.[49] The disastrous effect which these things have on the life of this young adolescent—Sébastien dies at the age of twenty—is Mirbeau's deliberate illustration of the dangers of alienating the individual from his natural course.

We meet Sébastien first as a healthy, fun-loving eleven-year-old. His pompous father, who keeps the ironmongery in the village of Pervenchères, is a pleasant enough character, described by Mirbeau with the kind of comic irony he was to employ later throughout *Les Vingt et un jours d'un neurasthénique*. Monsieur Roch has perhaps been guilty of neglecting his son, but at least he has allowed Sébastien a measure of freedom, and Sébastien's upbringing has been far less repressive than that of either Jean Mintié in *Le Calvaire* or Jules Dervelle in *L'Abbé Jules*. It is left to the Jesuits to perform this work of deformation and repression, and the greatest mistake Monsieur Roch makes is to confide his son to their tender care for the sake of his own vanity.

Throughout his life Mirbeau reproached the Jesuits for the kind of education they had tried to force upon him, and for the adverse effect their efforts had had upon his character.[50] In making the Jesuits responsible for the serious damage done to Sébastien, however, Mirbeau was expressing far more than merely personal animosity towards a particular religious sect; by illustrating the dangerous menace of education in the hands of the priesthood, Mirbeau was undermining the validity of religion itself, and was giving voice to the anticlerical feeling which was daily growing stronger in France, and which the extreme Left—and the anarchists in particular—were fomenting at that very time.[51]

In the very opening paragraphs of the novel, in a passage which, through over exaggeration, almost loses the significance of the truth it contains, Mirbeau accuses the Jesuits, with their religious superstition, of exploiting the abjection and poverty of their area of Brittany:

> Aucun décor de paysage et d'humanité ne leur convenait mieux pour pétrir les cerveaux et manier les âmes . . . De tous les pays bretons, le taciturne Morbihan est demeuré le plus obstinément breton, par son fatalisme religieux, sa résistance sauvage au progrès moderne, et la poésie, âpre, indiciblement triste de son sol qui livre l'homme, abruti de misères, de superstitions et de fièvres, à l'omnipotente et vorace consolation du prêtre.[52]

The novel is riddled with such outbursts of anticlericalism, of the 'haine de la prêtrise' which Mirbeau shared with so many of his contemporaries—many of whom knew what Jesuit college was like, having passed through it themselves—and it is hardly suprising that Mirbeau should invest Sébastien with this same hatred, as he noted in his diary:

> Enfin, j'ai l'horreur du prêtre, je sens le mensonge de ses consolations, le mensonge du Dieu implacable et fou qu'il sert; je sens que le prêtre n'est là, dans la société, que pour maintenir l'homme dans sa crasse intellectuelle, que pour faire, des multitudes servilisées, un troupeau de brutes imbéciles et couardes . . . .[53]

Sébastien, endowed with an abnormal sensitivity, is made to suffer horribly by the Jesuits. His only friend, the taciturn and thick-skinned Bolorec, suffers similar hardships but accepts them with quiet indignation. When Sébastien has been corrupted by the sensual Father de Kern, and has proved a disappointment to the Jesuit, he and Bolorec find themselves expelled from college on the grounds that a homosexual relationship has developed between them; and when Sébastien returns home in disgrace, we are able to measure the damage that has been done in the three years he has spent at Vannes. The diary which he keeps gives us a clear insight into the confused moral and mental state of this unfortunate victim of man's inhumanity. Sébastien shows himself to be incapable of forming normal relationships with people, especially with members of the opposite sex, like his childhood sweetheart Marguerite Lecautel. He is no longer the carefree self-confident child he once was; he is unstable, easily bored, misunderstood and disliked by his neighbours, and he is pursued by erotic nightmares which bring back all the horror of his days in Jesuit college. All this is a direct result of his three years in Vannes.

Beneath this marred existence however, we catch the occasional glimpse of what might have been if Sébastien had not been intellectually stunted by his education in Jesuit college. In his diary he struggles painfully to see clearly through the veils of prejudice and through the complexes the Jesuits have integrated into his personality; his generosity and his concern for the underprivileged make him feel the iniquity of the morality and the hollowness of the religion of his Jesuit teachers, and yet he is unable to formulate his own opinion—he cannot carry though his revolt to a true expression of himself:

> Révolte vaine, hélas! et stérile. Il arrive souvent que les préjugés sont les plus forts et prévalent sur des idées que je sens généreuses, que je sais justes. Je ne puis, si confuse qu'elle soit encore, me faire une conception morale de l'univers, affranchie de toutes les barbaries, religieuse, politique, légale et sociale, sans être aussitôt repris par ces mêmes terreurs religieuses et sociales, inculquées au collège.[54]

The parallel between Sébastien and the young Mirbeau is obvious, and there can be little doubt that the character of Sébastien became a means whereby Mirbeau could explain, to his own satisfaction at least, his paradoxical conduct earlier in his life. Had he lived, Sébastien might ultimately have found himself, as Mirbeau did. As it was, his humanitarian impulses and his potentially anarchistic temperament proceeded little further than this grandiloquent apostrophe, inspired by the resigned submissiveness of the population of Pervenchères:

> Y a-t-il quelque part une jeunesse ardente et réfléchie, une jeunesse qui pense, qui travaille, qui s'affranchisse de la lourde, de la criminelle, de l'homicide main du prêtre, si fatale au cerveau humain? Une jeunesse qui, en face de la morale établie par le prêtre et des lois appliquées par le gendarme, ce complément du prêtre, dise résolument: 'Je serai immorale, et je serai révoltée.' Je voudrais le savoir.[55]

When one day he receives a letter from his schoolfriend Bolorec, who is plotting to bring about a proletarian revolution, Sébastien thinks again of his own concern for the poor and the underprivileged, and he regrets his inability to communicate with the common people. He remembers, for example, how he tried in vain to explain to the poor population of Pervenchères that public charity was simply a means used by the rich to perpetuate poverty and justify their wealth:

> ... la charité, voilà le secret de l'avilissement des hommes! Par elle, le gouvernant et le prêtre perpétuent la misère au lieu de la soulager, démoralisent le coeur du misérable au lieu de l'élever. Les imbéciles, ils se croient liés à leurs souffrances par ce bienfait menteur, qui de tous les crimes sociaux est le plus grand et le plus

monstrueux, le plus indéracinable aussi. Je leur ai dit: 'N'acceptez pas l'aumône, repoussez la charité, et prenez, prenez, car tout vous appartient.' Mais ils ne m'ont pas compris.[56]

Sébastien is not able, as Bolorec is, to commit himself totally to the popular cause, and he is obliged to lead a tortured life of indecision. His mind is clear however, on one important point: the stupidity of militarism and its corollary, war between nations. This novel more than any other—*Le Calvaire* included—expresses Mirbeau's horror of war and his opposition to nationalistic patriotism. The ultimate fate which Mirbeau reserves for Sébastien is a meaningless death in a war he does not understand for a cause he knows nothing about. And before he goes off to war to die—supreme irony this—Sébastien is allowed to speak his mind in a passage which sums up not only Mirbeau's feelings, but also those of all those who were campaigning for the abolition of war:

> Je comprends que l'on se batte, que l'on se tue, entre gens d'un même pays, pour conquérir une liberté et un droit: le droit à vivre, à manger, à penser; je ne comprends pas que l'on se batte entre gens qui n'ont aucun rapport entre eux, aucun intérêt commun, et que ne peuvent se haïr puisqu'ils ne se connaissent point.[57]

The futility of Sébastien's death, in the arms of Bolorec, with whom he has met up again on the battle-front, fills the taciturn revolutionary with cold anger; and as he stumbles away into the smoke, bearing his friend's shattered body, he mutters dark threats of revenge on the world which has done this to an innocent youth.

It is tempting to agree with the critic Maxime Revon, who interprets the two friends as different aspects of Mirbeau's own personality: Sébastien the idealist, warm and generous, and Bolorec the revenge-seeking revolutionary, intent on making society pay for the death of the idealism personified by Sébastien. It is difficult not to see Sébastien as the younger Mirbeau, generous in impulse, but holding back through the reticence of prejudice, and Bolorec as the older Mirbeau, the revolutionary, the anarchist intent on making up for all the time that his indecisive self had lost.[58] Whether this be the case or not, *Sébastien Roch* was certainly the novel into which Mirbeau put most of himself, a novel where he invites the reader to discern his philosophy of life, that amoral but humanitarian anarchism which was becoming more and more pronounced.

Such then was the novel which Mirbeau dedicated to the 'Maître vénérable et fastueux du Livre Moderne', Edmond de Goncourt; and though Goncourt did not exactly share Mirbeau's extremist views, least of all when the anarchists began to throw bombs about, he greatly admired the fine prose style of his younger friend, and *Sébastien Roch* remained his favourite of Mirbeau's works. Their friendship clearly transcended political considerations, and Mirbeau remained a regular visitor to Goncourt's Grenier.[59]

The anarchists however, and Jean Grave in particular, were more interested in the sociological content of *Sébastien Roch* than in its literary merits, and they were quick to reprint the various sections of the novel which expressed ideas akin to their own. It had not long been published in book-form—it first appeared serially in *L'Echo de Paris* from January to April 1890—when the literary supplement of *La Révolte* published a section of it under the title 'La Guerre', closely followed by another under the title 'La Patrie', and then a third, 'Psychologie sociale'.[60] These extracts, and the very fact of their republication in an anarchist journal, illustrate the gulf that separated Mirbeau from his former reactionary self. His three 'novels of revenge' not only enabled him to unburden himself of the painful memories of his youth, but by their defence of individualism and by the suppressed anger of their condemnation of the forces which repress man's natural instincts, these books brought him to the forefront of the anarchists' propaganda, and were an earnest of the stand Mirbeau was soon to take on their behalf.

Notes

1 Pierre Borel, *Le Vrai Maupassant*, (Genève: Cailler, 1951), p. 72.
2 Mirbeau and Alice Regnault, whose real name, Augustine Alexandrine Renard, formerly Toulet, appears on the marriage certificate, were married by special licence at Westminster Register Office on 25 May 1887. They married in England to escape the wagging tongues. In 1886 Alice Regnault had published a novel, *Mademoiselle Pomme*, and she followed it up in 1888 with *La Famille Carmettes*. It is possible also that she was the writer of *Jean Marcellin*, a novel published in 1885 under the pseudonym (?) Albert Miroux. This book is mistakenly attributed by the Bibliothèque Nationale catalogue to Mirbeau himself, whose name appears on the half-title page of the B.N. copy.
3 Edmond [and Jules] de Goncourt, *Journal*, vol. 14 (Monaco: Les Editions de l'Imprimerie Nationale, 1956), p. 80.
4 *Cf.* R. de Bury, 'Dix lettres de Paul Bourget à Octave Mirbeau', *Le Mercure de France*, No. 153 (1 January 1922), pp. 279–80; also 'Lettres inédites de Paul Bourget à Octave Mirbeau', *Sur la Riviéra*, 18 April 1922.
5 'Le Calvaire', *La Nouvelle Revue*, 1 January 1887.
6 *La 628–E8* (Paris: Fasquelle, 1908 edition), pp. 394–5.
7 Quoted from 'Un Conflit littéraire', *Le Petit Caporal*, 24 November 1886.
8 *Ibid.*
9 *Cf.* particularly H. de Pène, 'Autour d'un chapitre', *Le Gaulois*, 26 November 1886, and Serpenoise, 'Chronique parisienne: les sacrilèges', *La Revanche*, 26 November 1886.
10 Quoted from *Les Ecrivains*, vol. 2, pp. 267–8. Reclus distinguished between politi-

cal patriotism, which involved an obligatory respect for the State, and popular patriotism, the individual's natural feeling for his place of origin. See E. Reclus, *L'Evolution, la révolution et l'idéal anarchique* (Paris: Stock, 1914 edition), pp. 113–14.
11 Jules Huret, 'Octave Mirbeau', in *La Grande Encyclopédie*, vol. 23 (Paris: Société Anonyme de la Grande Encyclopédie, 1899), p. 1099.
12 See A. H. Wallace, 'The fatal woman in French literature of the nineteenth century' (unpublished Ph.D. thesis, University of North Carolina, 1960); also Mario Praz, *The Romantic Agony* (London: Fontana, reprinted 1966).
13 In *Le Petit Bottin des lettres et des arts* (Paris: Giraud, 1886), p. 98: 'MIRBEAU (Octave). A défendu l'impressionisme, secoué les cabotins et les paltoquets de lettres.'
14 *La Justice* was Clemenceau's left-wing newspaper, on which Geffroy was an early collaborator.
15 Part of this correspondence has been published: 'Lettres à Claude Monet', *Les Cahiers d'Aujourd'hui*, No. 9 (1922) pp. 161–76.
16 'Sur M. Félix Vallotton', [Preface to the catalogue of an] *Exposition de peintures de Félix Vallotton . . . 10 au 22 Janvier 1910* (Paris: Galerie E. Druet, 1910), p. 4.
17 See G. Geffroy, 'Octave Mirbeau et les artistes', *La Dépêche de Toulouse*, 23 February 1917. A more recent article has gone part way to reconstructing Mirbeau's eminence in the artistic life of late nineteenth-century France: F. Cachin, 'Un Défenseur oublié de l'art moderne', *L'Oeil*, June 1962, pp. 50–5 and 75.
18 Mirbeau's library contained French translations of Büchner, Darwin and Spencer, as well as original editions of the works of Guyau.
19 H. Mondor, *Vie de Mallarmé* (Paris: Gallimard, 1941), p. 530.
20 See 'Lettres à Claude Monet', *op. cit.*
21 *L'Abbé Jules* (Paris: Fayard, 1904 edition), p. 102.
22 *Ibid.*, p. 16.
23 *Ibid.*, p. 101.
24 A. Adès, 'Octave Mirbeau à Cheverchemont', *Les Nouvelles Littéraires*, No. 589 (27 January 1934).
25 See J. Montérier, 'Symbolisme et anarchie', *Revue d'Histoire Littéraire de la France*, April 1965, pp. 233–8.
26 See F. Fénéon, *Oeuvres plus que complètes* (Genève: Droz, 1970), vol. 1, pp. lviii–lxvi and 222–36; vol. 2, pp. 910–42.
27 'Kervilahouen', *La Revue Indépendante*, January 1887, pp. 25–8.
28 When Fénéon was tried on suspicion of anarchist activities in 1894, Mirbeau wrote two articles in Fénéon's defence: 'Félix Fénéon', *Le Journal*, 29 April 1894, and 'Potins!', *Le Journal*, 7 May 1894.
29 *L'Abbé Jules*, p. 102.
30 *Les Temps Nouveaux, Supplément Littéraire* (hereafter *T.N.(S.L.)*), No. 38 (January 1897), No. 46 (March 1897) and No. 47 (March 1897).
31 See Jean Grave, *Le Mouvement libertaire sous la 3e République* (Paris: Les Oeuvres Représentatives, 1930), p. 71.
32 *Ibid.*, p. 88.
33 The offices of *La Révolte* were raided many times by the police, especially in 1894, and very little of the confiscated material ever found its way back. Reasons of security and space also obliged Grave to destroy large quantities of documents himself.
34 Kropotkin, *op. cit.*, p. 34.
35 E.g. Jean Grave, 'Soyons logiques', *Le Libertaire*, No. 18 (14 March 1896): 'Le suffrage universel est un moyen d'étouffer l'initiative individuelle que nous proclamons et que nous devons, bien au contraire, chercher à développer de toutes nos forces.'

36 *T.N.*, No. 48 (26 March 1898). Even after Grave had written his own abstentionist manifesto, *Si j'avais à parler aux électeurs* (1902), he continued to reprint Mirbeau's article in large quantities, notably in an edition of 40,000 in 1902. H. Zoccolli tells us that the article was translated into many different languages: *Die Anarchie* (Leipzig: Maas & Van Suchtelen, 1909), pp. 383-4. Sébastien Faure continued to use it even after Mirbeau's death. See Appendix for full text.
37 At Mirbeau's death in 1917, his two police dossiers (BA/1190 and EA/52) contained no fewer than 180 separate documents. (Bureau des Archives et du Musée, Préfecture de Police, Paris— B.A.M.P.P.)
38 Kropotkin, *op. cit.*, p. 27.
39 In a letter to Geffroy, dated 31 December 1888, Mirbeau wrote with typical self-denigration: 'Mon roman est commencé, et c'est infiniment idiot' (F.G.B.A.).
40 *Cf.* particularly the pessimistic letter to Mallarmé (May/June 1889), quoted in Mondor, *op. cit.*, pp. 553-4.
41 See Herbert, *op. cit.*, p. 23. An interesting sidelight on Mirbeau's time in Levallois-Perret, hot-bed of anarchist activity, is that it was here in 1931 that the parisian authorities chose the street which bears Mirbeau's name. It is a narrow, untidy and insignificant street, lying now within the Paris boundary, not far from the rue Rivay where Mirbeau lived in 1889. Ironically, the street was formerly the rue de la Révolte, and it runs parallel to the rue Louise Michel. Mirbeau's 'memorial' is thus closely linked, whether by design or coincidence, with the nineteenth-century anarchist movement in Paris.
42 Vindex, 'Bibliothèque anarchiste', *T.N.*, No. 22 (28 September 1895).
43 *La Guerre* (Bruxelles: Bibliothèque des Temps Nouveaux, [c. 1903]).
44 'Prélude', *Le Figaro*, 14 July 1889. Reproduced in *La Révolte*, No. 45 (27 July 1889), and again later, in pamphlet form, with 'La Grève des électeurs' in 1902.
45 On 2 July 1889 Mirbeau wrote to Geffroy: 'Je ne puis rester plus longtemps dans cet enfer . . .' (F.G.B.A.).
46 'La Grande Kermesse', *Le Figaro*, 18 July 1889. Reprinted in *La Révolte (S.L.)*, No. 6 (19 October 1889).
47 *Ibid.*
48 Mondor, *op. cit.*, pp. 553-4.
49 That Mirbeau intended the Jesuit college to be seen as a microcosm of society is clear from the following passage: 'Les collèges sont des univers en petit. Ils renferment, réduits à leur expression d'enfance, les mêmes dominations, les mêmes écrasements que les sociétés les plus despotiquement organisées.' *Sébastien Roch* (Paris: Fayard, 1913 edition), p. 32.
50 In 1902, in reply to an *enquête* on education conducted by the *Revue Blanche*, Mirbeau wrote of his own Jesuit education: 'De cette éducation qui ne repose que sur le mensonge et sur la peur, j'ai conservé très longtemps toutes les terreurs de la morale catholique. Et c'est après beaucoup de luttes, au prix d'efforts douloureux, que je suis parvenu à me libérer de ces superstitions abominables, par quoi, on enchaîne l'esprit de l'enfant, pour mieux dominer l'homme plus tard. Je n'ai qu'une haine au coeur, mais elle est profonde et vivace: la haine de l'éducation religieuse.' *La Revue Blanche*, 1 June 1902, p. 175.
51 See J. Maitron, *Histoire du mouvement anarchiste en France, 1880-1914* (Paris: Société Universitaire d'Edition et de Librairie, second edition 1955), pp. 469-71.
52 *Sébastien Roch*, p. 121.
53 *Ibid.*, p. 99.
54 *Ibid.*
55 *Ibid.*, p. 100.
56 *Ibid.*, pp. 103-4. Such criticism of public philanthropy was a favourite anarchist

theme, and one which Mirbeau was later to develop into a full-scale play, *Le Foyer* (1908).
57 *Sébastien Roch*, p. 121.
58 Paul Claudel (himself not unsympathetic towards anarchism at this time) may well have been influenced by the Sébastien–Bolorec duality in the creation of his remarkably similar pair Simon Agnel–Cébès in *Tête d'or* (the proofs of which Mirbeau read in 1892). I am indebted to Professor G. F. A. Gadoffre of Manchester University for pointing out this striking resemblance.
59 On Mirbeau's friendship with Goncourt, see Schwarz, *op. cit.*, pp. 67–74, and *id.*, 'Une Amitié ignorée: Edmond de Goncourt—Octave Mirbeau', *The French Review*, Special Issue No. 2 (winter 1971), pp. 97–105.
60 *La Révolte (S.L.)*, No. 34 (10 May 1890), No. 36 (24 May 1890) and No. 40 (21 June 1890).

Chapter III
From the 'social question' to the defence of anarchism (1891–3)

> Je ne crois qu'à une organisation individualiste. Sous quelque étiquette que l'Etat se présente et fonctionne, il est funeste à l'activité humaine et dégradant: car il empêche l'individu de se développer dans son sens normal.
>
> (Mirbeau, in *L'Ermitage*, 1893)

The literary interest in the popular cause, dating back to the naturalists, took on a more precise form in the 1890s as a result of the pre-eminence of the social question. Urban themes, increasingly popular in art,[1] proliferated in works of literature; suggestions for social reform and overt political discussions were worked into many plays and poems, whilst the steady flow of literature depicting the plight of the working classes showed no sign of abating. Zola, Rosny, Descaves, Ajalbert, Verhaeren, Richepin, Eekhoud, Adam, Curel and Jullien were some of the leading novelists, poets and playwrights whose works reflect the importance of the social question in late nineteenth-century France—few writers, in fact, remained totally unaffected.[2] Some, like Anatole France, were actually drawn out of their aesthetic aloofness to society by the intensity of this intellectual interest in the social question.[3] Mirbeau was by no means alone in his critical view of the principles which still controlled French society at that time; in his deepening preoccupation with socialist theory, and particularly with its extreme expression—anarchism—Mirbeau was simply one of many artists and writers whose idealism looked beyond the evils of contemporary social organisation to a world in which the faults they analysed and criticised would be done away.

In an important article published in *La Plume*'s special number on socialist literature in 1891, the symbolist writer and anarchist sympathiser André Veidaux placed Mirbeau, along with Zola, Cladel and Richepin, in the forefront of the movement towards a socially-conscious literature and wrote: 'L'ironie superbe de Mirbeau flagelle parmi les plus triomphants des trissotins de la bourgeoisie.'[4] And in thus pin-pointing Mirbeau's satirical opposition to the middle class as his contribution to the discussion of the social question, Veidaux was also putting his finger on the essential element of Mirbeau's anarchism at this time. Like the terrorists who were soon to follow, Mirbeau's opposition to the bourgeois republic and his attacks against the fabric of society were initially negative, a means of clearing the ground before a new start could be made—as Veidaux concluded, with reference to Mirbeau and his like: 'Ce sont ces pionniers infatigables, ces critiques d'élite, qui préparent la Révolution prochaine.'[5]

Mirbeau's individualism had manifested itself first in his refusal to submit to discipline, and later in his 'revolutionary' taste in art; it had motivated even his political gropings, for Mirbeau, reactionary or revolutionary, always supported the opposition or the minority, by instinct; and now in 1891 his anarchism, directed and modified by contact with the theories of Kropotkin and Reclus, was finding clearer expression in the social criticism which all his works contained. Lucien Descaves, himself not unsympathetic to anarchist philosophy at this time, styled Mirbeau 'mon ami Octave Mirbeau ouvreur de brèches',[6] and it was evidently Mirbeau's work as an iconoclast which endeared him to Descaves as well as to the anarchists, who gladly reprinted his work.

In four short years Mirbeau had established himself as one of the leading *hommes de lettres* of his day.[7] His first three novels, written in quick succession, had earned him the reputation of a fearless and stylish exponent of left-wing ideas, and he was now able to sit back and enjoy the quiet seclusion of his country home on the banks of the Seine, tending his flowers, trying his hand at painting, receiving his friends, reading widely—especially scientific and sociological textbooks—and only occasionally making a sortie into the capital. It seems that he had put so much of himself into his first three novels that, for the moment, he had nothing further to offer except the articles by which he earned his daily bread. It would appear though that in February 1892 he was working on a fourth novel, and Goncourt's diary contains an echo of the difficulties Mirbeau was experiencing with it.[8] In fact, it was not until 1899 that his next novel *Le Jardin des supplices* appeared in print. It was not only that Mirbeau had exhausted his source of literary inspiration but also that during the years between *Sébastien Roch* and *Le Jardin des supplices* his polemical opposition to society became so intense that he was unable to create a sustained and coherent work of fiction, and he was obliged to fall back heavily on his talents as a journalist. From 1891 to 1898 we need to consult Mirbeau's personal letters and to examine in detail the ephemeral articles into which he poured his burning convictions if we wish to recreate a picture of his attitude to the political and social conditions of the waning century.

Mirbeau's literary silence during his years at Pont-de-l'Arche and later at Carrières-sous-Poissy, where he moved early in 1893, did not mean, however, that he had cut himself off entirely from the world of creative art and from the literary activity of Paris. His celebrated article on Maeterlinck (August 1890), his attendance at the inauguration of a statue in honour of Flaubert in Rouen (November 1890), his attendance at the Moréas banquet (February 1891), his defence of Goncourt against the unwarranted criticisms of Robert de Bonnières (March 1891), and his successful efforts to help Gauguin realise his dream of emigrating to the South Seas,[9] are examples which illustrate how even in voluntary isolation Mirbeau was able to keep his finger on the pulse of the artistic life of France.

Mirbeau's time at Pont-de-l'Arche was, however, characterised most by his idealistic reflections on social organisation and reform. When Jules Huret came to Les Damps in 1891 to interview Mirbeau in the course of the celebrated *Enquête sur l'évolution littéraire*, Mirbeau at first appeared critical of and cynical about contemporary literature;[10] but in a letter to Huret after his visit, when Mirbeau had had more time to think, he toned down his cynicism and expressed the belief that literature, and art in general too, could and would become great again if only it became socially conscious:

> Oui, mon cher ami, l'art doit être socialiste, s'il veut être grand. Car qu'est-ce que cela nous fait les petites histoires d'amour de M. Marcel Prévost, et ses petites combinaisons. Ce n'est plus rien, c'est de la marchandise, comme des balles de coton, des caques de harengs; encore ces marchandises-là sont utiles, et celles de M. Marcel Prévost ne sont utiles à rien, puisqu'elles n'évoquent aucune beauté, aucune pensée, aucune lueur . . .[11]

Mirbeau's criticisms of the type of literature represented by the novels of Marcel Prévost had already been expressed in a full-length article which the anarchists endorsed sufficiently to reprint: 'Amour, amour'. The article showed quite clearly how Mirbeau associated the sorry state of French literature with the decadence of society in general; Mirbeau expressed his regret that literature was not progressing in step with the sciences; he criticised the public for demanding silly love-stories instead of ideological and thought-provoking literature; and deploring the infrequency of works of art with sociological themes, he added: 'Des oeuvres comme *Germinal*, où Zola nous montre le terrible et étrange fantôme de la question sociale, sont rares'. Literature, concluded Mirbeau, must therefore undergo a transformation: it must shake off the prejudice which had held it back for so long, and it must play its part in the regeneration of society, which he went on to describe in the following grimly prophetic words: 'Nous sommes à une période historique et probablement à la veille de grandes transformations . . . des événements se préparent, plus considérables qu'aucun de ceux qui se sont accomplis dans le passé.'[12] Mirbeau was thus suggesting that a literature of social utility would help to prepare humanity to face the upheavals which the progress of the sciences would produce in the not too distant future.

In replying to Huret's *Enquête* that literature needed to become increasingly orientated towards the discussion of social problems, Mirbeau was by no means a voice in the wilderness. J.-H. Rosny *aîné* suggested that literature could be renewed only by a wider comprehension of the social evolution of society and by an awareness of scientific and industrial progress.[13] Gustave Geffroy also told Huret that he thought it possible that literature would become socialistic, and even went so far as to suggest that Mirbeau might turn out to be one of the leaders of such a movement.[14] Others like Paul Bonnetain expressed similar ideas in their replies to Huret, and many of those who were interviewed spoke of Mirbeau as an outstanding writer. The extent of Mirbeau's reputation, particularly as a socially-conscious writer, can be seen from the frequency with which his name recurred during Huret's interviews, and also from the way in which Mirbeau's own reply to Huret was given prominence in *La Plume's* special number on 'socialist' literature in May 1891.

Mirbeau had developed his conviction that literature and art had a vital role to play in the life of society from his own interpretation of the social philosophers he had spent so much time reading in the quietness of his home in Pont-de-l'Arche. It is difficult to say whether Guyau's *L'Art au point de vue sociologique* (1889) or certain chapters of Kropotkin's *Paroles d'un révolté* had the greater influence on him at this time, or whether this honour fell to the small, sociologically-orientated literary magazines like *L'Ermitage* and *Les Entretiens Politiques et Littéraires*, which Mirbeau avidly devoured during his leisure moments.[15] It is probable that none of these, in fact, had as great an influence on him as Jean Grave's *La Révolte* and its literary supplement, which Mirbeau had been receiving for some time already in 1891.

In this cleverly-produced anarchist propaganda journal Jean Grave gave evidence of his brilliant gifts as a newspaper editor and publisher. *La Révolte* contained well-written, interesting material, and all its news, opinion and theory was highly readable. The literary supplement, containing many of the same ideas in literary form, came as the icing on the cake. There can be no doubt that Jean Grave and his newspapers made a deep impression on Mirbeau, who found himself at one with Grave on so many points as he familiarised himself, by means of *La Révolte*, with the philosophy of the extreme Left.[16]

The subject matter of Mirbeau's regular articles in the daily press was becoming increasingly radical as a result of his reading, and he himself was now indulging in a kind of voluntary propaganda for doctrines of the most extreme variety. Articles like 'Les Abandonnés',[17] in which a socialist mayor of a small village tries to organise the poor into a communal anarchist family, and 'Jean Tartas',[18] in which we meet an anarchist philosopher who tirades against the legal system and against capitalist society, are two examples which indicate Mirbeau's growing preoccupation with anarchist ideology. Such was the extent to which Mirbeau saturated himself with it in fact, that even in an article on the vexed question of hunting rights Mirbeau's anarchism breathes through every line when he writes in defence of the poacher: 'Je connais le braconnier, et je l'aime, comme j'aime tous les révoltés . . . Les forêts de l'Etat sont un patrimoine commun, le braconnier en possède une parcelle au même titre que le chasseur riche.'[19] Jean Grave's approving comment on this article—'Cette page sur le braconnier nous paraît admirable'—shows how there was much common ground between him and Mirbeau even before they met.

Mirbeau's sympathy for the working classes, and his conviction that capitalist society would one day give way, perhaps violently, to a better, freer, and more harmonious world, were demonstrated in his declaration of solidarity with the proletarian gatherings on May-day 1891. The year 1890 had seen the first international socialist demonstrations on the day which was to become traditionally the workers' day, and in 1891 the newspaper *La Bataille* sent its reporters out to seek the opinions of likely sympathisers. Mirbeau's reply was a clear statement of his revolutionary philosophy:

> Rien ne peut plus arrêter le mouvement social vers la destruction de l'oligarchie autoritaire et capitaliste. Si peu que la science ait encore pénétré dans les masses populaires, elle a cependant assez projeté de lumière pour montrer à tous la disproportion monstrueuse qui existe entre ce que nous pouvons, ce que nous devons être, et ce que nous sommes. Le jour où les travailleurs . . . seront unis dans une pensée de défense commune—et ce jour approche . . .—il n'y a pas d'armées, si nombreuses et disciplinées soient-elles, qui puissent empêcher ce qui doit arriver. Pour qui réfléchit, pour qui ose entrevoir l'avenir, le 1er mai est destiné à devenir, une année ou l'autre, une date primordiale dans l'évolution de l'humanité.[20]

The suggestion of violence and the reference to armed troops are no doubt allusions to the disturbances at Fourmies during the May-day demonstrations there. The left-wing press deplored the savageness of the repression which had been exhibited, and of course such reactionary brutality was all grist to the propaganda mill.

The authorities did not, however, take all the criticism which was levelled at them lying down. An anonymous article entitled 'Viande à mitraille', which appeared in *La Révolte* of May, and which exhorted soldiers like those sent to Fourmies to refuse to fire on innocent people, was pursued by the law with extreme vigour, so that Jean Grave, as editor of the paper in which the article appeared, was put on trial and found guilty of incitement of the armed forces to rebellion. The severity of the sentence—Grave was jailed for six months—indicates how sensitive the authorities were becoming at this time, and it also shows just how close Mirbeau, with his talk of a violent transformation of society, was himself coming to falling foul of the administrators of law and order.

It was from his prison cell in Sainte-Pélagie, in July 1891, that Grave wrote to Mirbeau about a quarrel he was having with the Société des Gens de Lettres. Grave had been deliberately careful to seek prior permission from most of the authors he reprinted in his literary supplement, and yet in the summer of 1891 the Société des Gens de Lettres saw fit to file an action against Grave claiming payment for his use of copyright material. The letter which Grave wrote to Mirbeau on this subject is the earliest in the surviving correspondence between them,[21] and the confidence with which Grave placed his case before Mirbeau indicates the faith he had in Mirbeau's sympathy. Grave made no bones about asking for Mirbeau's help in the form of an article which might bring public attention to his plight:

> . . . vous savez que notre pauvre *Révolte*, toute seule, a bien peu d'échos. Je viens vous demander, si vous croyez que le bon droit soit de notre côté, si vous pourriez porter la question dans la grande presse?[22]

In this first serious test of his sympathy towards the anarchist cause, Mirbeau was not found wanting. In one of the most eloquent and convincing articles which he ever wrote, Mirbeau outlined the dispute between Grave and the Société des Gens de Lettres, praising the former for his generous intellect, and reproaching the latter for its meanness and stupidity. Mirbeau's praise for *La Révolte* shows how much he now based his own anarchism on rational, scientific ideas and not on the sentimentalism of the Abbé Jules, nor on the fanatical sectarian prejudices of the terrorists, for he wrote in *L'Echo de Paris*:

> *La Révolte* est l'organe le plus indépendant, le plus pur des doctrines anarchistes, un

organe d'action, oui; mais aussi un organe d'idées qui ne se perd pas dans le vague des sentimentalités, ni dans l'inconsciente brutalité des provocations inutiles et des coups de main hasardeux. Il sait où il va, il va droit son chemin. Il est très au fait de la philosophie, de la science moderne, et s'inspire de leurs découvertes, de leurs applications «morales» pour préparer la venue d'une société nouvelle, normale, basée non plus sur le mensonge et l'arbitraire, mais sur la raison et la justice.

Mirbeau based his defence of *La Révolte* on the value of its contribution to the improvement of society; he reserved his bitter sarcasm for the society which made such an important work appear to be a criminal offence, and concluding in favour of Grave and *La Révolte*, Mirbeau added:

Il va de soi que la *Révolte* est de ces personnes et de ces Idées qui sont, à l'avance, vouées à toutes les rigueurs de la Justice. Mais ni M. Montagne, ni la Justice n'en seront plus riches pour cela, car, comme le disait gaiement M. Grave: «Là où il n'y a rien, le diable perd ses droits».[23]

The article was, in fact, so biased in favour of the anarchists that Grave at first expressed unwillingness to reprint it in his literary supplement.[24] But he was naturally very grateful to Mirbeau for responding to his appeal, and he kept him closely informed of the new developments in the affair. In his first letter of thanks Grave told Mirbeau how he had received a reply from Zola, retracting permission to reprint his work on the grounds that such permission had been granted prior to his membership of the Société des Gens de Lettres, of which he was now president. Zola's *volte-face* gave Grave good reason for including him in the reproaches he levelled at the Société des Gens de Lettres, which he described to Mirbeau as 'cette association de gribouilleurs rétrogrades qui envisagent la littérature comme un commerce d'épicerie'.[25] Grave, still serving his six-month jail sentence, also told Mirbeau that he was not afraid to face the possibility of a longer spell in prison if it would serve to unmask the venality and pettiness of this group of writers.

Mirbeau replied to Grave's letter in the following terms:

Non, l'article n'est pas trop élogieux; il est ce que vraiment je pense de votre oeuvre, du courage, de l'intelligence et de la foi que vous mettez à la défendre. J'aurais voulu mieux faire, mais je l'ai écrit cet article, dans un mauvais moment . . . la question n'est pas épuisée. Comptez que je serai toujours avec vous.

And with reference to the Société des Gens de Lettres, Mirbeau added: 'On les sent tout de même embarrassés. Peut-être n'oseront-ils pas poursuivre. Cela vaudrait mieux, car vous avez autre chose à faire que de passer votre vie en prison.'[26]

It was in this letter, too, that Mirbeau revealed that *La Révolte* was not the only anarchist journal he read and admired, for in a postscript he asked Grave: 'Est-il indécent de vous demander qui fait le *Père Peinard*? Je trouve cela curieux, très bien fait, d'une saveur rude.' *Le Père Peinard*, founded in 1889 by Emile Pouget, was written in an altogether different style from Grave's more sophisticated journal. The sub-title of Pouget's paper was 'les reflecs d'un gniaff', its cover showed an old cobbler in various attitudes of defiance, and it was written entirely in slang. It was very much the anarchist 'workers' rag'; but it appealed to Mirbeau by its directness and because of its fearless and virulent criticisms of the State, the army, the judiciary and the clergy. The deliberate coarseness of its approach was akin to Mirbeau's calculated recourse to obscenity and over exaggeration: both Pouget and Mirbeau intended to degrade the objects of their criticism by drowning them in a flood of abuse.

In his next letter to Mirbeau, Grave answered the enquiry about *Le Père Peinard*, gave a short résumé of Pouget's career as an anarchist, and mentioned one or two of his leading collaborators on the paper. Referring to the dispute with the Société des Gens de Lettres, Grave said he was more hopeful of the outcome. The publicity given to the affair by Mirbeau's article had begun a vigorous discussion of the question in the press, and Grave had especially noted an interview given by Henry Becque, 'qui n'est pas tendre pour la Société des Gens de Lettres', and which gave him reason for optimism: 'Allons, l'affaire se dessine on ne peut mieux. Je pense que le coup aura été rude pour la société, et Zola apprendra qu'on ne goûte aux honneurs qu'en y laissant un peu de dignité!'[27] It appears from this letter, and also from Grave's later memoirs, that another of Mirbeau's friends, Jean Ajalbert, himself a novelist of no mean reputation, who also happened to be a barrister, had expressed his willingness to defend Grave in the approaching court case. In a further letter Grave related to Mirbeau how Ajalbert had succeeded in having the case put back until the end of October, and expressed his confidence that the Société des Gens de Lettres would be morally routed. Grave was clearly not unaware of the debt he owed to Mirbeau for the strength of his position, for he wrote: 'il est même probable que, sans vous, [la presse] ne s'en serait pas occupée, encore une fois, merci.'[28] Indeed, the storm of protest and the wave of sympathy for *La Révolte* which was sparked off by Mirbeau and which filled the French press for many weeks, was directly instrumental in causing the Société des Gens de Lettres to withdraw its legal action and thus concede a moral defeat at the hands of the anarchist journal and its intrepid editor, who had won his case from a prison cell.

It was while Grave was in prison, between July and December 1891, that he began grouping together into book form various articles which had previously appeared in *La Révolte*. When he had partially completed the manuscript he sent it to Reclus and, as Kropotkin had done in a similar situation in 1885, asked Reclus to write a preface. Reclus replied that he was not 'assez entraîné' to write a preface, and that all he could do was to suggest the title: *La Société mourante et l'anarchie*. The sympathy which Mirbeau had shown over the dispute between Grave and the Société des Gens de Lettres caused Grave to think immediately of asking Mirbeau to write the preface for his book, and Mirbeau's enthusiastic response gave him reason once again to be grateful, as he noted in his memoirs: 'Je me retournai du côté de Mirbeau, et lui demandai de bien vouloir s'en charger. Il ne se fit nullement prier et accepta tout de suite, d'une façon tout à fait encourageante et gracieuse.'[29] As things turned out, Grave had to wait almost eighteen months before his book appeared in print with Mirbeau's preface in June 1893; but, as he himself admitted, it was worth waiting for: 'Quant à la préface, il tint parole. Elle était magnifique.'[30]

The main reason for the delay was Mirbeau's poor state of health. The eighteen months which passed from Mirbeau's promise to write Grave's preface until the fulfilment of that pledge were some of the unhappiest of Mirbeau's life. The severe winter of 1891, which he spent in his large and draughty country house, did not improve the feverish colds and rheumatic pains which now increasingly afflicted and depressed him. The destruction of his valuable flowers and shrubs, which he looked upon as his children,[31] only added to his gloom, for he spent much time and money on his gardens, and his moods often mirrored the success or failure of his horticultural efforts. It seems too that the relationship between Mirbeau and his wife, who was a rather tyrannical woman, and who ultimately confirmed Mirbeau in his misogyny, was steadily deteriorating.[32] There were difficulties also with the servants;[33] and Pissarro—a frequent visitor to Les Damps—made reference in one of his letters to Grave to the trouble which Mirbeau was having with his knee.[34] Mirbeau was on the verge of a breakdown when he wrote in October 1892, by way of apology to Grave about the delay with his preface:

> Ne m'en veuillez pas de mon silence. Vous ne pouvez comprendre, je ne comprends pas moi-même ce que j'ai, et quelle crise d'affreuse tristesse, sans cause, je traverse, depuis près d'un an. Je ne fais plus rien . . . plus rien . . . Et pourtant je ne suis pas paresseux. Je suis malade.[35]

Yet Mirbeau, in his brighter moments, was still as keen as ever to write the preface for *La Société mourante*. When he had read the manuscript for the first time he wrote to Grave:

> ... j'ai lu, très sérieusement, votre livre. Je le trouve très bien; d'une abondance et d'une logique admirable.
> Rien ne me heurte dans vos idées, et je serai très heureux de dire, dans une préface, ce que je pense de vous, et des idées que vous représentez.

And in an attempt to convince Grave of his enthusiasm and of his willingness, Mirbeau added:

> Ce que je trouve d'unique dans votre livre, c'est qu'il est impossible d'y relever une faute de logique; et c'est plein de clarté! ...
> Excusez-moi encore, et comptez sur moi. Je suis votre ami.[36]

In spite of the delay in publication which resulted from Mirbeau's incapacity, Grave showed himself very patient and understanding. In reply to Mirbeau he wrote: 'C'est à moi à m'excuser d'être venu vous troubler dans vos préoccupations et votre travail. Je pensais bien que votre silence était motivé par une cause sérieuse à vous personnelle ...'[37] The months that followed saw an exchange of letters concerning various details of the content, format and possible publisher of the book,[38] and soon the epistolary acquaintance between Mirbeau and Grave blossomed into friendship. Although they had still never met in person they began, in 1892, to address one another as 'mon cher ami', and it was on this subject that Mirbeau wrote to Grave:

> Si j'accepte ce titre? Je crois bien que je l'accepte, et de grand coeur, je vous assure. Et j'espère bien que ce titre d'ami que nous nous donnons mutuellement, nous le rendrons plus fort par une connaissance meilleure et prochaine de nous-mêmes.

And referring to *La Société mourante*, to which Grave wanted to add three more chapters, Mirbeau continued:

> Vous avez raison d'ajouter ces chapitres; et aussi celui de l'Influence des Milieux. Cela corsera encore davantage votre livre, et lui donnera même encore plus d'unité. De cette façon, il sera tout à fait complet: un vrai manuel des doctrines anarchistes.[39]

Mirbeau's assurances to Grave were not however able to make him produce the long-awaited preface; and Grave had still received only promises when, in April 1892, he found himself once more in prison—this time on the pretext of an unpaid fine. As always though, Grave sought to turn the situation to profit, and remembering the way in which Mirbeau had drawn the attention of the press to his affair with the Société des Gens de Lettres, Grave wrote to Mirbeau once more to give him a detailed description of the harrowing conditions prevailing in the prison depot, in the hope that Mirbeau might be able to work it into an article on *L'Echo de Paris*.[40] Mirbeau, perhaps feeling a little guilty about his delay over Grave's preface, obliged within only a few days, for his next article, 'Les Petits Martyrs', contained extensive quotations from the text of Grave's letter. This article, complying as it did with Grave's implied request, and containing severe criticisms of the hypocritical philanthropists like Jules Simon, who pretended that such terrible prison conditions as those described by Grave did not exist, demonstrated quite clearly that Mirbeau, in spite of the non-appearance of his preface for Grave's book, was still very much at one with anarchist philosophy. Indeed his own conclusions in this article tallied perfectly with Grave's, for Mirbeau wrote with reference to society: 'C'est contre elle qu'il faudrait déployer toutes les énergies d'une lutte sans merci, au lieu de s'ingénier à la consolider, à la hérisser de défenses meurtrières et d'homicides lois.'[41]

Though Grave's book did not appear in print as soon as he had hoped, the year 1892 saw another important anarchist publication: *La Conquête du pain* by Kropotkin, which was published in France in April of that year, and which soon attained world-wide circulation, making many friends for the anarchist cause by the sincerity of its tone and the logic of its arguments.[42] Its publication also offset some of the adverse publicity which the Ravachol affair was bringing the anarchists at this time. Both Mirbeau and his friend Pissarro read Kropotkin's book and were touched by it. Pissarro wrote to Mirbeau in the summer of 1892:

> I have just read the book of Kropotkin. I must confess that, if it is utopian, it is in any case a beautiful dream. And, as we have often had the example of utopias which have become realities, nothing prevents us from believing that this may well be possible one day, unless man founders and returns to complete barbarism.[43]

Pissarro and Mirbeau often discussed anarchist ideology during the painter's regular visits to Les Damps; and the execution of Ravachol, whom Mirbeau had discussed in an article which he sent for publication to Zo d'Axa's *L'Endehors*, would no doubt be a talking-point for the two friends during Pissarro's protracted stay at Pont-de-l'Arche in September 1892. Meanwhile, it seems, Grave had been trying, unsuccessfully, to get in touch with Mirbeau to bring up the question of the preface once again. He had written four times without reply, and when he turned up at Les Damps in search of his manuscript he was informed that Mirbeau was not in, even though Grave had deliberately written to say he would be coming.[44] In desperation Grave wrote to Pissarro, knowing that the artist often visited Mirbeau, and within a few days he received a reply from Mirbeau, in which Mirbeau apologised profusely for Grave's inconvenience, and blamed the maid for playing tricks on them all. Grave was so relieved to hear from Mirbeau—he thought Mirbeau might have lost the manuscript and might be afraid to tell him!—that he was willing to blame the postal service for the apparent non-arrival of his earlier letters, and regretted any rudeness he might have exhibited. The endangered friendship was thus rescued at the eleventh hour, and Pissarro seems to have played his part as go-between in this bizarre and unsatisfactory affair.[45]

During all this difficult period, however, Mirbeau continued to produce his regular weekly articles for *L'Echo de Paris*, and occasionally for *Le Figaro*, though he terminated his collaboration on the latter in October 1892. His articles betrayed the depression through which he was passing; and yet, though they were often marred by the effects of his physical and mental strain—his exacerbated criticisms of society became unbearably nihilistic at times—his articles still revealed his idealistic and utopian sympathy with the revolutionary cause, and his articles were still very suitable material for reprinting in the anarchist press.

Mirbeau's state of mind and body seem to have improved after his removal early in 1893 to the Clos St-Blaise at Poissy. An operation on his troublesome knee in April of that year, and the return of the warmer weather, also helped to dispel for the time being at least the unpleasant memories of the previous months, and he began to think seriously of fulfilling his promise to Grave. Even while he was still at Les Damps, he wrote to Grave in more optimistic mood: 'Cher ami, / Je vais vous envoyer la *Préface* ces jours-ci. / J'espère qu'elle vous plaira.' And he was able to speak of his mental and physical trouble as a thing of the past: 'Excusez-moi, de ces longs retards. J'ai passé par d'affreuses douleurs, qui m'enlevaient jusqu'au pouvoir de me distraire d'elles en travaillant.'[46]

In April 1893, Mirbeau was informed by Pissarro that *La Société mourante* had been accepted for publication by Stock, and the writing of the preface became his immediate preoccupation. It was finished by May, and it more than compensated Grave for the length of time he had had to wait. In six pages Mirbeau expressed the concern of a whole generation of intellectuals over the state of contemporary society, and showed just what it was in anarchist ideology that appealed to so many of his fellow writers and artists, and caused them to believe that the anarchists had the answer to the perplexing social question.

The preface was cast in the form of a dialogue between the author and a friend, and this provided Mirbeau with a convenient means of presenting certain arguments in a more logical form.[47] The author's friend, like Mirbeau himself, aspired to what was simple, great and beautiful, but he was often hindered by the prejudices which his education had impressed upon his personality. Like Mirbeau too, he was preoccupied with anarchist ideology, and could see, unlike many people, that it did not consist solely of blowing things to pieces:

> Il y entrevoit, au contraire, dans un brouillard que se dissipera, peut-être, des formes harmoniques et des beautés; et il s'y intéresse comme à une chose qu'on aimerait, une chose un peu terrible encore, et qu'on redoute parce qu'on ne la comprend pas bien.[48]

It was because the author's friend did not entirely understand certain aspects of anarchist doctrine that he and the author often discussed the question of anarchism in an attempt to resolve the problems. The author's friend was evidently well-read on the theoretical side—and here Mirbeau was revealing, albeit indirectly, the main sources of his own knowledge of the subject—for the preface explains:

> Mon ami a lu les admirables livres de Kropotkine, les éloquentes, ferventes et savantes protestations d'Elisée Reclus, contre l'impiété des gouvernements et des sociétés basées sur le crime. De Bakounine, il connaît ce que les journaux anarchistes, çà et là, en ont publié. Il a travaillé l'inégal Proudhon et l'aristocratique Spencer. Enfin, récemment, les déclarations d'Etiévant l'ont ému.[49]

The preface continued with an attempt by the author to resolve some of the uncertainties in the mind of his friend, and put forward Grave's new book as a manual of anarchist thought which his friend could not possibly misunderstand:

> Ce livre est un chef-d'oeuvre de logique. Il est plein de lumière. Ce livre n'est point le cri du sectaire aveugle et borné; ce n'est point, non plus, le coup de tam-tam du propagandiste ambitieux; c'est l'oeuvre pesée, pensée, raisonnée, d'un passionné, il est vrai, d'un «qui a la foi», mais qui sait, compare, discute, analyse, et qui, avec une singulière clairvoyance de critique, évolue parmi les faits de l'histoire sociale, les leçons de la science, les problèmes de la philosophie, pour aboutir aux conclusions infrangibles que vous savez et dont vous ne pouvez nier ni la grandeur, ni la justice.

Grave's book, made up of twenty-two chapters covering all aspects of anarchist philosophy, left no stone unturned in its attempt to provide a clear and comprehensive guide to anarchism. The development of anarchist theory, the problems of its relationship to practice, the nature of man, the questions of property, family, authority (legal, governmental, military and moral), of patriotism, of colonialisation, and of race relations, all these things were discussed in detail in the three hundred pages of Grave's book; no one who had read it could say that they no longer understood what anarchism really was. The friend in the preface readily admitted that he agreed with much of what Grave had to say, particularly with reference to the state:

> L'Etat pèse sur l'individu d'un poids chaque jour plus écrasant, plus intolérable. De l'homme qu'il énerve et qu'il abrutit, il ne fait qu'un paquet de chair à impôts. Sa seule mission est de vivre de lui, comme un pou vit de la bête sur laquelle il a posé ses suçoirs . . . Assassin et voleur, oui, j'ai cette conviction que l'Etat est bien ce double criminel.

The discussion between the author of the preface and his friend gave Mirbeau the opportunity to expound more than one point of view with regard to anarchist doctrine; and little by little the friend's conception of the principal theories was clarified, until, in true anarchist fashion, he was able to say:

> L'anarchie, au contraire, est la reconquête de l'individu, c'est la liberté du développement de l'individu, dans un sens normal et harmonique . . . Je sais cela . . . et je comprends pourquoi toute une jeunesse artiste et pensante,—l'élite contemporaine—regarde impatiemment se lever cette aube attendue, où elle entrevoit, non seulement, un idéal de justice, mais un idéal de beauté.

There was still one thing, however, perplexing the author's friend; and because it was the most vital and the most vexed question of all Mirbeau had deliberately left the discussion of it until the end of his preface: it was the question of the use of violence as a means of attaining a state of anarchy (i.e. absence of government). The author's friend put the problem in this way:

> —Eh bien, une chose m'inquiète et me trouble; le côté terroriste de l'anarchie. Je répugne aux moyens violents; j'ai horreur du sang et de la mort, et je voudrais que l'anarchie attendît son triomphe de la justice seule de l'avenir.

The author of the preface—now speaking clearly for Mirbeau himself—began his comments on this aspect of anarchist ideology with a question of his own: '—Croyez-vous donc . . . que les anarchistes soient des buveurs de sang?' The author, and Mirbeau himself, plainly did not believe such to be the case; and to demonstrate his confidence in the humanity of the anarchists, the author of the preface pointed to the example of Kropotkin—known as 'the gentle anarchist'—and asked again: 'Ne sentez-vous pas, au contraire, toute l'immense tendresse, tout l'immense amour de la vie, par qui le coeur d'un Kropotkine est gonflé?' Because he was convinced that the motives of the majority of the anarchists were pure and that their ultimate aims were for the good of humanity, Mirbeau was prepared to accept the inevitability of violent confrontations between the anarchists and the defenders of the traditions and institutions which they condemned. As he so often did, Mirbeau thought of this question in terms of an image from nature: the paradox of the destructive but fructifying rainstorm, which broke down large trees and yet caused the earth to bring forth in abundance; and the author of the preface concluded, within the terms of the image: 'Il ne faut pas trop, voyez-vous, s'émouvoir de la mort des chênes voraces . . .'

La Société mourante et l'anarchie was finally published, complete with Mirbeau's preface, in June 1893, at the high-water mark of the discussion of the social question in France and of the wave of sympathy of the intellectuals with the anarchist 'solution'. It was in May of the same year that *La Plume* produced its special number on anarchism, for which Mirbeau had been commissioned to write an article entitled 'L'Art et la littérature anarchiste'; and though, owing to the mounting pressure of his work, he was unable to produce it in time, the very fact that Mirbeau was asked by *La Plume* to write such an article shows how much he was then regarded as the leading intellectual anarchist sympathiser. Mirbeau had been one of the first to join this movement of sympathy; his novels, his short stories, and his articles had even helped to create it in the first place. His preface to Grave's book—an act of courage in itself, in view of the prison sentences that were being handed out liberally at that time—has even greater meaning in the context of the intellectual climate of 1893 than it does when viewed in isolation. It was very much a logical step in Mirbeau's own intellectual evolution, for the social question had become pre-eminent in his own life, and his defence of Grave, in the affair of the Société des Gens de Lettres and in the preface to *La Société mourante*, was as much a part of his social consciousness as the creative works and articles in which he expressed his own libertarian ideals and those of a growing number of his contemporaries.

Notes

1 See R. L. and E. W. Herbert, 'Artists and anarchism', *The Burlington Magazine*,

vol. 120, No. 692 (November 1960), p. 480, where it is pointed out that during the 1880s the neo-impressionists Seurat, Signac, Luce and Pissarro shifted their attention from rural to urban subjects. The same development is noticeable in Mirbeau's work, from the rural setting of the *Lettres de ma chaumière* (1885) to the industrial backcloth of *Les Mauvais Bergers* (1897).
2 See D. Knowles, *La Réaction idéaliste au théâtre depuis 1890* (Paris: Droz, 1934), pp. 408–11. 1891 seems to have been the time when Zola's socialistic 'messianism' began; *cf.* also J. Robichez, *Le Symbolisme au théâtre* (Paris: L'Arche, 1957), p. 17.
3 See J. Levaillant, *Les Aventures du scepticisme* (Paris: Colin, 1965), p. 414.
4 'De l'évolution de la philosophie et des lettres vers le socialisme', *La Plume*, No. 49 (1 May 1891), p. 143.
5 *Ibid.*
6 In the dedication of Descaves' *Les Emmurés* (1894). Descaves recounts his own contact with the anarchist movement in *Souvenirs d'un ours* (Paris: Les Editions de Paris, 1946).
7 In recognition of this fact, Goncourt added Mirbeau's name to the list for his future Academy in July 1890, in place of Zola, who was seeking election to the Académie Française.
8 Goncourt, *op. cit.*, vol. 18, p. 100. Mirbeau also mentions this fourth novel in a letter to Geffroy dated 10 February 1892 (F.G.B.A.).
9 See Mondor, *op. cit.*, pp. 589–96.
10 'La littérature? Demandez donc plutôt aux hêtres ce qu'ils en pensent.' J. Huret, *Enquête sur l'évolution littéraire* (Paris: Charpentier, 1891), p. 217.
11 *Ibid.*, p. 436.
12 'Amour, amour', *Le Figaro*, 25 July 1890. Reprinted in *La Révolte (S.L.)*, No. 47 (9 August 1890).
13 Huret, *Enquête*, p. 232.
14 *Ibid.*, pp. 238–9.
15 *Ibid.*, p. 213.
16 Fernand Vandérem also points out the influence of Jean Grave on Mirbeau at this time. *Gens de qualité* (Paris: Plon, 1938), p. 137.
17 Reprinted, from *L'Echo de Paris*, in *La Révolte (S.L.)*, No. 48 (16 August 1890).
18 Reprinted, from *L'Echo de Paris*, in *La Révolte (S.L.)*, Nos. 49 and 50 (23 and 31 August 1890).
19 'Dans la forêt', *La Révolte (S.L.)*, No. 31 (11 April 1891). Reprinted from *L'Echo de Paris*.
20 'Opinion d'Octave Mirbeau sur le 1er mai', *La Bataille*, 2 May 1891.
21 From what Grave says in his memoirs it seems certain that he and Mirbeau had already corresponded before July 1891; see Grave, *Le Mouvement libertaire*, p. 88.
22 Letter from Grave to Mirbeau, dated 21 July 1891 (Bibliothèque Publique et Universitaire de Genève—B.P.U.G.).
23 'A propos de la Société des Gens de Lettres', *L'Echo de Paris*, 3 August 1891. Reprinted in *La Révolte (S.L.)*, No. 49 (22 August 1891). See Appendix for abridged text. Montagne was the secretary of the society, and was directly responsible for the legal action.
24 Letter from Grave to Mirbeau, dated 3 August 1891 (B.P.U.G.).
25 *Ibid.*
26 Letter from Mirbeau to Grave, undated but *c.* 4–6 August 1891 (I.F.H.S.).
27 Letter from Grave to Mirbeau, dated 7 August 1891 (B.P.U.G.). It would be interesting to know to what extent Becque's attack on the Société des Gens de Lettres was motivated by his friendship with Mirbeau, who had previously taken a stand on Becque's behalf against the Académie Française. See A. Arnaoutovitch,

Henry Becque, vol. 3 (Paris: P.U.F., 1927), pp. 181 and 210–11.
28 Letter from Grave to Mirbeau, dated 22 August 1891 (B.P.U.G.).
29 *Le Mouvement libertaire*, p. 83.
30 *Ibid.*, p. 85.
31 'Mes enfants, quoi!' Letter from Mirbeau to Grave, undated but *c*. 1891 (I.F.H.S.).
32 Goncourt noted in his diary in December 1891 (*op. cit.*, vol. 18, p. 100) concerning the Mirbeau *ménage:* 'Le torchon commencerait à brûler.' The short story 'Mémoires pour un avocat', in *La Pipe de cidre* (Paris: Flammarion, 1918), written in 1894, is one of the many clear indications we have of Mirbeau's marital problems.
33 See the letter to Grave, reproduced in his *Le Mouvement libertaire*, pp. 84–5, where Mirbeau apologised to Grave, who had been turned away from Les Damps by 'cette petite fille, si sotte . . . qui nous joue, gaminement, souvent de pareils tours'.
34 Letter from Pissarro to Grave, dated 9 April 1893. C. Pissarro, *Letters to his Son Lucien* (London: Kegan Paul, 1944), p. 517.
35 Grave, *Le Mouvement libertaire*, p. 85. (Original in I.F.H.S.).
36 Letter from Mirbeau to Grave, undated but probably late 1891 (I.F.H.S.).
37 Letter from Grave to Mirbeau, undated but probably late 1891 (B.P.U.G.).
38 Mirbeau tried unsuccessfully to persuade his own publisher Charpentier to print the book.
39 Letter from Mirbeau to Grave, undated but probably early 1892 (I.F.H.S.). In this letter Mirbeau also asked Grave for the address of another leading anarchist, Charles Malato, from whom he had received a letter. Unfortunately, neither Malato's letter nor Mirbeau's reply have yet come to light.
40 Letter from Grave to Mirbeau, dated 28 April 1892 (B.P.U.G.).
41 'Les Petits Martyrs', *L'Echo de Paris*, 3 May 1892. Reprinted in *La Révolte (S.L.)*, No. 35 (28 May 1892).
42 Kropotkin's main theme in *La Conquête du pain* (Paris: Publications de *La Révolte*, 1892) was that the abolition of the ancient system of privileges would bring about the equal distribution of natural resources and man-made products, with the result that there would be plenty for all.
43 Quoted from Herbert, *The Artist and Social Reform*, pp. 186–7.
44 See Grave, *Le Mouvement libertaire*, pp. 83–5.
45 Apart from the explanation Mirbeau offered, there are several other possible explanations of the affair, even apart from the unlikely possibility that Mirbeau might be deliberately ignoring Grave's letters. During the short reign of terror inaugurated by Ravachol earlier in 1892, the police kept a particularly close watch on Grave and his correspondents, and did not shrink from tampering with the mail, as for example in the case of Mirbeau's article on Ravachol, the first version of which was 'lost' in the post; see 'Aventures postales', *L'Endehors*, No. 52 (1 May 1892). Another possibility is that either Mme Mirbeau or the maid, or both, were intercepting Grave's letters to Mirbeau. The fictional 'Mémoires pour un avocat' (1894) is the story of a man whose wife disapproves of his friends and drives them away; it seems almost certain that this tale is only thinly disguised autobiography. We know for example that in June 1893 Mme Mirbeau put an end to the regular visits of the painter Camille Pissarro, who was one of the friends who shared Mirbeau's libertarian ideals; see Pissarro, *op. cit.*, pp. 209–10.
46 Letter from Mirbeau to Grave, early 1893 (I.F.H.S.). The postscript to this letter was grimly prophetic: 'J'espère bien que toutes ces affaires ne vont pas vous causer d'ennui.'
47 It is possible that the form of the preface was based on Mirbeau's frequent conversations with Pissarro. See Appendix for full text.
48 *La Société mourante*, p. vi. The eight quotations which follow in the text are all from

the same edition, pp. vi-ix.
49 Etiévant was an anarchist convicted of theft in 1892 and sentenced to five years in prison. *La Révolte* published his 'Déclarations' in October 1892, and again in pamphlet form in 1893. Etiévant placed the responsibility for his actions at society's door.

Chapter IV
The extreme limits (1892–4)

> Les bienfaits du régime actuel en France à l'heure présente, c'est d'être tantôt volé, tantôt assassiné, tantôt dynamité.
>
> (Edmond de Goncourt)

Mirbeau's epistolary contact with the leading anarchist propagandist Jean Grave during the years 1891 to 1893 must be seen against the background of the anarchist movement as a whole; theoreticians like Grave and intellectual sympathisers like Mirbeau did not operate in isolation from the rest of the movement—they had practical effects on the physical deeds of those who read their writings as much as on their intellectual attitudes. It was the delicate relationship between the theory and practice of anarchism which made the early 1890s a crucial point in the history of the movement, and which brought the anarchists into the public eye in a way which was more sensational than many of them had bargained for.

Anarchist propaganda, from the beginning of the movement onwards, was made up of three separate parts, which often overlapped, and any one of which a particular anarchist might choose as his 'speciality'. Propaganda by the written word was the area in which Mirbeau's friend Jean Grave specialised, producing anarchist newspapers in Paris for over thirty years. Propaganda by the spoken word was the forte of Louise Michel, and later of Sébastien Faure, both of whom were known to Mirbeau, (the latter particularly during the Dreyfus Affair). Propaganda by the deed (*par le fait*) was the domain of a few fanatical adherents like Henry, Ravachol and Caserio, with none of whom Mirbeau was personally acquainted. It was this latter type of propaganda which not only brought the anarchists most publicity during the years 1892–4 but also brought about, by the repression which it provoked, the break-up of the anarchist movement in France and the dispersion of its militants into many different areas of activity.

L'Ere des attentats, as this period of anarchist terrorism is known, is the phenomenon for which the French anarchists are usually remembered in the history books. And yet, ironically, at this very time the leaders of the anarchist movement were beginning to doubt the efficacy of violence as a means of attaining the desired end. In 1891 Kropotkin wrote:

> Ce n'est pas par des actes héroïques que se font les révolutions . . . La révolution, avant tout, est un mouvement populaire . . . Ce fut . . . l'erreur des anarchistes en 1881. Lorsque les révolutionnaires russes eurent tué le Tsar . . . les anarchistes européens s'imaginèrent qu'il suffirait désormais d'une poignée de révolutionnaires ardents, armé [sic] de quelques bombes, pour faire la révolution sociale . . . Un édifice basé sur des siècles d'histoire ne se détruit pas avec quelques kilos d'explosifs.[1]

The association in the mind of Kropotkin between violence and the Russian nihilists of the 1870s and 80s is of capital importance, for it is clear that Russian terrorism had an early influence on the anarchist movement in Europe. When the anarchist movement was in its infancy in France, many of the theoreticians had actually advocated the use of violence;[2] they soon realised however that more subtle means were called for; and in 1886 the following declaration appeared in the anarchist press: '. . . ce serait, croyons-nous, se perdre dans l'illusion et l'utopie que de croire que des actes semblables peuvent devenir l'objet d'une propagande raisonnée, active et continue.'[3] This statement was representative of the opinions of an increasing number of anarchist thinkers, and by 1892, when the terrorist 'epidemic' began, not one of the leading anarchists was advocating such acts of violence as a viable means of bringing about the anarchist revolution.

Jean Maitron, the historian of the anarchist movement in France, explains the period of anarchist terrorism from 1892 to 1894 as 'une manifestation attardée d'un état d'esprit déjà ancien . . . avec un retard d'une décade sur la théorie'.[4] And though the theoreticians might disclaim responsibility for the actions of fanatics like Emile Henry, it was nevertheless they who had sown the seed, and it was their fierce verbal criticisms of society which bore fruit in the short, sharp period of acts of aggression and revenge.

The extreme limits of anarchism—the physical violence employed by a fanatical handful of anarchists—created a very delicate problem for the leaders of the anarchist movement, for they were held responsible by the law and by the general public for the revolutionary fervour which inspired these terrible deeds. Yet while Reclus chose to suspend his judgement on the question of violence, Kropotkin came down in favour of non-violence, and Jean Grave even described the terrorists as 'idiots' and 'knaves',[5] and wrote:

> Nous ne sommes pas de ceux qui prêchent les actes de violence, ni de ceux qui mangent du patron ou du capitaliste . . . ni de ceux qui excitent les individus à faire telle ou telle chose, à accomplir tel ou tel acte . . . Nous nous bornons à tirer les conséquences de chaque chose, afin que les individus choisissent d'eux-mêmes ce qu'ils veulent faire.[6]

The terrorists themselves, however, were quite adamant about the influence which the theoreticians had had on their actions. Virtually all of them claimed to be disciples of Kropotkin and Reclus, while the newspapers of Jean Grave had done much to foment the discontent of those who took their opposition to society to a violent extreme.

Mirbeau himself could not deny that he had played his part, during the decade preceding the terrorism of Henry, Vaillant and Ravachol, in stirring up animosity towards the traditions and institutions which these men attacked in such a literal way. Whichever aspect of Mirbeau's social criticism we like to choose, we always find that it had its counterpart in anarchist doctrine. All of Mirbeau's work was essentially anti-bourgeois; the extremes of wealth and poverty which Mirbeau saw in an increasingly materialistic society excited his anger, as in the short story 'L'Oiseau sacré', and his pity, as in 'Le Pauvre Pêcheur'; and tales like these soon found their way into the anarchist press. Mirbeau made no secret either of his opposition to the State; the article 'Le Rôle de l'Etat' reveals how completely Mirbeau had read and absorbed the second chapter of Kropotkin's *Paroles d'un révolté*. Mirbeau's rejection of republicanism and his impatience with parliamentarianism were regularly expressed in articles like 'Rêverie' and 'Sur un député', both of which were reprinted in *La Révolte*'s literary supplement; and in a letter to Geffroy in May 1891, Mirbeau anticipated by over two years the bomb which the anarchist Vaillant was to throw into the Chambre des Députés in December 1893, for Mirbeau described the French parliament as 'cette chambre d'odieux imbéciles . . . qui feront explosion, magnifiquement, un de ces jours'. And he added, with sinister confidence: 'Cela, je le sais, j'en suis sûr. Et ce sont les événements,—qui approchent—qui allumeront la mèche.'[7]

Mirbeau agreed with the anarchists in their belief that the world was evolving, through a series of cataclysmic events, towards a desirable and more perfect state. Like all the left-wing revolutionary movements of the nineteenth century, marxism included, anarchism taught, from a study of the history of civilisation, that each revolution brought the ideal nearer to realisation; and from the 1880s onwards, when the term 'decadent' began to be applied in earnest to French society,[8] it was commonly believed, in intellectual circles at least, that another revolution was imminent, and that this might be the greatest of them all. Anarchists, marxists, socialists, and even many right-wing intellectuals shared the conviction that France was on the verge of a cataclysmic upheaval. Speaking for the anarchists, Kropotkin expressed it thus:

> Décadence et décomposition des formes existantes et mécontentement général; élaboration ardue des formes nouvelles et désir impatient d'un changement; élan juvénile de la critique dans le domaine des sciences, de la philosophie, de l'éthique, et fermentation générale de l'opinion publique . . .
> . . . Tel fut toujours l'état des sociétés à la veille des grandes révolutions.[9]

The English philosopher Herbert Spencer, whom Mirbeau had read thoroughly, had also foreseen the possibility of another revolution;[10] and though some anarchists saw such a revolution in terms of a necessary and gradual evolution of society rather than as one great insurrection, the feeling that society must soon disintegrate was widespread, and it was an important factor in the appeal of anarchism to the intellectual élite of the 1890s.

Artists like Pissarro genuinely expected a speedy end to contemporary society;[11] writers of the young generation like Camille Mauclair and André Veidaux confidently shared this view;[12] and the office of *L'Endehors* was typical of many of the *avant-garde* milieux in 'prophétisant de terribles chambardements, très écoutés par les jeunes gens'.[13] Mirbeau, who to some extent had felt the influence of this philosophy before he espoused the anarchist cause—his article 'La Fin' painted a horrifying picture of the *grand soir*, which he hoped would sweep away the government of Jules Grévy in 1883![14]—endorsed the anarchists' view of the nearness of a revolution, and in 1891 he told Jules Huret:

> L'esprit de révolte fait des progrès, et je m'étonne . . . que les misérables ne brûlent pas plus souvent la cervelle aux millionnaires qu'ils rencontrent . . . Oui, tout changera en même temps, la littérature, l'art, l'éducation, tout, après le chambardement général . . . que j'attends cette année, l'année prochaine, dans cinq ans, mais qui viendra . . . j'en suis sûr![15]

The terrorist attacks of 1892 to 1894 were not, however, greeted by Mirbeau or by the anarchist press as the dawn of the revolution everybody seemed to be expecting, and neither the theoreticians of anarchism nor their intellectual sympathisers seemed willing to accept the practical consequences of anarchist doctrine. Jean Maitron points out that no anarchist newspaper ever made unreserved praise of any act of terrorism, and that most anarchists believed that individual terrorism did their cause more harm than good.[16]

To be fair to the theoreticians in their uncomfortable position during the terrorist epidemic, there was certainly more behind these acts of violence than a mere putting into practice of primitive anarchist doctrine; each of the terrorists, in fact, on careful scrutiny, can be seen to have had additional and often more significant motives for the deed. The criminal tendencies of Ravachol, the suicidal nature of Vaillant, the vanity and egotism of Henry, and the slightly unhinged mentality of Caserio, all these facets of their characters contributed to turning each of these anarchists into a terrorist. Each one of them too, was motivated by a desire for revenge. Ravachol explained his deadly explosions as vengeance for the harsh sentences passed on the anarchists after a riot in 1891 at Clichy; Caserio's assassination of President Carnot was intended as revenge for Ravachol's execution; Vaillant's bomb-throwing in the Chambre des Députés was his own personal revenge on the society which had kept him in miserable poverty; and Henry's Café Terminus bomb was vengeance for the execution of Vaillant.

Yet though there were such personal factors involved in the terrorism of the 1890s, the theoreticians and the intellectuals of anarchism could not exonerate themselves from ultimate blame. And though Mirbeau may have deplored the violent excesses of anarchist terrorist vengeance, he had nevertheless been guilty himself of equivalent acts of revenge in his writings. The autobiographical aspect of Mirbeau's works revealed the personal nature of his opposition to the society in which he was brought up, and the violence of so much that he wrote showed how intensely disillusioned, impatient, and angry he felt. Mirbeau's attempts to undermine society in his writings, his criticisms of capitalism, of clericalism and of militarism, his exploitation of scandal and obscenity as a means of unsettling the smugness of the bourgeoisie, his exposure of vice, injustice and of tyranny, were all part of his desire to see these things done away with and replaced by something better; and all these aspects of his work tied him in closely not only with the theoreticians who shared his views and used his literary and journalistic celebrity to boost their propaganda, but also with the terrorists, who translated these ideas into deeds, with such unfortunate results.

On 11 March 1892 a bomb exploded in the boulevard Saint-Germain, destroying the apartment of the law-court president Benoît, who had directed proceedings at the recent trial of the Clichy anarchists; miraculously, no one was hurt by the explosion. Just over two weeks later another bomb wrecked the building in the rue de Clichy where the advocate-general Bulot lived—it was he who had conducted the prosecution at the recent anarchist trial; again there was no one killed, but the damage was great and public consternation reached fever pitch. Both these bomb attacks turned out to be the work of one man, an anarchist of Dutch extraction, whose real name was Koenigstein but who went under the alias of Ravachol. Until the time of these two bombs Ravachol's crimes had been more a question of self-interest than of anarchist propaganda; over a period of six years he had committed theft, desecration of tombs and even murder, and had succeeded in remaining undetected. Ravachol's immunity to capture, however, deserted him shortly after the second of his anarchist bombs; he was arrested as he sat in the café–restaurant Véry, where he had aroused the suspicion of a waiter by preaching anarchism to him and boasting about the effectiveness of the recent bombs.

Ravachol was an enigmatical character—James Joll observes that we are just as puzzled by him as his contemporaries were[17]—and it is not clear to what extent his acts were motivated by anarchist convictions, or how much of it was purely self-interested criminality. What is clear, however, is that once arrested he made the most of his position, for by his insistence that he was a genuine anarchist, by his calculated replies, and by his unruffled manner in the courtroom, he was able to make anarchism front-page news,[18] and laid great claims to be regarded by the anarchists as an apostle and martyr for the cause.

Public opinion was amazed and horrified when Ravachol escaped the death penalty. Mirbeau, who had sensed the gathering tide of sympathy for Ravachol in anarchist circles, and who was bitterly opposed to the death sentence whatever the crime, greeted the outcome of this first Ravachol trial with an article in *L'Endehors* (1 May 1892), and used the occasion to attack the society which had engendered men like Ravachol and provoked them to such extreme revolt. 'Ravachol', of which the first draft was 'lost' in the post,[19] demonstrated Mirbeau's sympathy for the anarchist cause even during his period of personal difficulty, and it was greeted with great enthusiasm by the anarchist press; when *La Révolte* reprinted the article a few days after its first publication in *L'Endehors* the editorial comment read:

> Nous sommes heureux d'emprunter à notre confrère l'*Endehors*, ces belles paroles sorties du coeur. C'est une occasion pour nous de témoigner à ces camarades . . . la sympathie profonde que nous éprouvons pour eux et la joie que nous avons de nous solidariser pour le bon combat.
> La persécution nous rapproche et nous unit. Des accents comme ceux de Mirbeau, font de nous des frères, et nous vous tendons, nous vous serrons la main.[20]

Mirbeau's article began by discussing the reason for Ravachol's escape from the death sentence. Was the jury afraid as the right-wing press maintained, or had the jury sensed the justice in the cause which Ravachol thought to advance? Mirbeau himself would evidently rather believe the latter; though he could not say for certain, he sensed that the members of the jury were less intimidated than the press believed, and he thought that perhaps they had listened to 'la voix de l'Idée future, de l'idée dominatrice qui le spécialise, cet acte, qui le grandit'. Yet Mirbeau was careful not to make it appear that he condoned the violence to which Ravachol had resorted; he preferred to evade the practicalities of Ravachol's conduct, and chose to intellectualise the affair, by theorising about the role of violence in the evolution of humanity towards the anarchist society of the future. In words which prefigured the preface to *La Société mourante*, which Mirbeau was to write a year later, he summed up his true feelings about Ravachol, and in doing so he revealed the sincere humanitarianism behind the anarchist beliefs which he shared with those theoreticians who had now rejected acts of violence as a valid means of propaganda:

> J'ai horreur du sang versé, des ruines, de la mort. J'aime la vie, et toute vie m'est sacrée. C'est pourquoi je vais demander à l'idéal anarchiste ce que nulle forme de gouvernement n'a pu donner: l'amour, la beauté, la paix entre les hommes. Ravachol ne m'effraie pas. Il est transitoire comme la terreur qu'il inspire. C'est le coup de tonnerre auquel succède la joie du soleil et du ciel apaisés. Aprés la sombre besogne, sourit le rêve d'universelle harmonie, rêvé par l'admirable Kropotkine.

In any case, continued Mirbeau, how could society possibly have cause for complaint?—'Elle seule a engendré Ravachol. Elle a semé la misère: elle récolte la révolte. C'est juste'—and by way of example, Mirbeau pointed to the massacres of the 1871 Commune and of Fourmies, and to the slaughters perpetrated in the name of colonialism; and he asked—with much justification: 'En face de ces tueries continuelles et de ces continuelles tortures, qu'est donc ce mur qui se lézarde, cet escalier qui s'effondre?' The evident prosperity of contemporary civilisation had given the poor and hungry an increase awareness of their plight—who could blame them for seeking revenge, or for demanding their share of the common heritage? What government could hope to resist the demands of an enlightened and insistent populace?

By this point in the article, Mirbeau had left the debate about Ravachol far behind; he was now looking to the future, where in his idealism he saw the transformation of society effected largely through the renewal of the individual social consciousness:

Nous touchons au moment décisif de l'histoire humaine. Le vieux monde croule sous le poids de ses propres crimes. C'est lui-même qui allumera la bombe qui doit l'emporter. Et cette bombe sera d'autant plus terrible qu'elle ne contiendra ni poudre ni dynamite. Elle contiendra de l'Idée et de la Pitié: ces deux forces contre lesquelles on ne peut rien.[21]

Mirbeau's view of the Ravachol affair, then, kept the significance of the terrorist's act in proportion; there was little room in Mirbeau's anarchism for any aesthetic exaltation of the gesture of defiance. Many anarchists agreed with his evaluation of Ravachol, though others—and especially the literary sympathisers—preferred to join in the hysterical canonisation of the terrorist, who was subsequently tried, convicted and executed for a number of crimes which had had very little to do with the anarchist doctrines he claimed to promote. The punishment meted out to Ravachol, however, served to turn the criminal into a martyr, for writers like Schwob and Barrucand began to compare Ravachol to Socrates and to Jesus Christ,[22] Paul Adam declared loudly that a saint had been born and a new era had begun,[23] and even *La Révolte* absolved Ravachol of blame because of his anarchist motives.[24] But Mirbeau held his peace, and would go no further than the rational and level-headed view of Ravachol which he penned before the terrorist had been made to pay for his crimes, and at a time when it seemed Ravachol had escaped the death sentence.

In June 1893 Jean Grave's *La Société mourante et l'anarchie* was published, accompanied by Mirbeau's 'magnificent' preface. On 6 November that same year the Paris première of Ibsen's *Enemy of the People*, attended by Mirbeau and preceded by a lecture from the anarchist–poet Laurent Tailhade, was the occasion for a stormy demonstration of anarchist feeling, for the play lent itself to an anarchistic interpretation, and the ageing Ibsen was regarded, by the anarchists at least, as a leading literary exponent of libertarian ideals. Within a week of this sensational première at the Théâtre des Bouffes-du-Nord, the wave of anarchist terrorism, which had somewhat abated since the execution of Ravachol, returned with renewed ferocity. On 13 November the anarchist Léauthier stuck his cobbler's knife into a harmless middle-class gentleman in a café on the avenue de l'Opéra; on 29 November the anarchist Marpeaux killed a policeman; and finally, on 9 December, at four o'clock in the afternoon, a bomb thrown by the anarchist Vaillant exploded in the crowded Chambre des Députés, injuring forty-seven people—including Vaillant himself—and miraculously killing none.

The fact that Vaillant, when he was brought to trial, mentioned the names of both Mirbeau and Ibsen in support of his act is sufficient in itself to suggest a definite cause and effect relationship between the writings of the intellectuals and the terrorism of the 1890s;[25] the fact that the terrorist epidemic broke out again so soon after the publication of Grave's book, and particularly after the Ibsen première, undoubtedly serves to corroborate this view. This at least was how the right-wing press interpreted the situation, as Jules Dietz declared in the *Journal des Débats* immediately after Vaillant's bomb:

> Cette guerre de sauvages se prêche ouvertement dans certains journaux, dans les réunions publiques . . . Et tout cela s'accomplit sous l'oeil des autorités qui ne veulent ou ne savent ou ne peuvent ou n'osent rien faire.[26]

Such repressive talk as this, and the fact that the government itself had been directly threatened by Vaillant's bomb, was sufficient to spur the authorities to sterner action against the terrorists, and against the theoreticians, whose disciples the terrorists often claimed to be. Vaillant's bomb was in fact the beginning of the end for the anarchist movement in France: it sparked off a movement of reaction which led to the dispersion, imprisonment or expulsion of almost all the leading militants, and it assured the government of sufficient parliamentary support to write new laws into the statute book—the so-called *lois scélérates*, aimed at the press, at secret associations and at the possession of explosives—laws with which the authorities were not only able to repress much anarchist activity, but were also empowered to interfere with the civil liberties of many who had little or nothing to do with the recent acts of anarchist terrorism.[27]

One of the first to suffer under the new laws was the Dutch writer and anarchist sympathiser Alexandre Cohen. It was initially uncertain whether he had been imprisoned or simply deported, but his treatment was so unjust that even Zola, who was anxious at this time to dissociate himself from those writers who openly sympathised with anarchism, was incensed by it and went as far as to visit the Minister of the Interior M Raynal in an attempt to plead Cohen's case, but without success.[28] Mirbeau used the affair as a pretext for commenting on the frightening rapidity of the elaboration and implementation of the new laws, and wrote in *L'Echo de Paris*:

> On a, les uns disent expulsé, les autres, emprisonné Alexandre Cohen. Peut-être l'a-t-on déjà guillotiné! Si la rapidité dans l'application des lois terroristes correspond à la rapidité de leur fabrication, cette hypothèse n'a rien que de très vraisemblable.

This article revealed Mirbeau at his satirical best. Cohen, it seemed, had been suspected of many heinous crimes, on the evidence of a copper tube found in his possession! Assuredly, parliament would sleep easier now that such a dangerous enemy had been neutralised! And after evoking the memory of his three or four meetings with Cohen, whom he remembered as a hard-working, intelligent and modest writer of talent, Mirbeau concluded with an attack on the press, which to his way of thinking was responsible for all the repressive agitation which had led to such folly as the persecution of this harmless Dutchman: 'En vérité, je ne sais pas où nous allons, vers quels océans de bêtise, vers quelles forêts d'inconcevables ténèbres! Chaque jour, dans les journaux, on lit des choses de plus en plus stupéfiantes.'[29]

As for the unfortunate Vaillant, his trial was a travesty of justice. Not only was his lawyer given insufficient time to prepare a defence but also the hearing itself was expedited, and the harsh death sentence—on a man who had not killed anyone—was carried out within a few weeks of the hasty trial.[30] Though Vaillant's sincerity as an anarchist was never called into question, and though he too, like Ravachol, became a 'martyr for the cause' by virtue of his death, it was becoming increasingly apparent, to the theoreticians at least, that far from advancing their cause, such acts of terrorism were strengthening the power of the government—which was only too glad to be able to distract public attention from the compromising Panama affair. This was clearly Mirbeau's greatest cause for concern, for in his article about the expulsion of Cohen, he ironically compared contemporary France to czarist Russia, and this was a point of view shared by many of those who thought of anarchism as a serious political philosophy, and not merely as an excuse for criminality or as a fashionable outlet for dilettante individualism.

One intelligent and egotistical young anarchist who had no doubts about the long-term efficacy of acts of violence was a twenty-two-year-old named Emile Henry. Within a week of Vaillant's execution on 5 February, this well-educated son of the bourgeoisie had avenged the death of the latest anarchist martyr by a bomb which killed one person and injured twelve others in the crowded Café Terminus at the side of the Gare Saint-Lazare. Henry's exceptional intellect and his extreme self-confidence brought a new note into the debate about anarchism which was filling the press, dismaying some and intriguing others. Henry was essentially an egotist; his calculated and premeditated murders were not the result of a criminal mind, nor were they motivated by personal despair or hardship. Henry was what Paul Bourget called a 'victime du livre'—like Robert Greslou in Bourget's *Le Disciple* (1889), Henry had allowed his reading to go to his head, and his imagination had fed on what seemed to be perfectly harmless books. From Rabelais' *Abbaye de Thélème,* from Stendhal's *Le Rouge et le noir,* from Zola's *Germinal* and Barrès' *Le Culte du moi,* Henry had distilled his own romantic cult of anti-social individualism, and when fused with anarchist ideology, this created a brand of anarchism of an intense and highly volatile nature. The declarations Henry made during his trial and the letters he wrote from his prison cell reveal a clinical mind and a talent for oratory and prose-writing such as few anarchists could boast. His insolent bearing in court and his unruffled acceptance of the inevitable death sentence caused many anarchists and anarchist sympathisers to rally to his support, and even in our own time Henry is remembered as the prototype of a certain brand of intellectual anarchist militant.[31]

Mirbeau was not among those who expressed sympathy for Emile Henry. Instead he witnessed with alarm the gathering tide of repression; he warned of the consequences of playing into the hands of the government by insensing public opinion; and he grieved at the denial of the elementary civil rights of many who were totally unconnected with the acts of terrorism. Alexandre Cohen was one such, and then Mirbeau's friend Jean Grave became another.

Grave was arrested in January 1894 as a direct consequence of the new laws passed immediately after the Vaillant scare. He was used to being arrested without charges, but this time he was being prosecuted for his book *La Société mourante*, which had appeared over seven months before! He was still in prison when Vaillant was executed on 5 February, and was awaiting trial on these trumped-up charges when Henry's bomb came along to make his hopes of an early release extremely unlikely. Mirbeau was fully aware of the delicacy of Grave's position, and of the damage Henry had done to Grave and the anarchists generally; and writing in defence of Grave Mirbeau made a thorough condemnation of the terrorism of Emile Henry—a condemnation which met with the approval of many clear-sighted anarchists. The article began:

> Un ennemi mortel de l'anarchie n'eût pas mieux agi que cet Emile Henry, lorsqu'il lança son inexplicable bombe, au milieu de tranquilles et anonymes personnes, venues dans un café, pour y boire un bock, avant de s'aller coucher. L'ineptie de cet acte est telle que beaucoup de gens, à imagination romanesque, soupçonnèrent, en lui, au premier moment, une ingérence policière . . . Si l'on s'en tenait au fameux précepte criminaliste qui veut que, dans un crime commis, l'on recherche d'abord celui à qui le crime profite, ce soupçon apparaîtrait vraisemblable et motivé. Car le gouvernement triomphe, par cette bombe qui, avec un merveilleux opportunisme, semble justifier, dans l'esprit de ceux qui ne réfléchissent pas, les sanglantes répressions d'hier, les mesures violentes de demain.[32]

Mirbeau's fears, and the fears of those who, like Charles Malato, agreed with him,[33] were ultimately proved to be justified. The government felt so much public support behind it at this time that the police were authorised to make scores of arrests and hundreds of searches daily. Criminals, militants, philosophers and sympathisers were lumped together and treated alike—Mirbeau's own house was searched early in 1894, and it was later rumoured that a warrant had been made out for his arrest[34]—and the legal authorities spent the first half of 1894 preparing the briefs on the massive trial of anarchists which took place in August of that year: the so-called Procès des Trente.

Though Mirbeau thought it ultimately wise to leave France for a while in the early summer of 1894,[35] he did not keep silent during these months of repression and suspicion, nor did he allow the government to pursue its course without maintaining his vociferous opposition. At great risk of falling victim to the conspiracy complex which had possessed the French authorities from the time of Vaillant's bomb, Mirbeau continued to speak out for those who had been implicated in crimes they knew little or nothing about. Mirbeau was not unaware either that he himself was on the wanted list, as this rather nasty report by police officer Legrand—obviously enjoying the *chasse à l'anarchiste*—illustrates:

> Plusieurs anarchistes se croient filés et il y a une sorte de délire de persécution policière qui est un cas pathologique nouveau, digne d'observation. Il n'est pas jusqu'à M. Mirbeau qui n'en soit un peu atteint.[36]

Aware though he certainly was of police interest in his activities, Mirbeau was by no means intimidated. The imprisonment of Grave, Zo d'Axa, Fénéon, and Faure, and the expulsion of Alexandre Cohen not only failed to silence him but actually seemed to galvanise his efforts, and found him not only campaigning in their favour, but also attacking with renewed vigour the society, and particularly the government, which was responsible for such injustice. On the day before Emile Henry's execution Mirbeau wrote a virulent article condemning the stupidity and the inefficacy of the leading politicians of the day; and referring to the President of the Republic Sadi Carnot, Mirbeau wrote:

> . . . ç'a toujours été un des plus grands étonnements de ma vie de voir que l'on s'obstinait à payer d'une somme d'argent aussi considérable un homme aussi inutile, et, parfois, aussi ridicule, qu'est le président de la République française.[37]

This article—'A l'Elysée'—was an extension of an article Mirbeau had written earlier in *L'Echo de Paris*, and which had found its way into Mirbeau's police dossier, where certain passages had been heavily marked in the margin. 'Egalité, fraternité . . .', as the article was called, was ostensibly a discussion of governmental agricultural policy; but it was really an excuse for Mirbeau to speak his mind about Sadi Carnot. It was written early in February 1894, at the time when Vaillant's fate lay in the President's hands. Mirbeau, who had more sympathy for Vaillant than for all the other terrorists put together[38]—the death sentence for a man who had not committed murder seemed to Mirbeau to be the extremest act of barbarity possible—expressed the conviction that both Jules Grévy and Napoléon III would have had enough tolerance and pity to spare Vaillant; but with Sadi Carnot, Mirbeau felt sure, Vaillant was certain to die, as Mirbeau said:

> M. Carnot, lui, n'est pas un philosophe, et il n'a pas de pitié . . . Il ignore complètement la générosité, et il ne sait pas que la générosité n'est pas seulement une façon de sentir, mais aussi une façon de comprendre, et que, dans bien des cas, elle est un acte d'habileté supérieure et un ressort de grand politique . . .[39]

Mirbeau little knew when he wrote 'A l'Elysée' that within a matter of weeks this politician whom he had so maligned with his pen would fall victim to an anarchist's knife. Just as the bomb which Vaillant threw into the Chambre des Députés had been a grim fulfilment of the words which Mirbeau had written to Geffroy two years before the event, so the assassination of President Carnot on 24 June 1894 by the Italian anarchist Caserio was an extension—albeit unbalanced and fanatical—of the sentiments which Mirbeau had expressed, not only in these two articles, but also in his letters, his private conversations, and even in his novels. The parallelism between Mirbeau's own anarchism and the terrorism rampant in Paris in the closing years of the nineteenth century (in spite of Mirbeau's disapproval of the use of violence) is striking enough for us to appreciate why the French authorities kept a close watch on him: a watch which ceased only with his death over twenty years later.

Though Caserio's coup proved to be the last of the terrorist acts of that traumatic period, and though the repression which ensued resulted in the dislocation of what little organisation the anarchists had relied upon, the influence of the anarchist cult—for such it was—was deeper and more far-reaching than either contemporary commentators realised or subsequent critics have been prepared to concede.[40] The number and quality of all the writers and artists who were touched in some way by anarchism in late nineteenth-century France is in itself a phenomenon not justifiably overlooked. A philosophy which could attract, however ephemerally, writers as disparate as Barrès, Mirbeau and Claudel, artists like Pissarro and Luce, and politicians and thinkers like Léon Blum, is at least worthy of examination as an element in the spirit of the age.

The anarchist ideal was susceptible of so many variations, each of which complied by its very individuality with the anarchist 'rule' of individual freedom, that many otherwise dissimilar minds were able to find themselves in contact with one another beneath the anarchist umbrella—in Mirbeau's own words: '. . . l'anarchie a bon dos. Comme le papier, elle souffre tout.'[41] The wave of sympathy among the intellectuals in France in the 1890s was partly the work of the progress of humanitarian and socialistic demands for the amelioration of society; it was partly the result of a state of mind so often attendant upon the end of an age: the awareness of decadence, and the élitist desire to rise above the mediocre; it was partly the child of the revolutionary spirit exemplified twenty years earlier by the Paris Commune; it was partly a hangover from the utopian romanticism of the second quarter of the century; it was partly the by-product of the rapid technological and industrial developments; it was partly an assertion of the ego, an aesthetic pose, a nihilistic refusal to conform, a desire to escape, a gesture of defiance, an excuse for self-gratification; and in addition to all this it was a question of fashion: anarchism was essentially à la mode. All or any of these factors were sufficient to cause many writers, artists and thinkers to express in their way of life, their conversation, their works or their deeds, some form of sympathy with one or more aspects of anarchist philosophy.

It affords an interesting insight into the human intellect to know that this wave of sympathy for anarchism was never so high as when the anarchist fortunes were at their lowest ebb. Mirbeau himself, though he had long been a supporter of the anarchist cause and had other reasons for his intellectual approval of anarchist doctrine, was undoubtedly confirmed in his defence of anarchism by this instinctive movement to take sides with the weaker party—as he wrote later in *La 628-E8*:

> Et puisque le riche—c'est-à-dire le gouvernant—est toujours aveuglément contre le pauvre, je suis, moi, aveuglément aussi, et toujours, avec le pauvre contre le riche, avec l'assommé contre l'assommeur, avec le malade contre la maladie, avec la vie contre la mort.[42]

The persecution of the anarchists, in the early months of 1894 in particular, was a great stimulus to their intellectual counterparts; and, as Zola remarked, such persecution only served to fortify the doctrine.[43] For this very reason, many right-wing intellectuals, totally opposed to anarchism, counselled restraint in the use of repressive measures against the anarchists; but by 1894 the authorities were not prepared to listen to counsels of moderation.

The instinctive, temperamental aspect was as much a part of Mirbeau's anarchism as his rational endorsement of the political theory, and it tied him in with many of his fellow sympathisers. Claudel, Mauclair, and many of those who, for example, added their names to the list of writers who protested at the sentence passed on Jean Grave for his *La Société mourante*,[44] found in anarchism, as Mirbeau did, an outlet for their frustration at the state of society, and a means of expressing their refusal to accept or conform to the *status quo*.[45]

Mirbeau did not meet on common ground with many other anarchist sympathisers, however, in that he did not adopt the artistic pose which constituted the anarchism of so many writers. The symbolists in particular, as the *avant-garde* of French literature, greeted anarchism as the social counterpart of their own revolutionary aesthetic. Gourmont, Régnier, Saint-Pol-Roux, and even Fénéon—who was nevertheless prepared to risk his neck for his anarchist sympathies—fell into this category of writer for whom anarchism was an aesthetic rather than a sociological complement to their literary activity. Barrès, Tailhade and Jarry had their own variations on this same kind of anarchism, and it hardly resembled Mirbeau's anarchism at all. Mirbeau shared their intense individualism, and he was not altogether free from the suspicion of dilettantism;[46] but his anarchistic protests were intimately related to the social realities which motivated them. With that disarming frankness which is the hallmark of Mirbeau's autobiographical style, he wrote in *La 628–E8*:

> Sans pose, sans littérature, sans arrière-pensée d'ambition, puisque je n'en attends aucune place, aucun mandat, aucune décoration,—j'ai grand'pitié du malheur humain. Chaque jour, de plus en plus, je m'indigne que,—quelle que soit l'étiquette, même la plus rouge, sous laquelle ils arrivent au pouvoir,—les hommes de pouvoir, par seul amour du pouvoir, fassent de l'inégalité sociale, soigneusement cultivée, une méthode toujours pareille de gouvernement . . .[47]

It was almost certainly because Mirbeau's anarchism was nearest to the reality of the social problems of the age that the anarchists made more use of Mirbeau's writings than of any other single literary author. It was for the same reason, too, that Mirbeau was known not only to the police but also to the literary world and to the general public as a genuine supporter of the anarchist cause. As early as 1891 *La Plume* had regarded Mirbeau as an established writer in sympathy with libertarian ideals: in the number of *La Plume* devoted to socialist literature, in addition to the important quotation from Mirbeau's reply to Huret's *Enquete* and the article by Veidaux which spoke of Mirbeau as a pioneer revolutionary, there was also an anti-patriotic poem which was dedicated to Mirbeau by its young author P.-N. Roinard.[48] Mirbeau's articles on behalf of Jean Grave in his fight against the Société des Gens de Lettres in 1891, his article about Ravachol in *L'Endehors* in 1892, the publication in June 1893 of *La Société mourante*, with Mirbeau's preface, and the general tone of all his writings, stamped Mirbeau very clearly in the public mind as a serious anarchist sympathiser. So much so that when, in January 1894, *Le Figaro* devoted one issue of its literary supplement to a discussion of anarchism, Mirbeau was featured prominently among those who were spoken of with distaste by the editors of this conservative newspaper.[49]

When in the following month, immediately after Grave's trial, another of Mirbeau's former forums *Le Gaulois* decided to conduct an *enquête* on literary sympathies for anarchism, it was to Mirbeau that the paper first turned for an opinion.[50] Mirbeau was so well known as an anarchist sympathiser that in July 1894 this fact could be used as the basis of a humorous skit on the whole anarchist affair: the supplement of *La Revue Blanche*, *Le Chasseur de chevelures*, published a collection of cynical witticisms entitled 'Réflexions anarchistes', which was dedicated to Mirbeau by the author Paul Masson.

Mirbeau clearly deserved this reputation as an anarchist sympathiser, for he never shrank from the opportunity either of expressing his own libertarian views or of defending those who chose to express theirs also. Apart from his defence of Cohen, Mirbeau took up his pen in the cause of many writers who had been accused, either by the authorities or by the critics, of expressing dangerous, revolutionary ideas, or of having anarchist sympathies. In April 1891, for example, Remy de Gourmont wrote a highly anti-nationalist article, 'Le Joujou patriotisme', for which he was subsequently dismissed from his post at the Bibliothèque Nationale. Mirbeau, who had read many of Gourmont's articles in *Le Mercure de France*, and had recognised the anarchistic ideals which they shared in common, particularly on this question of militant patriotism,[51] sprang immediately to Gourmont's defence with a forceful article in *Le Figaro*: 'Les Beautés du patriotisme'. Patriotism, at least of the type encouraged by the militant nationalists, was in Mirbeau's view, as it was for Gourmont, 'un des meilleurs agents de la gouvernable ignorance, un des moyens les plus sûrs de retenir un peuple dans l'abrutissement éternel'.[52] Mirbeau's article was once again so redolent of anarchist philosophy that Jean Grave had no hesitation in reprinting it in the literary supplement of *La Révolte*.[53]

Mirbeau was also quick to spring to the defence of Anatole France in 1893. France, whose social awareness seems to have developed quite suddenly in 1892,[54] had set about expressing his own social opinions in the words of an eighteenth-century priest, the Abbé Coignard. *Les Opinions de Jérôme Coignard*, which were nothing less than a denunciation of the vices of parliamentary democracy, of the abuses perpetrated by the legal authorities, and of the exploitation of humanity by the militarists and the colonialists, appeared initially in serial form in *L'Echo de Paris*, on which Mirbeau was a collaborator, and where no doubt France and Mirbeau began their long and fruitful friendship. The opinions of the Abbé Coignard could not fail to delight Mirbeau; they were so anarchistic that one critic has written of them: 'Elles furent lues avec surprise et scandale, et it fallait admettre que Kropotkine et Jean Grave n'avaient jamais rien soutenu de plus subversif que ce que disait, dans une meilleure langue, Jérôme Coignard.'[55] How appropriate it was then that the whole work should be dedicated to Octave Mirbeau—for France wrote, when the last part of *Les Opinions* was published: 'Je tiens à honneur de saluer dignement le maître de Jacques Tournebroche, que nous ne reverrons plus. Et, pour qu'il soit manifeste que je fais l'éloge d'une âme généreuse, je dédie ces lignes à Octave Mirbeau.'[56]

It was hardly surprising that *La Révolte*, to which France was now a subscriber,[57] should want to reprint the whole chapters from *Les Opinions* in its literary supplement; and from July 1893 onwards sections from France's work often appeared in the anarchist press side by side with articles by Mirbeau. It was for this reason particularly, that when *Les Opinions* appeared in book form at the end of 1893 France was spoken of by conservative critics in the same terms as Grave, Mirbeau and even sometimes Zola, who were all regarded as 'revolutionaries' of differing shades. It was to these critics that Mirbeau reacted vigorously when, writing in defence of France, his 'cher collaborateur', he spoke of *Les Opinions de Jérôme Coignard* as 'un livre où . . . dans le style merveilleux qui lui est particulier, Anatole France remue des questions philosophiques dont on n'a pas idée dans les groupes parlementaires'.[58]

Mirbeau's sincerity in his anarchist sympathies was however exemplified most particularly in his dealings with Jean Grave. In a letter to Grave written in the latter half of 1893,[59] Mirbeau had agreed that a cheaper, paperback edition of *La Société mourante* was a good idea, and he had given Grave advice as to how to persuade the publisher to agree to such a move. In the event Mirbeau's advice turned out to be both good and bad: Grave had his cheap edition, in January 1894, but within a very short space of time bulk copies of the book were seized by the police from public bookstalls, the publishing house of Stock was raided and all its copies of the book were confiscated, while Grave himself was arrested and charged with incitement to unlawful acts. Grave and Mirbeau, it seems, had played into the hands of the authorities; the one-franc edition of *La Société mourante*, containing an additional chapter—a perfectly anodine article called 'La Méthode expérimentale'—officially constituted a new publication, and was therefore liable to prosecution under the recent legislation. As Grave himself said, this was 'pure jesuitry' on the part of the authorities,[60] but it was nevertheless to cost Grave over a year's jail.

Mirbeau was horrified at Grave's arrest, and wrote to him:

> Vous pensez si j'ai été affligé, autant que stupéfait de votre arrestation. Il n'est pas possible qu'elle soit maintenue. Il n'est pas possible que malgré tous les défilés ténébreux où l'on va essayer de vous faire passer, que votre innocence n'éclate au grand jour.

This same letter also contained reassurances to Grave that he had friends who would not desert him, and Mirbeau himself promised to do all in his power on Grave's behalf. He wrote too of his intention to publish an article on Grave, and described the effect which these numerous arrests were having in the literary world: 'La presse est terrorisée, mais je ne désespère pas de faire sur vous, un article qui montre l'homme que vous êtes et que nous aimons.' To reassure Grave yet more Mirbeau insisted that even those who were not anarchists had a favourable opinion of him as a man and as a philosopher. Félix Dubois, for example, who was responsible for the adverse write-up on anarchism in *Le Figaro*, had told Mirbeau: 'Dieu sait si je suis anarchiste, mais j'ai de M. Grave une vraiment grande admiration. C'est un des plus beaux, un des plus nobles caractères que j'aie rencontrés.'[61]

Within a few weeks of this letter Mirbeau had succeeded in having an article on Grave published, in Xau's *Le Journal*. The press in general may have been intimidated by the stringent measures taken by the government—the *lois scélérates* contained a clause relating to those who even condoned anarchist activities—but Mirbeau was not prepared to stand by and watch injustice being done. 'Pour Jean Grave' was a very subtle and yet a very frank expression of sympathy for an anarchist who was evidently regarded by the authorities as a public danger. The main theme of Mirbeau's argument was that Grave ought to be distinguished from the criminal fanatics like Emile Henry, and ought to be admired and respected as a logician and philosopher. To this end Mirbeau embarked upon a condemnation of Emile Henry which showed clearly that he had very little sympathy for the terrorists. It had been suggested that Henry had been used by the police as an *agent provocateur* in order to bring anarchism into disrepute, but Mirbeau was quite clear in his own mind that this was not so, for he wrote: 'J'aime mieux croire que cet Emile Henry ne prit, en cette occasion, conseil que de lui-même, sans obéir à d'autres suggestions que celles de sa propre folie.'

In 'Pour Jean Grave' Mirbeau also strongly criticised those criminals who sought to glamorise their crimes by claiming to be anarchists, and he deplored the way in which common criminals such as this had been confused with philosophers like Kropotkin and Reclus; anarchist bombs were most dangerous of all to anarchism itself, for they provoked an explosion of human stupidity which inflicted 'wounds which could never heal'. The delicate situation of Jean Grave had been seriously jeopardised by Henry's bomb, and in an attempt to reassure the jury, Mirbeau gave a short biographical sketch of the man they would be asked to find guilty of crimes against humanity and against the State. The lowly origins of Grave, his self-education, his gentleness of character and the keenness of his intellect—Mirbeau brought all these elements into play as evidence of Grave's sincerity and of his innocence of the charges being laid at his door. As for *La Société mourante*, Mirbeau expressed ironical surprise that it should suddenly be found to constitute a public danger, whereas it was in fact 'une oeuvre de critique sociale, un livre de pure philosophie, et non pas un pamphlet'.

Mirbeau wondered whether Grave would be found guilty; the trial was only a few days away and Mirbeau could not help fearing the worst: 'Tout est à craindre, car nous sommes dans un moment de peur où tout est confondu dans une même haine, et la bombe du criminel isolé, et l'idée qui marche, impassible et lente, à travers les siècles.' Unwilling, however, to end the article in a minor key, Mirbeau expressed his belief that whatever the outcome of the trial Grave would carry on working and would continue the struggle undeterred; and he looked forward to the day when Grave would once again be a free man: 'De cette tombe qui est une prison, il reviendra, grandi, parmi les vivants, et mieux armé encore pour la lutte intellectuelle.'[62]

Grave's trial took place on Saturday 24 February 1894. Mirbeau was present for the whole of the proceedings, having received the previous day a summons to appear as a witness for the defence.[63] Surprisingly, it was the first time he had ever set eyes on Grave. Mirbeau was called to the witness-box immediately after Elisée Reclus, whose writings Mirbeau had long admired and who witnessed warmly in favour of Grave by saying that he was 'une âme d'élite . . . un homme remarquable . . . un des rares hommes qui n'aient jamais menti'.[64] When Mirbeau took the stand he was first asked whether he was the author of the preface to *La Société mourante,* to which he replied: 'C'est exact. J'ai été séduit par l'élévation d'idées que j'y ai rencontrée, par les hautes et nobles préoccupations de Jean Grave, et je suis ici pour témoigner de mon estime pour lui.'

The questioning was then taken up by Grave's lawyer, Emile de Saint-Auban, who asked Mirbeau how he came to write the preface and what he thought of Grave and his book. In reply Mirbeau described his long epistolary relationship with Grave, and declared:

> Je le considère comme un apôtre et un logicien tout à fait supérieur. Il pousse la logique jusqu'au bout, et c'est pourquoi il arrive à des conclusions . . . extrêmes. Mais il ne faudrait pas en détacher de phrases séparées pour en juger l'esprit. Un livre est une harmonie, et on peut faire dire à une phrase séparée le contraire de ce qu'elle signifie.

In reply to a further question from the president about the opinion of the world of literature concerning Grave, Mirbeau continued: 'Il y a beaucoup de mondes des lettres depuis l'Académie jusqu'au *Chat-Noir*; mais enfin, parmi les littérateurs en général, il est considéré comme un homme très sérieux.'

Thus far Mirbeau had answered confidently and competently—perhaps because the questions had been relatively straightforward. But then the advocate-general, Bulot, put a question to Mirbeau which was intended to come right to the heart of the debate about the use of violence, for, alluding to the section in Mirbeau's preface which discussed this problem, Bulot declared: 'M. Mirbeau répond aux scrupules des futurs anarchistes qu'il n'y a pas grand mal à ce que l'orage abatte quelques chênes voraces s'il vivifie les humbles plantes. Que M. Mirbeau veuille bien m'expliquer ce passage.' The question was deliberately calculated to throw Mirbeau off balance and perhaps even to implicate him in the 'crimes' for which Jean Grave was himself on trial. Mirbeau's presence of mind, however, did not desert him; he answered the question boldly, by reiterating the same attitude to the use of violence which he had expressed in his preface: he regretted the need for violence, and yet he accepted the inevitability of at least some of it, but not the indiscriminate terrorism of Ravachol and Henry:

> C'est un fait historique que les révolutions ne sont fondées que sur la mort,—par exemple 1793. Personnellement j'ai horreur de la mort, et, d'ailleurs, ce n'est pas d'hier que j'ai réprouvé la propagande par le fait. Lors de l'attentat de Ravachol, j'ai publié un article dans ce sens dans un journal *l'Endehors*.

Mirbeau was followed into the witness-box by two other writers, Paul Adam and Bernard Lazare, both of whom expressed their admiration for Grave and insisted that Grave was not in favour of the use of violence as a means of propaganda. Paul Adam went so far as to declare that he would have been happy to have written such a book as *La Société mourante*. But the testimonies of Reclus, of Mirbeau, of Adam, and of Lazare all proved fruitless for, though the jury did not comply with Bulot's demands for the greatest severity and found Grave guilty with extenuating circumstances, at the end of the short trial Grave was fined 1,000 francs, which he was naturally unable to pay.

The verdict came as a great shock to the artistic and intellectual milieux sympathetic to anarchism. Grave had committed no physical act of violence; he was not a criminal; he was essentially a writer and a philosopher; and many intellectuals realised that there was an important principle at stake in the jailing of a man on ideological grounds.[65] So much so, that on the Monday following the trial 130 writers published a letter of protest in *L'Echo de Paris*, endorsing the opinions of Reclus, Mirbeau, Adam and Lazare, and deploring the sentence on Grave. This movement of indignant protest did not die out quickly, for the left-wing papers were full of references to the shameful treatment of Grave, and they did not give up the fight for his release until January 1895 when, after the accession of Félix Faure to the presidency, Grave was released under a general amnesty for political detainees.

Mirbeau himself was utterly dejected by the outcome of Grave's trial. On the day after the court proceedings, he had this to say to the reporter from *Le Gaulois*:

> Voilà Grave, par exemple, un homme admirable, qui s'est fait lui-même, Grave, un doux, un résigné, qui réprouve la propagande par le fait; on l'a confondu avec les autres, on l'a envoyé aux assises, condamné! . . . Hélas, il a un défaut, Grave! un défaut qui, peut-être, dans la circonstance, lui a joué un mauvais tour: il est trop logique. Pauvre Grave! un homme si droit, si juste, si honnête. Son procès, c'est celui de la pensée, sous prétexte d'anarchie aujourd'hui. Demain, un autre prétexte remplacera celui-ci.[66]

In the weeks that followed Mirbeau was haunted by the sentence passed on Grave. In *Le Journal* he openly voiced his fear that the violence of the anarchist fanatics had merely been the pretext for the repression of freedom of thought and of expression. Mirbeau reminded his readers how Grave's book had been discussed on a serious, philosophical level by almost every newspaper in Paris when it first appeared in 1893, and he reproached the authorities for their 'legal trickery' in prosecuting the second edition as they did. Grave's lawyer Saint-Auban had clearly understood the significance of this move, as Mirbeau wrote: 'Il a compris . . . que ce n'était pas la personnalité de Grave qu'on traînait sur le banc d'infamie, que ce n'était pas même une idée, mais l'Idée, la honte de penser et le crime de le dire.' Never, Mirbeau concluded on a note of pessimism, had he felt so helpless as he did at Grave's trial; never had he felt how pointless it was being a great philosopher like Grave or a great defender of justice like Saint-Auban.[67]

In his general feeling of pessimism, and with his fears about the future of the basic human liberties, Mirbeau proved himself once again to be something of a prophet; for though he could only suspect it, the authorities were indeed preparing to bring to justice all those whose ideas did not conform to what they regarded as the socially acceptable norm. The wording of the *lois scélérates*, and the evidence of the secret files brought to light in particular by Jean Maitron, show how it was clearly the intention of the authorities, armed with the new laws, not only to punish the active anarchists but also to deal with those writers and journalists who expressed their sympathy with the anarchist cause.[68]

One such writer who, like Mirbeau, stood in danger under the new laws, himself became, by a coincidence which many unkind people found appropriate, the victim of the next anarchist coup. This was the poet Laurent Tailhade, whose semi-apocryphal comment on the Vaillant explosion had epitomised the dilettante anarchism of so many young writers of the time.[69] On 4 April 1894 Tailhade was dining in the restaurant Foyot when a bomb exploded on the window ledge by his table. Tailhade lost an eye and was lucky to escape with his life. Given the climate of suspicion in which this event occurred, it was natural that the authorities should speculate about this coincidence; but to suggest, as some did, that Tailhade was carrying explosives around with him when he went out to dinner with a lady-friend was just a little too much for Tailhade's friends to swallow. A headline in *Le Gaulois*, which read 'M. Laurent Tailhade serait-il complice?' provoked Mirbeau to write an article in Tailhade's defence. Mirbeau cast this in the form of a short sketch in which a witness in the Foyot affair recounted Tailhade's 'abnormal' behaviour to the commissioner of police. It seemed so ridiculous to Mirbeau to accuse Tailhade of complicity that he chose to adopt a humorous tone: everything which one would normally expect someone to do at dinner—go to the washroom, sit down next to a friend, order dinner, etc.—all these things were noted down by the police as evidence of abnormal behaviour and as proof of Tailhade's complicity![70]

But while Mirbeau was taking an ironical view of the rumours of Tailhade's involvement with the anarchists in the Foyot affair, the authorities were proceeding towards their determined end, and were preparing a large-scale trial of anarchists as the prelude to the repression of all the anarchist sympathisers. With this in view they began to step up the number of arrests they made; over one hundred philosophers, militants, sympathisers and terrorists—including a number of common criminals—found themselves in prison in 1894 awaiting trial for their association with the anarchist movement. It was not until the August of that year that twenty-five of them, along with Grave, who was already serving a two-year sentence, and four others who were tried *in absentia*, appeared in court in what became known as the Procès des Trente. Reactionary retribution, it seemed, was about to exact its pound of flesh.

It was the inclusion of the literary and artistic critic Félix Fénéon among the number of the accused at the Procès des Trente that was to anger the world of literature and was to give the trial a significance and a colour which it would otherwise have lacked. Fénéon, it seemed, was acquainted with the anarchist Louis Matha, and through him, with Emile Henry; and while it seems certain that Fénéon knew little or nothing about Henry's bomb outrages before they happened, it is probable that the flask of mercury and the detonators which were found in his bureau at the War Office had once been in the possession of Henry, whose flat was cleared by Matha before the police arrived shortly after Henry's arrest on 12 February 1894. For this reason, and for his collaboration on *L'Endehors* and his friendship with Alexandre Cohen and the German anarchist Kampfmeyer, Fénéon—the 'éminence grise du mouvement symboliste' as he has been called[71]—was arrested on 25 April, and taken to Mazas jail, where he remained until his trial in August.

Fénéon's pungent wit, and the glowing tributes which were paid to him at his trial by witnesses as well respected as Mallarmé, have now become almost legendary;[72] but at the time of his arrest nobody could foresee that Fénéon and most of the other defendants would be acquitted, and he stood in need of all the support his friends could muster. Mirbeau, one of Fénéon's closest colleagues, thought Fénéon's arrest so outrageous that he devoted his next two articles in *Le Journal* entirely to his friend. The first, entitled simply 'Félix Fénéon',[73] compared the incriminating evidence found in Fénéon's office to the mysterious tube for which Cohen had been criminally hounded from the country. Cohen's 'tube' had turned out to be a walking-stick; and as Fénéon himself declared at his trial, mercury could be used for making barometers as well as explosives! Endorsing what Bernard Lazare had already said about Fénéon as an artist, Mirbeau added his own impressions of him as a friend; and from the ironical opening to this article Mirbeau passed into a mood of melancholy reminiscence, recalling Fénéon's last visit to Poissy, relating how highly Fénéon's colleagues regarded him, and concluding by describing the sad scene in the Fénéon family household now that the head of the house had been taken so abruptly away.

Altogether different was the second article which Mirbeau devoted to Fénéon's cause. In 'Potins' Mirbeau adopted an aggressive tone with the authorities, whose actions he deplored. A man could not be taken away to prison, Mirbeau insisted, and be subjected like a thief or an assassin to endless forensic examinations and legal inquisitions without a very good reason which ought to be made plain to those who demanded to know. If justice wished to survive at all then the authorities who administered it must disclose their reasons and their evidence and not just keep Fénéon in solitary confinement without bringing any charges. The police, insinuated Mirbeau, were more interested in caretakers' gossip than the reliable testimony of those who really knew Fénéon, like himself; and Mirbeau could not hide his bitterness towards those who perverted justice when he remarked: 'Celui qui a vu l'oeil du juge, a vu le fond de la désespérance humaine.' Mirbeau also summarily dismissed the allegation that Fénéon was a Prussian spy. This, he maintained, was simply another ruse to keep Fénéon behind bars longer: 'Lorsque l'on a rien à dire de quelqu'un, arrêté par erreur ou par simple dilettantisme, on l'accuse d'être un espion. C'est vague, c'est souverain sur l'esprit des foules et cela contente tout le monde'—everybody that is save those who, like Mirbeau, demanded that justice be done, and who were confident that the police would soon reach the point where 'après avoir tout essayé, tout tenté, tout retourné, elle est bien obligée d'ouvrir, à la victime, les portes de la prison . . .'.[74]

Once again, time proved Mirbeau to be right in his judgement; for in spite of all the efforts of the police and the legal authorities, they were unable to prove the accusations brought against twenty-seven of the defendants, and Fénéon walked away from the court as a free man.

The outcome of the Procès des Trente, conducted in such an atmosphere of repression and fear, was a surprise to most onlookers; but the police had clearly overstretched themselves. The moderation shown by the jury corroborated the view of those who maintained that persecution and repression only encouraged fanaticism and resistance, for it soon became apparent after the trial that the intensity of the period of terrorist propaganda had subsided. It was almost as if the trial had come six months too late—it now appears as the afterglow of a phenomenon already in decline. The anarchist movement itself, temporarily stunted, was soon to revive and show its constructive strength in the fields of anarcho-syndicalism, libertarian education and communal anarchist colonisation. The fanatics had now had their day, their dilettante supporters had had their moment of fashionable revolt, and anarchism began to slip gratefully out of the adverse public limelight. At least Mirbeau could claim that he had resolutely and consistently defended the genuine anarchist credo, and could justifiably feel that he had brought a little common sense into the hysterical atmosphere of this period during which the extreme limits of anarchism had been reached.

Notes

1 *La Révolte*, No. 32 (18 March 1891).
2 *Cf.* Maitron, *op. cit.*, pp. 101–2.
3 *Le Révolté*, No. 20 (4 September 1886).
4 Maitron, *op. cit.*, p. 252.
5 Max Nettlau, *Elisée Reclus: Anarchist und Gelehrter, 1830–1905* (Berlin: Der Syndikalist, 1928), p. 241.
6 Grave, *La Société mourante*, pp. 210–11.
7 Letter from Mirbeau to Geffroy, dated 11 May 1891 (F.G.B.A.).
8 See K. W. Swart, *The Sense of Decadence in Nineteenth-century France* (The Hague: Nijhoff, 1964).
9 *Paroles d'un révolté*, p. 27.
10 See *L'Individu contre l'Etat* (Paris: Alcan, 1885).
11 See T. Natanson, *Peints à leur tour* (Paris: Albin Michel, 1948), p. 62.
12 C. Mauclair, *Servitude et grandeur littéraires* (Paris: Ollendorff, third edition 1922), p. 115, and A. Veidaux, 'Philosophie de l'anarchie', *La Plume*, No. 97 (1 May 1893), p. 191.
13 A. Salmon, *Souvenirs sans fin*, vol. 1 (Paris: Gallimard, 1955), p. 167.
14 *Les Grimaces*, No. 12 (6 October 1883).
15 Huret, *Enquête*, p. 218.
16 Maitron, *op. cit.*, p. 246.
17 J. Joll, *The Anarchists* (London: Eyre and Spottiswoode, 1964), p. 134.
18 E. Joannès summed up the significance of Ravachol's terrorism in these terms: 'Extension prodigieuse du mouvement anarchiste depuis les actes de Ravachol. Les intellectuels sont à l'Idée.' 'Historique des faits', *La Plume*, No. 97 (1 May 1893), p. 214. Though he did not entirely approve of the use of violence, Mirbeau himself said of anarchist terrorism: '. . . il me faut bien reconnaître que cette propagande par le fait a attiré l'attention sur les idées, a servi le mouvement anarchiste. On n'en parlait pas du tout autrefois, on en parle maintenant.' 'Réponse d'Octave Mirbeau à l'enquête sur l'anarchie', *Le Gaulois*, 25 February 1894.

19 Cf. Chapter III, note 45. The full text of 'Aventures postales' is reproduced in the author's M.A. thesis, p. 272.
20 *La Révolte*, No. 32 (7 May 1892).
21 'Ravachol', *L'Endehors*, No. 52 (1 May 1892). See Appendix for full text.
22 Cf. Mauclair, *op. cit.*, p. 115, and *L'Endehors*, No. 64 (24 July 1892).
23 'Eloge de Ravachol', *Les Entretiens Politiques et Littéraires*, No. 28 (July 1892).
24 See Maitron, *op. cit.*, pp. 210–11.
25 *L'Echo de Paris* of 12 January 1894 quoted Vaillant as saying at his trial: 'Toutes les forces gouvernementales actuelles n'empêcheront pas les Reclus, les Spencer, les Ibsen, les Mirbeau, de semer les idées de justice et de liberté . . . et ces idées, accueillies par les malheureux, fleuriront en actes de révolte . . .'.
26 *Journal des Débats*, 10 December 1893.
27 Cf. E. Pouget and F. de Pressensé, *Les Lois scélérates de 1893–1894* (Paris: Les Editions de la Revue Blanche, 1899).
28 R. Ternois, *Zola et son temps* (Paris: Les Belles Lettres, 1961), p. 326.
29 'A travers la peur', *L'Echo de Paris*, 26 December 1893. Reprinted in *La Révolte* (S.L.), No. 17 (6 January 1894).
30 The novelist–lawyer and anarchist sympathiser Jean Ajalbert was chosen by Vaillant as his counsel, but Ajalbert refused in the hope of drawing attention to certain irregularities in the legal proceedings. The brief was finally accepted by Fernand Labori, who later defended both Dreyfus and Zola. See J. Ajalbert, *Les Mystères de l'Académie Goncourt* (Paris: Ferenczi, 1929), p. 171.
31 Barrès, Fénéon, and even Clemenceau (who was sympathetic to anarchism at this time) were known to admire Henry. In our own days, the secretary of the Anarchist Black Cross, Stuart Christie, who attempted to assassinate Franco, has more than once expressed himself in Henry's words; cf. 'Their violence and ours', *Daily Telegraph Magazine*, No. 212 (25 October 1968).
32 'Pour Jean Grave', *Le Journal*, No. 510 (19 February 1894).
33 Malato said in *Le Matin* of 28 February 1894: 'Je partage entièrement l'appréciation d'Octave Mirbeau: l'acte d'Emile Henry . . . a surtout frappé l'anarchie.'
34 See Pissarro, *op. cit.*, p. 245.
35 According to a letter to Geffroy, dated 24 May 1894 (F.G.B.A.), Mirbeau was intending to leave for London on 25 May, shortly after Henry's execution.
36 Extract from a report by the *3e Brigade de Recherches*, dated 30 March 1894. Dossier BA/1190, Item 12 (B.A.M.P.P.).
37 'A l'Elysée', *Le Journal*, 20 May 1894.
38 'Vaillant, par exemple, un homme intelligent . . . un homme qui, assurément, n'est pas méprisable . . . tout cela, c'est la faute au républicanisme, ce régime absurde qui détruit tout, renverse tout, rabaisse l'homme jusqu'à la bête!' 'Réponse d'Octave Mirbeau à l'enquête sur l'anarchie', *op. cit.*
39 'Egalité, fraternité . . .', *L'Echo de Paris*, 6 February 1894.
40 Only Jean Maitron, in the historical field, and Roger Shattuck, in the artistic field, have ascribed any degree of importance to the anarchist movement.
41 'Pour Jean Grave', *op. cit.*
42 *La 628–E8*, p. 308.
43 Cf. Ternois, *op. cit.*, p. 327.
44 *L'Echo de Paris*, 26 February and 3 March 1894.
45 Claudel described his own sympathy for anarchism in these terms: 'Je trouvais dans l'anarchie un geste presque instinctif contre ce monde congestionné, étouffant, qui était autour de nous . . .'. Quoted from G. Gadoffre, *Claudel et l'univers chinois* (Paris: Gallimard, 1968), p. 49. On Mauclair's anarchist sympathies, see his *Servitude et grandeur littéraires*, p. 115.

46 Many modern critics see little more than fashionable dilettantism in any of the literary sympathy for the anarchism of the 1890s. *Cf.* for example E. Carassus, *Le Snobisme et les lettres françaises de Paul Bourget à Marcel Proust, 1884–1914* (Paris: Colin, 1966), pp. 370–90.
47 *La 628-E8*, p. 307.
48 'La Patrie', *La Plume*, No. 49 (1 May 1891).
49 *Le Figaro*, *Supplément littéraire*, 13 January 1894. Special number on anarchism, prepared by Félix Dubois.
50 'Réponse d'Octave Mirbeau à l'enquête sur l'anarchie', *op. cit.*
51 On Gourmont's anarchism, see particularly G. S. Burne, *Remy de Gourmont. His Ideas and Influence in England and America* (Carbondale: Southern Illinois University Press, 1963), pp. 20–8.
52 *Le Figaro*, 18 May 1891. Reproduced in *Les Ecrivains*, vol. I.
53 No. 41 (20 June 1891). The article also contained a few words on behalf of Ernest Gegout, a journalist with anarchist sympathies who had been jailed for criticising the government's latest legal reforms.
54 See J. Suffel, *Anatole France* (Paris: Les Editions du Myrte, 1946), p. 208.
55 *Ibid.*, p. 213.
56 *L'Echo de Paris*, 19 July 1893.
57 According to the subscription list seized by the police in 1894 (Archives Nationales, Carton F7 12506).
58 'A travers la peur', *op. cit.*
59 I.F.H.S.
60 *Le Mouvement libertaire*, p. 119.
61 Letter from Mirbeau to Grave, dated 13 January 1894 (I.F.H.S.).
62 'Pour Jean Grave', *op. cit.* See Appendix for full text.
63 The summons, an explanatory letter from Grave's lawyer Emile de Saint-Auban, and five letters from Grave to Mirbeau relating to *La Société mourante* are in the John Rylands University Library of Manchester (J.R.U.L.M.). The documents are bound in Mirbeau's own copy of Grave's later work, *La Société future* (Paris: Stock, 1895), which is inscribed in Grave's hand: 'A O. Mirbeau / en témoignage / d'inaltérable amitié / J. Grave'.
64 In addition to the official *Gazette des Tribunaux*, there are many sources, both partial and exhaustive, for the declarations made at Grave's trial. The most useful are: A. Bataille, *Causes criminelles et mondaines de 1894* (Paris: Dentu, 1895), A. Sergent, *Les Anarchistes: scènes et portraits* (Paris: Chambriand, 1951), E. de Saint-Auban, *L'Histoire sociale au Palais de Justice* (Paris: Pedone, 1895), as well as the daily papers of the period. *Cf.* also A. Billy, *L'Epoque 1900* (Paris: Tallandier, 1951), pp. 431–3. The quotations are here given from *Le Gaulois*, 25 February 1894.
65 Even the poet François Coppée, who was far from sympathetic to anarchism, deplored the sentence passed on Grave. See Carassus, *op. cit.*, p. 373.
66 *Le Gaulois*, 25 February 1894.
67 'Au Palais', *Le Journal*, 4 March 1894.
68 *Cf.* Grave, *Le Mouvement libertaire*, pp. 128–9.
69 There are several different versions of Tailhade's remark, but the gist of it was this: 'Qu'importe la mort de quelques vagues humanités, pourvu que le geste soit beau?'
70 'Une Déposition', *Le Journal*, 8 April 1894.
71 By J. U. Halperin in her introduction to Fénéon, *Oeuvres plus que complètes*, vol. 1, p. lvii.
72 Several of Fénéon's replies to the judge are reproduced in *ibid.*, pp. lx–lxii.
73 *Le Journal*, 29 April 1894.
74 *Ibid.*, 7 May 1894.

Chapter V
The journalist of revolt (1894-8)

> Romancier, critique d'art ou de moeurs, chroniqueur et essayiste, esthéticien et conteur, M. Octave Mirbeau est, toujours et avant tout, un révolté.
> (Bernard Lazare, in 1895)

The fashionableness of the anarchist sympathies of the 1890s waned in proportion to the fading of anarchist terrorism from the newspaper headlines and from the public consciousness. The end of the *Ere des attentats*, marked by the Procès des Trente, robbed such sympathies of the topicality of their snob-appeal, and the anarchist movement was left once again to its genuine adherents and to those intellectuals who, though they supported anarchism to a certain extent for the satisfaction it afforded their taste for individualism, had always understood anarchism rather as a logical and scientific political philosophy than as an aesthetic pose. There were, it is true, many writers who continued to sport anarchist sympathies for some time after the fashion had passed; but few of these could be taxed with dilettantism once the anarchist movement had moved into the shadows and was no longer regarded as a convenient mode of expression for the elegant and cultivated non-conformity which characterised the spirit of the dying century.[1]

While writers like Barrès, Claudel, Adam and Mauclair were passing on from their anarchist phase into nationalism, catholicism, militarism and monarchism, others like Tailhade, Lazare and Mirbeau were loth to relinquish their faith in the anarchist ideal. They continued to express in their differing ways many of the same sociological, intellectual and political views as the anarchists, who were beginning to seek success in new directions, and who were watched with interest by these writers who had not merely ridden the anarchist bandwagon until they could find some ideology more to their developing taste, as so many writers, especially among the young, had done during the years 1892 to 1894.

Mirbeau in particular remained sincere in his anarchist faith. In 1894 he was forty-six years old; he was a successful novelist (*Le Calvaire* had reached eleven editions in one year alone); he was a successful journalist (it has been said that a newspaper sold ten thousand extra copies when it contained an article by Mirbeau);[2] he was comfortably off, well-liked by his friends and colleagues, and highly regarded by those who mattered to him most of all; there was no external compunction on him to continue in his support for the anarchist cause. Many men in his position would have begun to covet honours and to fulfil their personal ambitions by frequenting the milieux to which his celebrity and his wealth could have admitted him. Yet outside the immediate circle of those artistic and literary friends who endeared themselves to him by their art and not necessarily by their politics, Mirbeau chose as his associates men like Faure, Geffroy, Clemenceau, Quillard, Grave and Malato—men who accepted the *status quo* as little as he did, and who sought to replace it with something more humane, more equitable and more desirable. By his middle forties Mirbeau was no longer subject to the whims of youth. He had come to anarchism as a result of his own moral and intellectual evolution, and on his way there he had in fact toyed with the very ideologies towards which many anarchist sympathisers, much younger than himself, were now themselves evolving. Mirbeau had found the niche which satisfied him, and the anarchist outlook was now as much a part of him as his tendency to exaggeration and his naïve enthusiasm.

Mirbeau had spoken the truth when he declared that none of Grave's ideas in *La Société mourante* shocked him in the least. Out of the impulsiveness and unruliness of his early manhood Mirbeau had fashioned an attitude to society in which most of the important principles of anarchism played an essential role. His anarchism was very much a question of temperament. Léon Daudet, a close friend of Mirbeau until the Dreyfus Affair, described Mirbeau in the following terms:

> Il détestait les gendarmes, les douaniers, les contrôleurs, les rentiers, les huissiers, les concierges, les domestiques. Il professait qu'un préfet est presque toujours un inverti et un incestueux, et qu'un ministre est, par définition, un voleur. Mais le démocratie lui était odieuse, les hommes de loi et les financiers le faisaient vomir. De sorte qu'il n'avait plus d'indulgence que pour les enfants, les vagabonds, les très jeunes femmes, cinq ou six peintres et sculpteurs, et les chiens.[3]

Even allowing for the evident over-simplification of Daudet's portrait of Mirbeau, this passage certainly casts light on the instinctive aspect of Mirbeau's anarchist sympathies.

There was, however, much more to Mirbeau's anarchism than this important, initial impulse of his personality. Superimposed upon this basis was a conscious, wholehearted endorsement of all the standard anarchist philosophy, which he made his own, reinterpreted in his own fashion, and which expressed itself, particularly in his years on *Le Journal*, in articles of a virulence rarely equalled before or since. The rejection of all authority (moral, economic or political), the criticism of man-made laws, of all types of government, of the venality of the press, of the exploitation of the poor, of the brutality of the police and of the military (at home as well as in the colonies), the need to encourage spontaneous associations of like-minded individuals, the desire for freedom of expression, for a more broadminded approach to education, and the emphasis laid on the power of art and beauty as teachers of natural morality and truth—these were the basic tenets of anarchist propaganda during the 1890s in France; and Mirbeau endorsed them all, and expressed them throughout his own work. These were ideas which appeared revolutionary in the context of the essential conservatism of the Third Republic, and as a result Mirbeau was seen by his contemporaries primarily as a writer in revolt against society as it then existed.[4] A careful examination of Mirbeau's contributions to *Le Journal* during the years 1894 to 1898 helps to show how closely bound up with anarchist ideology were the recurring themes of Mirbeau's journalistic output, and how much these themes drew their inspiration from the philosophy which Mirbeau had so fervently espoused.

While the literary world waited with interest,[5] and with a certain amount of regret,[6] for Mirbeau to break his literary silence, the general public and the influential, conservative critics preferred either to dismiss Mirbeau with uneasy contempt or to criticise him sharply for his lack of respect and his impetuosity. Mirbeau's admirers, however, took this 'respectable' disapproval of his works as a guarantee of their value—as Bernard Lazare wrote in 1895:

> Je crains bien que jamais on ne donne en prix dans les écoles le *Calvaire* ou bien *Sébastien Roch*, car ce sont des oeuvres fort dangereuses et susceptibles de détourner les bonnes âmes du droit chemin. Un meilleur sort leur est réservé. Si elles ne sont pas apostillées par les bienveillances officielles . . . on n'en viendra pas moins à elles, et elles auront cette inestimable récompense d'être des éducatrices et des initiatrices.[7]

The ideological war on the conventions of his age, which Mirbeau had declared in his first three novels, and which he was to intensify in his next novel *Le Jardin des supplices* (1899), was waged without interruption during the years of his literary silence, and particularly during his first four or five years as a regular contributor to *Le Journal*.

In the first place, Mirbeau's very collaboration on *Le Journal* was a direct consequence of his anarchist sympathies. Not that *Le Journal* was by any means a forum for anarchist propaganda; simply that Simond, the editor of *L'Echo de Paris*, on which Mirbeau was writing regularly until February 1894, was not as obliging as Xau, the editor of *Le Journal*, on the question of non-literary articles or of literary articles which bore the unmistakeable stamp of Mirbeau's polemical verve. One of Mirbeau's last regular contributions to *L'Echo de Paris* was the article in which he attacked President Carnot for his inclemency towards the anarchists, while the very first of Mirbeau's regular articles in *Le Journal* was his resounding defence of Jean Grave. It was largely in order to escape the editorial yoke that Mirbeau made the move to *Le Journal*, where he found a freer outlet for his revolutionary temperament.

Authority was perhaps the principle which Mirbeau attacked most consistently in all his writings, and particularly in his articles on *Le Journal*. And of all the tyrannies exercised by authority in its various manifestations of power, it was the authority of the law which met with Mirbeau's most unfailing opposition. The articles on Grave, Tailhade and Fénéon, all of which appeared in *Le Journal* in 1894, were criticisms of particular instances of legal tyranny, but Mirbeau devoted many other articles to more general attacks on the principle which lay behind such abuses of authority: the right of one person or group of persons to oblige others to comply with their demands. Nobody, Mirbeau maintained, had a right to impose his will upon another, for this was nothing short of exploitation, authoritarianism, and the death of the individual.

The most striking illustration of the abuses of legal authority was, in Mirbeau's view, the treatment received by the anarchists in 1894; and in a pointedly amusing sketch, 'Les Dessous des lois',[8] Mirbeau depicted the machinations going on behind the scenes to keep all those arrested in prison for as long as possible. The sketch consisted of a dialogue between M Raynal, the Minister of the Interior, and a leading *député*, M Pourquéry de Boisserin. Raynal was evidently worried about the rising number of prisoners he now had to cope with, but Boisserin reassured him: 'Quelques citoyens de plus ou moins, ce n'est pas une affaire.' Raynal still seemed afraid, however, of what the press might say if he did not soon come up with some charges against all these detainees, and he at least had a glimmer of conscience about the injustice of his methods when he admitted: 'Pour condamner quelqu'un, il faut, au moins un prétexte . . . Et il n'y en a pas!'—but again the cynical, reactionary reply was quick to flash back: 'Il y a toujours un prétexte, quand on veut . . . Bulot a de l'imagination et de la gueule . . . Il s'en tirera très bien.' As for the antidote to anarchism, continued Boisserin, there was always the possibility of further legislation along the lines of the *lois scélérates;* and he suggested four clauses which would look well in the penal code: that all criminal proceedings must be held *in camera*; that all accounts of anarchist trials must be banned; that newspaper reports of anarchist activities must be suppressed; and that the very word 'anarchy' and all its derivatives must be cut off from the French language and be used only on pain of punishment! These ideas now seem so extreme as to be faintly humorous, and yet it was not many months before at least one of Boisserin's reactionary suggestions was implemented, for during the Procès des Trente later that year the replies of Grave and Faure were struck from the record and publication of them was banned!

Behind the irony of Mirbeau's view of the internal workings of the Ministry of the Interior was his serious concern at the injustices being perpetrated in a country which boasted a free society and which was supposed to be the heir of the great Revolution of 1789. Mirbeau's indignation was sometimes so overwhelming that he was unable to couch his opinion in irony and spoke his meaning directly, in tones which left the reader in no doubt as to the genuineness of Mirbeau's libertarian zeal—as for example in 'Autour de la justice',[9] an article in which Mirbeau accused magistrates of being more worthy of public distaste than the dreaded executioner, since it is the judge who reasons and condemns, while the executioner merely carries out the judge's command. As for the lawyer—the one person who, in the opinion of Mirbeau, ought to be the counterbalance to the autocratic power of the judge—he was in fact no different: '. . . l'avocat s'en fait le plat auxiliaire, le complice traître, et le joyeux pourvoyeur.'

It was not only the legal profession, either, which Mirbeau despised, but also the antiquated, anomalous and authoritarian system which it purported to uphold. Mirbeau had himself been enrolled for three years in the Faculty of Law in Paris, his family was traditionally connected with the administration of justice, and during his own chequered career he had occasion to observe the law in action at close quarters. His antipathy towards legal authority was based, then, on first-hand knowledge, and it was this instinctive but well-founded animosity which constituted one of the firmest links between Mirbeau and the anarchist movement. The agreement between Mirbeau and Grave for example on this subject was manifest, and it was illustrated in two important short stories which Mirbeau published, with an interval of three years between them, in *Le Journal*: 'Le Petit Gardeur de vaches' and 'La Vache tachetée.[10]

'Le Petit Gardeur de vaches'—the story of a rich man accused of murdering a cowherd—was contrived by Mirbeau so as to place in the murderer's mouth a thorough condemnation of the authority of the law which sought to punish him. The murderer is presented as a sympathetic, free-thinking individual with genuine humanitarian ideals—he has written a book entitled *La Réforme judiciaire*, for which the upper class has ostracised him—and we learn how he was led to kill the cowherd in a fit of anger when he found him torturing a cat. In spite of these extenuating circumstances, however, the rich murderer has been treated by the police and by the magistrate as a homicidal robber, and they will accept no other explanation for the murder. The murderer's case illustrates the blindness of the law which by its very nature functions on the basis of notions about human actions and crimes which never correspond exactly to the particular case in point. Mirbeau's opinion of the law was being expressed by this sympathetic murderer when he addressed the jury in these outspoken terms:

> La Loi . . . capricieuse et vaine . . . change avec le temps, avec les gouvernements, avec les majorités parlementaires, avec le diable sait quoi! Les magistrats sont bornés, ignorants, routiniers, essentiellement romantiques et féroces, par indifférence, quand ils ne le sont pas par tempérament. Ils sont magistrats, enfin. D'ailleurs je ne puis admettre qu'un homme ait osé se dire, à un moment quelconque de sa vie: «Je serai juge!» Cela m'épouvante. Ou cet homme a conscience de la responsabilité effrayante qu'il assume, et, dans ce cas, c'est un monstre; ou il n'en a pas conscience, et, dans ce cas, c'est un imbécile. Imbéciles et monstres, voilà par qui nous sommes jugés, depuis qu'il existe des tribunaux![11]

'La Vache tachetée', written three years later, at the height of the Dreyfus Affair, was even more poignant than 'Le Petit Gardeur de vaches', and it was certainly far more sinister. The unfortunate Jacques Errant has been in a dark prison cell for a year and has no idea why. His jailer tells him that the courts are crowded with anarchists at the moment, and that Jacques need not fear for his life unless he has spoken the truth or has ever kept a spotted cow. When he finally comes up for trial, Jacques is in fact accused of owning a spotted cow, and is found guilty and sentenced to fifty years in the same solitary cell. Jacques' touching faith in French justice being understandably shaken, he asks the jailer how he can possibly own a spotted cow without knowing it, and receives the rather unsettling reply: 'Moi, je ne sais pas pourquoi je suis geôlier, la foule ne sait pas pourquoi elle crie: A mort! . . . et la terre pourquoi elle tourne! . . .' The surrealist humour of this tale is at once bathetic and terrifying; a world run along such lines would be nothing less than a continuous nightmare, and Mirbeau was trying to wake his readers up to an awareness of the capriciousness of the arbitrary laws which kept society in a state of subjection at the expense of justice and human happiness.

The ultimate degradation to which repressive legal authority could bring a society was exemplified for Mirbeau in the autocratic dictatorship of czarist Russia, and he was afraid lest France should follow that example. On an issue which was always an anarchist hobby-horse—anarchist terrorism originated of course in Russia, in the fight of the early nihilists against the Czar—Mirbeau expressed himself on a number of occasions during these years of revolutionary journalism on *Le Journal*,[12] and spoke of his fears for the future of free society. In 'Sous le knout' for example—an article inspired by Mirbeau's reading, in a Franco-Belgian libertarian journal, *La Société Nouvelle*, of extracts from a book on Siberia—Mirbeau described Russia as 'un pays malheureux où, depuis si longtemps, agonise tout ce qu'il y a de noble, d'intelligent et de généreux',[13] and deplored in that country the same capricious legal system as that which he criticised so much in 'La Vache tachetée'. The main theme of *Le Jardin des supplices*, on which Mirbeau was working spasmodically at this time, was in fact to be that Europe, and France in particular, had evolved a system of legalised torture which gave rein to all the unhealthy passions of humanity, encouraging the corrupt and corrupting the innocent.

What was worse, as Sébastien Faure pointed out, was that legal authority implied so much more than just itself, and depended for its smooth functioning upon the exercising of so many other tyrannies.[14] Laws were made essentially to protect the rich against the poor, the powerful against the weak, and it was in the field of economic tyranny that the law manifested its power most cruelly against the underprivileged. One of the main themes of Mirbeau's later novel *Le Journal d'une femme de chambre* was to be this very question of the unequal relationship between the rich and the poor, the master and the servant. Several of the novel's episodes on this subject date back in fact to Mirbeau's years on *Le Journal*. The scene in chapter fifteen of *Le Journal d'une femme de chambre* which takes place in Mme Paulhat-Durand's employment agency between a poor maid looking for work and her cruel prospective employer first appeared as a short story in *Le Journal* in 1895, and it illustrated the inhumanity of an economic system which gave so much power to one person over another.[15]

'Crescite', in which Mirbeau tells the sad tale of a gardener's wife who is forced to have an abortion because her mistress does not like children, was yet another article in which Mirbeau condemned the economic tyranny of a capitalist society;[16] and when, in the summer of 1894, Mirbeau read Edouard Conte's *Les Mal-vus*, he was delighted to find there the same concern with degrading effects which financial deprivation and economic inferiority had on the more unfortunate members of society. Conte's book-looked at the underworld of parisian life and concluded that society at large must take the blame for the vices and the crimes of the underprivileged. Mirbeau wrote of his enthusiasm for Conte's book, gave expression to his feelings of humanity and of pity towards the exploited and downtrodden, concluding with Conte that though the poison of corruption was ever-present in life, 'loin de l'atténuer, la société, avec ses lois d'inégalité, avec ses terreurs, avec ses injustices, le rend de plus en plus mortel'.[17]

Such articles as this not only demonstrated Mirbeau's abiding anarchism but they also assured him of the continued attentions of the police, who looked upon him as the natural successor to the imprisoned Jean Grave as the leading anarchist propagandist.[18] The members of the government were no doubt also kept informed of the often violent criticisms which Mirbeau levelled at them, as for example on the question of economic tyranny, and particularly in the articles which Mirbeau directed against the politician and economist Méline. In 'Protégeons-nous les uns les autres'[19] Mirbeau was savagely ironic about Méline's handling of the French economy, accusing him of destroying free enterprise and of failing to encourage the spontaneous growth so necessary for the stability of a nation. The tariff barriers which Méline brought in in 1892, and his creation of the Caisses du Crédit Agricole in 1894, were very popular with the *petite bourgeoisie*, but were vehemently criticised by all shades of left-wing opinion, as well as by the upper middle class, who stood to lose financially.

Mirbeau's preoccupation with the government's leading economic spokesman shows us how important he judged the running of the economy to be. The country's economy was of course controlled by the government, and it was in this control, exercised by parliament and the Cabinet, that Mirbeau saw the root cause of all society's trouble. Mirbeau's anti-parliamentarianism was reinforced by his desire to see a free economy. It may seem strange therefore, that among his friends, mostly artists and libertarians like himself, he should number the parliamentarian and future nationalist hero of France, Georges Clemenceau. In fact, the Clemenceau of 1895 and the Clemenceau of 1918 were poles apart. The Clemenceau of 1871 was a young libertarian idealist who had taken office as mayor of Montmartre under the Paris Commune; the Clemenceau of 1885 was admired for his revolutionary ardour by the ageing Vallès; the Clemenceau of 1895 was a socialist of the extreme Left who made common cause with the anarchists on many issues. The days were still far off when Clemenceau was to find himself in the seat of power, obliged to suppress industrial strikes or leading the military patriotism of France to bloody victory over her traditional German enemy. In 1895 Mirbeau had much in common with him.

Mirbeau had been introduced to Clemenceau by their mutual friend Gustave Geffroy, and there are many allusions in the Mirbeau–Geffroy correspondence to Clemenceau's visits to Mirbeau's home, particularly at Carrières-sous-Poissy. It was during these visits that Mirbeau was able to familiarise himself with the minutest details of parliamentary life—those details which provided him with ammunition for his articles and gave them the factual basis which made so many politicians feel uncomfortable when Mirbeau turned the spotlight on them. It is particularly significant that Mirbeau should choose to publish an article in praise of Clemenceau almost immediately after his friend had lost his seat in parliament, and was therefore no longer actively engaged in government, and that Mirbeau should look forward to a greater contribution to the good of society from Clemenceau once he had been released from the vanity of a parliamentary career.

As for Mirbeau's own opinion of politics, he expressed it unequivocally in this same article on Clemenceau: 'La politique, par définition, est l'art de mener les hommes au bonheur; dans la pratique, elle n'est que l'art de les dévorer. Elle est donc le grand mensonge, étant la grande corruption.'[20] And while Clemenceau would not go as far as Mirbeau in his rejection of parliamentarianism and of the principle of authority of any kind, he was clearly in agreement with some of the things Mirbeau said against certain facets of government policy and against individual members of the government. Clemenceau's articles in *La Justice*, many of which were collected together in book form under the title *La Mêlée sociale* (1895), reveal many points of contact with Mirbeau's ideas, and also with certain aspects of anarchist philosophy. A Mirbeau article entitled 'Nous avons un fusil', with its cutting remarks about government abuse of military strength to suppress left-wing demonstrations (a new gun had just been issued to the troops which made the Lebel rifles used in the Fourmies massacre redundant) was very much in line with the articles in which Clemenceau himself attacked government policies.[21]

Mirbeau's hatred of government exuded from almost every line he wrote, and this applied to government on the local as well as on the national level. The article 'O Rus!' for example, found him complaining bitterly, through the mouth of one of the characters in the story, about the incompetence and the indifference of local government officials; and with that sweeping exaggeration which was the hallmark of Mirbeau's style, he declared:

> L'administration française ne sert qu'à entraver l'initiative individeulle, décourager les gens de bonne volonté qui rêvent des améliorations, hérisser la vie de mille obstacles, contre lesquels, à la fin, on se lasse de lutter . . . un préfet ne répond jamais.[22]

Indignant protest and concerted action were the only possible means of shaking the government out of its ineffective lethargy. This was the message of another article, 'Tous cyclistes!',[23] in which a young man draws a parallel between the terrible state of French roads and the poor state of French society, and suggests that if everyone took up cycling they could bring about the downfall of the government by their united protests about the unsatisfactory roads! Though the form of this article, and many others like it, was rather puerile, the message was very clear; Mirbeau was fond of such childish allegory to express his social criticisms, and at least it had the merit of never masking what he was trying to say.

During the years immediately following the Procès des Trente the anarchist militants largely moved away from terrorism as a means of propaganda, and turned their attention to the grass roots of the industrial working class, in the trades unions and the so-called Bourses du Travail. But they still maintained the flow of written propaganda against the State and against the representatives of its power and authority, and one of the public figures who came in for most criticism of this kind was the prefect of police M Lépine. Hardly a day seemed to pass without some mention of him in the anarchist press, and police-baiting became a favourite pastime.[24] As early as the *Lettres de ma chaumière* Mirbeau had expressed his opinion of the low level of police mentality in the comic figure of Barjeot in the short story 'Un Gendarme';[25] but as time went on Mirbeau's humour turned to bitterness, at least with regard to the police, for he had seen the things of which they were capable during the recent years of anarchist propaganda. By 1895 Mirbeau's fictional characters were speaking of the police in the following terms:

> Avertir la police, la justice? . . . Jamais . . . Alors, méfiants, avec des regards de hyène, ils m'interrogeraient, et, fatalement, je tomberais dans le guet-apens de leurs questions insidieuses et louches . . . Ils iraient fouiller ma vie, toute ma vie . . .[26]

—and in 1896 Mirbeau's indignation at the oppressiveness of criminal law as administered by the police expressed itself in 'Pour M. Lépine', the pitiful tale of a poverty-stricken prostitute;[27] the title of the short story itself spoke eloquently of the bitterness that Mirbeau felt towards the chief of police for the unhappiness he caused in the lower échelons of society.

While the police, at the government's bidding, were oppressing certain sections of French society, the army, again under the direct control of the government, were pursuing the same nefarious policies on foreign soil; and here once more Mirbeau's opposition to imperialistic colonialism found him on common ground with the philosophers of the extreme Left. A chapter in *La Société mourante*, entitled 'La Colonisation', summed up all that the anarchists ever wrote on this question and expressed their contempt for the hypocrisy which covered the mercenary and militaristic motives of the 'civilising' invaders. None of Grave's ideas were lost on Mirbeau, who endorsed them in many an article on this subject in *Le Journal*. One such article was 'Paysage parlementaire'—reprinted by the anarchists—which contained Mirbeau's sarcastic comments on the news of General Gallieni's military successes in Madagascar, which would continue, Mirbeau foretold gloomily, 'jusqu'à l'extinction complète de cette race antipatriotique qui empêche Messieurs les militaires de coloniser en rond'.[28]

On other occasions again, Mirbeau's opposition to military colonialism expressed itself in a paroxysm of humorous over-exaggeration. This was the case in 'Maroquinerie', an important article in which Mirbeau relates an imaginary interview with General Archinard, the author of a new colonisation plan for the Sudan based on imperialist brutality. General Archinard's principles are quite simple, as he readily admits: 'Je ne connais qu'un moyen de civiliser les gens, c'est de les tuer . . .' Archinard's plan is also disarming in its simplicity: the skins of slaughtered negroes make fine leather, as the wall-coverings in his room demonstrate, and could be a most profitable by-product of a military invasion of the Sudan! Archinard is only sorry that public opinion is a little touchy about putting white skins to the same practical use, otherwise criminals and delinquents could be similarly disposed of to the country's greater profit. Mirbeau's narrator is of course suitably impressed, and declares: 'Cela me fait tout de même plaisir, et me remplit d'orgueil de revoir, de temps en temps, de pareils héros . . . en qui s'incarne l'âme de la patrie.'[29]

Mirbeau's chief complaint against all these manifestations of authority: legal, economic, political, and military, was that they exercised a tyranny over those who asked nothing more revolutionary than to be left alone to decide their own destiny. The same criticism was levelled by Mirbeau and the anarchists at the religious authorities of the day. The moral and intellectual dominance of the Church, particularly in the vital field of education, was the basic cause of much of the anti-clericalism of the anarchists, and especially by Sébastien Faure, with whom Mirbeau became closely associated in the years following the Procès des Trente and during the Dreyfus Affair.[30] Mirbeau's article 'Cartouche et Loyola' (1894) contained a full expression of his opinion of the injurious tyranny exercised in matters educational by the Church as well as by the paternalistic state. The article was inspired by the sudden dismissal from the experimental orphanage at Cempuis of Paul Robin, a malthusian educationalist of libertarian leanings. Reports of Robin's work and of the happy and enthusiastic response his methods produced in his children appeared sporadically in the anarchist press, which noted his efforts with no little interest. Mirbeau on his part accused the Church and the government of engineering Robin's dismissal, and spoke of the collusion of Church and State as 'la double pression des prêtres et des panamistes . . . Edifiante coalition, à laquelle personne ne peut résister aujourd'hui'. With polemical incisiveness also, he spotlighted the implications of Robin's dismissal and explained the policy behind the authorities' decision:

> Ils ont compris que de Cempuis, et des établissements fondés sur la meme philosophie de liberté et de dignité humaines, ne sortiraient plus les électeurs soumis et les fervents du mensonge religieux. Il fallait décourager tous les novateurs, et les novateurs ont été frappés dans la personne même de M Robin.[31]

Education was just one of the fields in which the anarchists, along with left-wing intellectuals of all denominations, demanded freedom from the tyranny of Church and State. The campaign for educational reform—which ultimately bore some fruit—was only one aspect of the anarchist struggle to bring about an entirely free society. The pages of *Le Journal* are full of articles by Mirbeau which reflect his own wish to bring such freedom into many different aspects of daily life. Whether we take his lone defence of the imprisoned Oscar Wilde—Mirbeau did not particularly like the English writer, but he maintained his right to follow his natural tendencies wherever they might lead him[32]—or whether we consider such short stories as 'La Folle',[33] in which a harmless old woman is removed to a lunatic asylum by a local government official who wants her land, or 'En attendant l'omnibus',[34] in which a young man is kicked and beaten by a crowd for daring to board a bus which the conductor had said was full, all these texts, and many more besides, bear witness to Mirbeau's desire to see more freedom in society.

In the Wilde affair, Mirbeau was horrified particularly at the servility of the press and its subjection to middle-class morality. He saw this as a further illustration of what he had long suspected: that journalism in general was the slave of those who held the purse-strings. Mirbeau had expressed this opinion as early as 1883 in an article entitled *Le Figaro*,[35] and he wrote a short story to illustrate his point in *Le Journal*.[36] The mediocrity and the venality of the press was one of Mirbeau's most constant themes; for him it was all part and parcel of the decadence of society of which he was convinced, and which caused him to hope that a sudden end to the middle-class Republic might soon usher in an era of social and artistic regeneration.

The Wilde affair also reinforced Mirbeau's opinion that middle-class artistic taste was lamentable in its mediocrity. The beauty of art, Mirbeau believed, transcended all considerations of narrow morality and even invalidated them; and one of the highest social functions of art was to re-educate, by exposure to truth and beauty, the minds of those who were hide-bound by the convention and tradition which was responsible for the petrification of society. Mirbeau had long been regarded as a leading spokesman for *avant-garde* French art, and many of his articles on art in *Le Journal* reveal the revolutionary character of his campaign to induce an awareness of the values of those artists he admired for the sincerity of their declarations of individuality and the quality of their representations of truth.

With the anarchists, Mirbeau agreed that the visual arts were potentially great teachers and moralisers in the highest sense.[37] By a two-way process art could not only give insight into the ideal, but could also reproduce and highlight the real, and thus fulfil a useful function above and beyond the expression of the artist's personality. Art for art's sake was all very well, but art could not be great unless it revealed something of value to humanity in its struggle to teach the ideal. It was because he believed this that Mirbeau refused to separate art from other fields of human culture and science, and it is for this reason that his art criticism was invariably anchored to social realities and was perhaps all the more readily understandable. His articles in *Le Journal* on Rodin, for example, whom Mirbeau had been among the first to admire and to champion in the 1880s, contained almost as much overt social criticism as they contained technical discussion of the sculptor's work;[38] and when the French government demonstrated its ignorance of the value of contemporary art in its clumsy handling of the magnificent collection of paintings which Gustave Caillebotte left to the nation in 1894, Mirbeau wrote an article in which he attacked centralised government with as much zeal as he expressed his enthusiasm for Caillebotte's taste.[39] Great art, such as that over which the State was hesitating, was one of the surest guides humanity had at its disposal to lead it out of contemporary mediocrity, and Mirbeau's campaigns on behalf of new artistic values was an essential part of his role as a social critic, for he saw how important an educative force the arts could be in their affirmation of truth, of beauty, of idealism and of individual sincerity.[40]

It is hardly surprising then, in view of the revolutionary nature of Mirbeau's articles in *Le Journal* during the years immediately following the Procès des Trente, that he should be regarded by the authorities as a threat to their conservative traditions. Mirbeau's continued contact with the anarchist movement cannot but have reinforced them in this view. The correspondence between Mirbeau and Grave went on, though at less frequent intervals, until at least the outbreak of the First World War; Mirbeau tried, unsuccessfully, to visit Grave in prison;[41] Mirbeau and Grave met regularly after the latter's release in 1895, and Mirbeau was both a subscriber and a collaborator on Grave's *Les Temps Nouveaux*;[42] Mirbeau's name continued to appear in the columns of most of the anarchist newspapers; there was even a question of him helping Sébastien Faure to found a newspaper after the Procès des Trente in 1894',[43] and the number and variety of Mirbeau's visitors kept the police very busy whenever they put him under surveillance. All these activities, and his association with so many artists, writers and social philosophers opposed like himself to the bourgeois Republic, formed the backcloth to the powerful and polemical articles he published in *Le Journal*. These articles not only expressed his personal revolt against almost every aspect of contemporary society, but also demonstrated, to the delight of a few and to the scandal of many, that Mirbeau had found in anarchism the attitude and the philosophy which suited him best, and that he had finally arrived, in these middle years of his life, at the term of his intellectual evolution. The novelist of revenge had become the journalist of revolt, and the combination of the two was making him a writer to be respected and feared, a force to be reckoned with in the literary, artistic and political milieux of the age.

Notes

1 There is a well-documented section on the snob-appeal of anarchism in Carassus, *op. cit.*, pp. 371–90. There was, of course, a great deal more to some of these anarchist sympathies than mere snobbery. For a brief summary of the more positive aspects of anarchism and its appeal in France during the years 1894 to 1914, see G. Woodcock, *Anarchism: A History of Libertarian Ideas and Movements* (Harmondsworth: Penguin Books, reprinted 1970), pp. 295–304.
2 B. Danielsson, *Gauguin in the South Seas* (London: Allen & Unwin, 1965), p. 43.
3 *Souvenirs*, vol. 2 (Paris: Nouvelle Librairie Nationale, 1926), p. 44.
4 Bernard Lazare's description of Mirbeau (reproduced at the head of this Chapter) just about sums up contemporary opinion of him: '. . . toujours et avant tout, un révolté'. *Figures contemporaines* (Paris: Perrin, 1895), p. 167.

5 *Cf.* Vandérem, *op. cit.*, p. 137.
6 *Cf.* Gourmont, *op. cit.*, p. 75.
7 Lazare, *op. cit.*, pp. 168–9.
8 *Le Journal*, 18 March 1894.
9 *Ibid.*, 24 June 1894. Reprinted in *T. N. (S.L.)*, No. 22 (October 1904).
10 *Le Journal*, 30 September 1895 and 20 November 1898.
11 Compare this with the following passage from *La Société mourante* (p. 96), and the extent of Mirbeau's oneness with Grave on the subject of law becomes apparent: 'Vous qui vous posez en juges sévères et infaillibles de cet homme qui a tué ou volé, savez-vous quels sont les mobiles qui l'ont fait agir? . . . Vous les hommes implacables qui lancez l'anathème sur le «justiciable» que la force publique amène à votre barre, vous êtes-vous jamais demandé si, placés dans le milieu et les circonstances où cet homme agit, vous n'auriez pas fait pis?'
12 In later years, especially after the turn of the century, Mirbeau participated in the anti-czarist movement in France.
13 *Le Journal*, 3 March 1895.
14 *La Douleur universelle*, p. 267: 'Qui dit loi dit délinquant—qui dit délinquant dit policier ou gendarme qui arrête, magistrat qui condamne, gardien de prison qui enferme et bourreau qui exécute. Tout l'ensemble ne fait qu'un.'
15 'Présentation', *Le Journal*, 19 May 1895. The *bureaux de placement* often came under attack from the anarchists who, like Mirbeau, regarded them as cattle-markets; *cf.* 'Les Bureaux de placement', *Le Libertaire*, No. 47 (3 October 1896).
16 *Le Journal*, 1 April 1894.
17 *Les Mal-vus*, *ibid.*, 3 June 1894. Reproduced in *Les Ecrivains*, vol. I.
18 Extract from a police report of 1894: 'C'est *Octave Mirbeau*, successeur désigné de Grave, que les compagnons ont en vue pour fonder un journal.' Mirbeau dossier BA/1190, item 11 (B.A.M.P.P.).
19 *Le Journal*, 25 February 1894.
20 'Clemenceau', *ibid.*, 11 March 1895. Reproduced in *Les Ecrivains*, vol. II.
21 'Nous avons un fusil', *Le Journal*, 22 April 1894. It is interesting to note the affinity, on this question of the French army's new gun, between Mirbeau and Alfred Jarry, an anarchist of a different sort, who wrote an amusing piece on the same topic: 'Les Fusils transformés', *La Revue Blanche*, 1 November 1901, pp. 383–4.
22 *Le Journal*, 15 April 1894.
23 *Ibid.*, 19 August 1894.
24 *Le Père Peinard*, which resumed publication in October 1896, was particularly abusive towards the police.
25 Reprinted by the anarchists in *La Révolte (S.L.)*, No. 7 (24 October 1890).
26 'Le Petit Pavillon', *Le Journal*, 15 September 1895. This short story was later incorporated into *Les Vingt et un jours d'un neurasthénique* (Paris: Les Belles Lectures, 1954 edition), pp. 185–92 (first published 1901).
27 *Le Journal*, 8 November 1896. Also in *Les Vingt et un jours*, pp. 281–92.
28 *Le Journal*, 11 November 1896. Reprinted in *T.N.(S.L.)*, No. 2 (May 1897).
29 *Le Journal*, 12 July 1896. This article was recommended by Jean Grave in *T.N.*, No. 12 (18 July 1896). It was also incorporated in *Les Vingt et un jours*, pp. 96–102.
30 On Faure's own successful attempt at running a libertarian school, see Maitron, *op. cit.*, p. 338.
31 *Le Journal*, 9 September 1894.
32 Wilde was arrested on 5 April 1895. The French press was generally unsympathetic, but Mirbeau wrote two articles in Wilde's defence condemning the hypocrisy of English puritan morality: 'A propos du *Hard Labour*', *ibid.*, 16 June 1895, and 'Sur un livre', *ibid.*, 7 July 1895. Though Mirbeau admired *The Picture of Dorian Gray*

for its exposure of the 'moral gangrene' of English society, he had no taste for Wilde's aestheticism; in fact, he satirised it in *Le Journal d'une femme de chambre* in the person of Lord Kimberley.
33 *Le Journal*, 25 March 1894. Reproduced in *La Vache tachetée* (Paris: Flammarion, 1918), pp. 137–44.
34 *Le Journal*, 27 September 1896. A few lines of this story are worth quoting for their typically Mirbellian irony, especially this comment by the narrator on the fate of the poor young man who dares to think for himself: 'Nous applaudîmes frénétiquement à cet acte de justice, à cette conquête du règlement sur les principes révolutionnaires, et, le calme s'étant rétabli, les voyageurs ayant repris chacun sa place, l'omnibus s'en alla, symbole de la paix sociale, affirmation triomphante de la hiérarchie . . .'.
35 *Les Grimaces*, No. 2 (28 July 1883).
36 'Interview', *Le Journal*, 19 January 1896. This short story was later expanded into a one-act play. The anarchist press was full of similar criticisms of French journalism; cf. for example the editorial by S. Faure in *Le Libertaire*, No. 62 (15 January 1897).
37 Kropotkin, in *Paroles d'un révolté*, pp. 66–7, had appealed to the young artists to help improve society by awakening it to true values, while Jean Grave and Emile Pouget gladly took advantage of the social consciousness of artists like Steinlen, Pissarro, Ibels, Willette, Luce and Signac to illustrate the philosophies expressed in their anarchist journals. Cf. Herbert, 'Artists and anarchism', *op. cit.*
38 'Auguste Rodin', *Le Journal*, 2 June 1895; 'A propos de la statue', *ibid.*, 30 August 1896; 'Préface aux dessins d'Auguste Rodin', *ibid.*, 12 September 1897.
39 'Le Legs Caillebotte et l'Etat', *ibid.*, 24 December 1894.
40 It was many years before Mirbeau came round to a more élitist view of art. Cf. 'Réponse d'Octave Mirbeau à l'enquête sur l'éducation artistique de public contemporain', *La Plume*, No. 333 (1 March 1903), p. 279.
41 According to an extract from a prison report, dated 10 September 1894, Mirbeau was refused permission to visit Grave in Clairvaux. Mirbeau dossier BA/1190, item 18 (B.A.M.P.P.).
42 Cf. Grave, *Le Mouvement libertaire*, p. 85.
43 Extract from police report on anarchist activity. Mirbeau dossier BA/1190, item 17 (B.A.M.P.P.).

Chapter VI
The Dreyfus passion (1898-9)

> Et que pouvons-nous faire maintenant que tous ces gens ont mis leur botte sur la justice?
>
> (Mirbeau in a letter to Zola, 1898)

During the years when he was publishing nothing save the fierce articles on *Le Journal*,[1] Mirbeau had been unable to produce a sustained work of literary creation. His feverish mind had been so occupied with the application of his anarchist ideas to the minutiae of the day-to-day life of society that he had been overfaced with subjects to write on, and the result had been the proliferation of short polemical pieces which earned for him a reputation as a journalist of revolt. His fourth novel was progressing very slowly due to his inability to concentrate his efforts over a long period upon the single theme which was required to give his novel a sense of unity and purpose. He confided his difficulties to his friend Monet:

> Je ne puis faire des livres et des articles en même temps. Il faut rompre trop souvent le courant de ses idées, cela vous rejette trop loin, en dehors de la préoccupation obstinée, qui doit s'attacher à la confection d'un livre.[2]

It was almost certainly for this reason that Mirbeau toyed in the meantime with the idea of trying his hand at writing a play, for he felt this might demand less protracted concentration and would give him the opportunity of expressing himself in a literary form sooner than if he waited for some inspiration to energise him into the completion of his fourth novel. Though he spent almost four years producing his first play, *Les Mauvais Bergers*,[3] he does not seem to have found it as difficult or as painful as he undoubtedly found the production of a novel, and it was with this play, in December 1897, that he finally broke a literary silence which had lasted for the best part of eight years.[4]

Mirbeau's fourth novel, meanwhile, had reached a point of stagnation. The parts of it which he had published as articles and short stories in *Le Journal* from 1894 onwards had shown that it was to be a more general criticism of society than any of his previous works; and it was perhaps the very diffuseness of Mirbeau's theme which was making it difficult for him to bring it to completion. 'Divagations sur le meurtre' for example (*Le Journal*, 31 May 1896), which later constituted the bulk of the preface to *Le Jardin des supplices*, was of such a general philosophical nature—it concerned murder as one of the fundamental principles of human society—that it is easy to see why Mirbeau struggled for so long to develop such a theme into a full-scale novel. It was only the full implication of the Dreyfus Affair, which horrified Mirbeau by its injustice and its cruelty, and the consuming passion which it awoke in him, which provided him with the stimulus he needed to complete his novel, to tie his free-ranging mind down to one central topic, and to give motivation and meaning to *Le Jardin des supplices*, the long-awaited follow-up to *Sébastien Roch*.

Until a fairly recent article,[5] the important part played by Mirbeau in the Dreyfus Affair and the contemporary notoriety he gained by it were virtually unknown, neglected by the historians of the Affair, and submerged in the silence of the archives of the period. The unearthing of many revealing letters from Mirbeau to Zola, and the combing of the contemporary newspaper files—particularly of *Le Journal* and *L'Aurore*—now enable us to grasp some idea of the passion with which Mirbeau embraced the cause of justice in the campaign for the rehabilitation of an innocent man. It is not intended in this chapter either to retell the Dreyfus Affair, or to provide an inventory of Mirbeau's dreyfusard activities, but rather to show, by highlighting certain aspects of Mirbeau's dreyfusard sympathies, that his active participation in the Affair was inspired by the same anarchistic temperament which had caused him to reject the traditions of his family, to write three novels of revenge against society, and to embrace libertarian ideals.[6]

Mirbeau's energetic defence of Dreyfus and of Zola was consequential upon and complementary to his anarchism, and it was a further opportunity for him to make a stand against the abuses of authority and to undermine the existing social structure. The anarchists were closely connected with the Dreyfus Affair, and Mirbeau was closely involved with them.[7] It was in fact Bernard Lazare, a friend of Mirbeau's and an anarchist sympathiser highly regarded by Jean Grave,[8] who was the first to suggest that Dreyfus had been condemned by a miscarriage of justice: his brochure *Une Erreur judiciaire. La vérité sur l'affaire Dreyfus* appeared in Brussels in 1896. It was not however until January 1898 that the anarchists accepted in any great numbers that there had been irregularities in the judicial proceedings against

Dreyfus. A meeting organised by the anarchist Sébastien Faure under the auspices of *Le Libertaire* on 8 January 1898 publicised the illegalities in Dreyfus' trial, and thus ante-dated by five days Zola's celebrated 'Lettre à M. Félix Faure', better known as 'J'accuse!' This meeting was the first outward manifestation of the support which the majority of the anarchists gave to the dreyfusard cause. Pouget, the editor of *Le Père Peinard*, like many libertarian intellectuals, at first refused to believe that a wealthy Jewish officer was worthy of his concern, and Grave was even slower in being converted to the cause of Dreyfus; but Faure firmly believed that an injustice had been done, that authority had abused its power, and that there was much to be gained from a frontal attack on the army and on the law on this particular issue:'. . . l'affaire Dreyfus', he said, 'n'est plus l'affaire Dreyfus . . . elle porte à l'ordre du jour la question sociale toute entière avec ses complexités.'[9]

It was because Mirbeau saw the Dreyfus Affair in exactly the same light as Sébastien Faure that he entered the lists on behalf of Dreyfus, and chose Faure, Lazare and Quillard—another literary anarchist sympathiser—as his closest associates in the fight for justice and for truth. In 1899, Faure suspended publication of *Le Libertaire* to found the dreyfusard *Le Journal du Peuple*, and Mirbeau was among the paper's earliest collaborators and a frequent visitor to its offices.[10] The articles which Mirbeau gave to Faure for publication in *Le Journal du Peuple* during 1899 contained the same characteristic combination of ferocity and pity as his articles in *Le Journal*. But now Mirbeau's criticisms had found a single peg on which to hang all their virulence, and his writings became all the more vitriolic because of it. Articles like 'Apologie pour vacher' for example,[11] as well as being diatribes against all forms of government, and against the principle of universal suffrage, contained highly personal attacks against important public figures—in this case against the War Minister Cavaignac, and on different occasions against Méline and other members of the cabinet: attacks which bordered on the libellous, and which might easily have been prosecuted as incitement to violence.[12]

That Mirbeau's participation in the Dreyfus Affair was motivated by his deep-rooted anarchistic principles, and not by self-interest or personal animosities and friendships, is clear from the fact that Mirbeau not only severed close relationships with those who would not support Dreyfus (like Léon Daudet), but also strengthened recently-formed acquaintances with dreyfusards (like Faure and Quillard), remade old friendships which had fallen into neglect and even into antipathy (like Zola's), and completely revised his unfavourable opinions of several whom he had formerly attacked (like Joseph

Reinach).[13] Mirbeau was not afraid either to shout his principles from the roof-tops, even though in so doing he laid himself open to the accusation of self-contradiction. When for example his anti-dreyfusard opponents tried to discredit him by reprinting fifteen-year-old articles from *Les Grimaces*—articles like 'Le Comte de Chambord',[14] which betrayed Mirbeau's reactionary origins—Mirbeau did not hesitate to reply in terms which bespeak the sincerity of a man who was genuinely ashamed of some of his former opinions.[15]

The renewal of Mirbeau's friendship with Zola was one of the most intriguing effects of the libertarian ideals which brought Mirbeau to support the cause of an innocent army officer. It was primarily because Zola chose to defend the man and the principles Mirbeau believed in that the lapsed friendship between the two naturalist novelists was remade, and on an entirely different and surer basis.[16] Mirbeau's first association with Zola had been in the days prior to the *Soirées de Médan*, when Mirbeau was clearly the disciple and Zola was the 'Cher Maître'. Mirbeau had then drifted away from Zola's circle, and had begun to express his independent opinions about Zola and his works, most of them favourable, but occasionally meeting with Zola's disapproval. In 1886 for example—the year of *Le Calvaire*—Mirbeau expressed his fervent admiration for *L'Oeuvre*,[17] and in 1887 he attacked those who criticised Zola's dramatisation of *Renée*, in an article which André Antoine recalled in his memoirs published almost fifty years later.[18] But as Mirbeau moved left, and as he listened to the adverse criticisms of Zola which he heard in anarchist circles,[19] and in the Grenier of Edmond de Goncourt—who reproached Zola for aspiring to the Académie Française—Mirbeau became more and more critical of Zola, until it looked as though their friendship was finished for good.[20] In 1887 for example, Mirbeau criticised *La Terre* in no uncertain terms, and by 1888 his admiration for Zola had virtually evaporated, as the title of a scathing attack on Zola suggested: 'La Fin d'un homme' (*Le Figaro*, 9 August 1888).

Mirbeau was not alone either in this swing against Zola. There were many young writers who agreed with Camille Mauclair that 'Zola était bien antipathique; il visait l'Académie et détestait les jeunes gens'.[21] Rosny *aîné* in particular, like Mirbeau a regular visitor to Goncourt's Grenier, had reason to dislike Zola, and was one of the five young writers who expressed their rejection of Zola's aesthetic credo in the celebrated *Manifeste des Cinq* of 1887.[22] A letter from Mirbeau to Rosny, written in 1890, shows how much Mirbeau now agreed with Rosny's assessment of Zola, for Mirbeau actually referred to Zola as 'un parfait imbécile'.[23] For almost ten years Mirbeau and Zola remained poles apart, and it was only a question of principles as important to Mirbeau as the Dreyfus Affair that could make him revise his excessive but nevertheless well-grounded animosity towards his former idol.

It was only a few days after the degradation of Dreyfus on 5 January 1895—an account of which Mirbeau heard from the lips of Léon Daudet—that Mirbeau first began to sense the possibility of a legal error in the Dreyfus Affair.[24] By the summer of 1896 Mirbeau and Zola were again on friendly terms;[25] and when Zola published the first of his articles directly concerning the Dreyfus Affair ('M. Scheurer-Kestner')[26] Mirbeau wrote Zola a warm letter of admiration which signalled the beginning of the renewal of their friendship. 'Oh! mon cher Zola,' Mirbeau wrote in almost breathless admiration, 'quel beau, quel brave, quel admirable article vous avez écrit hier! . . . Ç'a été une émotion qui a fait frissonner tous les coeurs qui ne sont pas encore pourris! Et c'est plus qu'une belle page, c'est un acte d'un beau courage.'[27] From this time on Mirbeau and Zola fought together for the ideals which Mirbeau had already campaigned for, and which he had mistakenly assumed to be of little interest to his more eminent colleague.

Though Mirbeau did not collaborate regularly on the pro-Dreyfus *L'Aurore* until August 1898, he was by then a regular visitor to the paper's offices. This came about because of his acquaintance with Vaughan (the owner), his friendship with Clemenceau (the editor), and because of the convictions he shared with *L'Aurore's* other *habitués*: Lazare, Gohier, Leyret, Quillard and France.[28] Mirbeau was present when Zola arrived on 13 January 1898 armed with his 'Lettre à M. Fèlix Faure', which he read to the enthusiastic group of writers and journalists. This was a decisive moment in Mirbeau's life, for in it he made a resolution which he kept to the last letter, for when he had listened in wrapt silence to the reading of 'J'accuse', he turned to Zola and declared with typical frankness:

> Mon cher Zola, je dois vous avouer que je n'avais pas jusqu'ici une grande admiration pour votre oeuvre. Mais après ce que vous venez de faire, à vos risques et périls, je suis votre homme; vous m'entendez, et, quoi qu'il arrive, je vous suivrai jusqu'au bout.[29]

As Camille Mauclair put it, 'J'accuse' 'parut racheter toutes les erreurs de caractère de Zola romancier et chef d'école'.[30] From this moment on the durability of Mirbeau's admiration for Zola was based upon the certainty that Zola now supported some of the principles which had long been dear to Mirbeau himself. 'Depuis *J'accuse*,' he said to Léon Daudet about Zola, 'c'est autre chose.'[31]

The offices of *Le Libertaire* and of *L'Aurore* were centres of dreyfusard activity which Mirbeau gladly frequented, for like the Affair itself, Mirbeau synthesised within himself the anarchism and the radicalism of these militant journalistic circles. It was for this reason perhaps that Mirbeau found himself at home most of all in the third centre of dreyfusard activity: the offices in the rue Laffitte of *La Revue Blanche*. It was on *La Revue Blanche* that anarchist and dreyfusard sympathies worked most closely together: Thadée Natanson, Léon Blum, Victor Barrucand and Félix Fénéon were the mainstays of the magazine, and like Mirbeau they carried their anarchism over into the fight for Dreyfus.[32] Small wonder then that Mirbeau was one of the most assiduous attenders at the war-councils of *La Revue Blanche*, for there he could meet with artists and fellow men of letters who like himself were motivated by a love of truth and justice to put their talent to practical use in the cause of an ideal. It was *La Revue Blanche*, with Félix Fénéon as editor, which published in February 1898 a declaration of protest against the legal proceedings taken against Zola;[33] it was *La Revue Blanche* which, in the same year, published in book form the violent dreyfusard diatribe of Urbain Gohier *L'Armée contre la nation*; it was *La Revue Blanche* which, on the occasion of the re-trial of Dreyfus, organised the concerted attendance of so many leading dreyfusards in 1899; and it was *La Revue Blanche* which, in the same year, published a book condemning the *lois scélérates* of 1894, by Pouget the anarchist, and by Pressensé, a militant supporter of Dreyfus. The atmosphere of the magazine itself was a very special cocktail of artistic refinement and of revolutionary ideology, and it was an atmosphere to which Mirbeau contributed as much as anyone else.[34]

It was amidst all this fervent activity, in his daily visits to the centres of the dreyfusard cause and his continuous contacts with the anarchists, the radicals and the republicans who had taken up cudgels on behalf of Dreyfus, that Mirbeau found the inspiration to complete and publish his fourth novel, *Le Jardin des supplices*. The basic thesis of this nightmarish novel is that society is organised in a way which encourages and fosters the animal instincts of humanity, giving free rein to the cruel and homicidal tendencies of man, and producing a world full of suffering, of exploitation and of death. This thesis was already established in Mirbeau's mind, and he had already committed it to print before the Dreyfus Affair came along to confirm it to his satisfaction and to provide the stimulus he needed to finish the full-scale work which was intended to demonstrate the truth of his thesis.[35] It is impossible to say how much of *Le Jardin des supplices* had actually been written before Mirbeau was gripped by the Dreyfus passion. The novel seems to have been conceived in three parts: the preface—in which Mirbeau explains his thesis—and the two distinct halves of the novel itself: *En mission*, which expounds the situation of the main character Eugène Mortain, and *Le Jardin des supplices*, in which Mortain is given a conducted tour of the eastern equivalent of a 'chamber of horrors' by his depraved companion Clara. All three sections contain some material that was written and published prior to Mirbeau's consuming interest in the Dreyfus Affair;[36] and this suggests that at least the novel's basic philosophy was well defined in Mirbeau's mind by early 1897. This would explain why there are few overt references to the Dreyfus Affair in *Le Jardin des supplices*, for Mirbeau evidently considered that the shape, plot and content of his novel which he had already partly prepared were sufficient commentary on the sorry state of affairs in France.

Such references as there are in *Le Jardin des supplices* to the Dreyfus Affair show clearly that the fate of Dreyfus convinced Mirbeau of the validity of his thesis that 'le meurtre est la plus grande préoccupation humaine';[37] and it was for this reason that his support for the Dreyfus cause was an instinctive one, a revolt against the homicidal and sadistic tendencies which Mirbeau depicts so horribly in his frenetic novel. As the Darwinian scientist in the long philosophical discussion which forms the key preface declares with regard to criminal law: 'En cette affaire, comme en toutes autres, ce sont les petits qui paient pour les grands.' It was against this law of society that Mirbeau revolted, and like many others he supported Dreyfus as much for his role of scapegoat as for anything else.

Joining in the discussion of the human murder instinct in the preface to *Le Jardin des supplices*, a Sorbonne philosopher points directly to the Dreyfus Affair as an example of humanity's dangerous tendency to revert to atavistic barbarism, and his words could be aptly applied to the scenes of sadistic carnage in Mirbeau's Chinese torture-garden: '. . . jamais, je crois, la passion du meurtre et la joie de la chasse à l'homme, ne s'étaient aussi complètement et cyniquement étalées . . .'

The correspondence in the mind of Mirbeau between the example of the Dreyfus Affair and the monstrous horror of the torture-garden was so close that the novel is imperfectly understood without an appreciation of the link between the two. The twenty-eight pages of the vital preface state quite clearly the moral thesis of the novel; Mirbeau's comments on French society in this section leave no possible doubt as to the sincerity of his desire to cleanse it of the evils which, in his presentation of the torture-garden, he describes in minute allegorical detail.[38] There is no doubt that in the main body of the novel Mirbeau plumbs the depths of horror and obscenity; and he does it with such emphasis and with such apparent relish, that the many accusations of depravity which have been levelled at him would seem to be well-founded were it not for the supporting evidence of the background against which the novel was written, evidence which must be taken into account if the preface has any meaning at all, and which alone can bring out the full weight of Mirbeau's vehement dedication of the book: 'Aux prêtres, aux soldats, aux juges, aux hommes, qui éduquent, dirigent, gouvernent les hommes, je dédie ces pages de meurtre et de sang.'

Le Jardin des supplices must be understood not as an exhibition of the morbid eroticism of a degenerate *fin-de-siècle* artist,[39] but as the impassioned cry of disgust of a man who loathed contemporary civilisation and who tried to exorcise its hold upon him by paying it back in its own cynical and sadistic coin. This at least was how Mirbeau's closest associates understood the novel;[40] and this no doubt was why, while awaiting his re-trial at Rennes, Captain Dreyfus himself asked for a copy of the book and read it with interest, and almost certainly with gratitude.[41] The feeling too would be mutual, for it was Dreyfus who had filled Mirbeau with passion sufficient not only to fill his life with single-minded zeal but also to bring to completion one of the most frenzied and one of the most disturbing books modern literature has ever produced.[42]

Whatever the unfavourable reactions of the contemporary literary critics—ostensibly on the grounds of pornography, but more probably because Mirbeau was a dreyfusard!—and whatever notoriety the novel may have gained since in the obscene literature of the western world, the morality of *Le Jardin des supplices* is sufficiently clear to be put beyond doubt. It resides in the very structure of the novel. The preface, so unfortunately ignored by most critics, explains the proposition: man is cruel to his fellow men, and human society in its present state encourages this cruelty while glossing it over with respectability and legality. Part One, containing an account of the narrator Eugène Mortain's life in parisian society and the halls of governmental power, reveals the callousness and the corruption of western life beneath the respectable exterior of honour and position. Part Two is in deliberate juxtaposition to the hypocrisy revealed in Part One, for it describes the unashamed practices of cruelty and the avidly cultivated decadence and corruption of the eastern world. Mirbeau is clearly equating the two societies, the important difference being in the question of the hypocrisy, the moral pretence which the western world seeks to preserve. Clara, who first appears to Mortain in western climes as an innocent young woman, and who only reveals her true sadistic tendencies once they reach the Orient, clinches this interpretation of the novel when she reproaches Mortain and his fellow Europeans for their hypocrisy:

> L'Europe et sa civilisation hypocrite, barbare, c'est le mensonge . . . Vous êtes obligé de feindre un respect extérieur pour des personnes, des institutions que vous trouvez absurdes . . . Vous demeurez lâchement attaché à des conventions morales ou sociales que vous méprisez . . . C'est cette contradiction permanente . . . qui vous rend tristes, troubles, déséquilibrés . . .[43]

The orientals at least were honest about the cruelty of their society.

Lest, after all these pointers, there should still be any doubt as to the morality of *Le Jardin des supplices*, Mirbeau brings the narrator himself to an understanding of the significance of the torture-garden through which he passes; and Mortain's expression of that understanding, coming as it does towards the end of the novel, ties together all the threads of the moral thesis of this unusual work:

> Alors, peu à peu, ma pensée se détache du jardin, des cirques de torture, des agonies sous les cloches, des arbres hantés de la douleur, des fleurs sanglantes et dévoratrices . . . Et l'univers m'apparaît comme un immense, comme un inexorable jardin des supplices.
> . . . Les passions, les appétits, les intérêts, les haines, le mensonge; et les lois, et les institutions sociales, et la justice, l'amour, la gloire, l'héroïsme, les religions, en sont les fleurs monstrueuses et les hideux instruments de l'éternelle souffrance humaine . . .
> Et ce sont les juges, les soldats, les prêtres qui, partout, dans les églises, les casernes, les temples de justice s'acharnent à l'oeuvre de mort . . .[44]

Notes

1 From 1890 to 1898 Mirbeau published no new books except the *Contes de la chaumière* (1894), which was merely a collection of short stories previously published in various newspapers, and which included several stories from the *Lettres de ma chaumière* of 1885.
2 'Lettres à Claude Monet', *op. cit.*
3 Mirbeau told Grave in a letter of July(?) 1893 (I.F.H.S.), that he was working on 'une pièce sociale et anarchiste', which was almost certainly an early version of *Les Mauvais Bergers*.
4 Mirbeau's literary silence does not seem to have damaged his reputation as a writer. In November 1894 for example, Cézanne is said to have regarded Mirbeau as 'the greatest writer of his time'. H. Perruchot, *Cézanne* (London: Perpetua, 1961), p. 245.
5 Martin Schwarz, 'Octave Mirbeau et l'Affaire Dreyfus', *The French Review*, December 1965, pp. 361–72.
6 Mirbeau's police dossiers show that he spoke or was present at scores of dreyfusard meetings, and on at least one occasion (Toulouse, 22 December 1898) he was the victim of brutal retaliation when he was dragged from the speaker's platform and

beaten, and was later shot at, along with the poet Pierre Quillard. See *L'Aurore*, 24 December 1898. As well as travelling all over France to whip up support for Dreyfus, Mirbeau visited Colonel Picquart in prison, and Zola in exile; he attended all the court hearings connected with the Affair and kept up a flow of invective in the pro-Dreyfus press. As Léon Blum later put it in his memoirs: 'Il s'était jeté à corps perdu dans la bataille . . . parce qu'il aimait l'action et la mêlée, parce qu'il était généreux, et surtout parce qu'il était pitoyable . . .'. *L'Oeuvre de Leon Blum*, vol. IV (Paris: Albin Michel, 1965), p. 546.

7 See S. Faure, *Les Anarchistes et l'Affaire Dreyfus* (Paris: Au Libertaire, 1898), and Maitron, *op. cit.*, especially chapter 2. Mirbeau's connections with the anarchists during the Affair are amply illustrated by his two police files. These reveal that Mirbeau was a founder-member of the revolutionary coalition of anarchists and radicals who banded together in October 1898 in anticipation of a right-wing coup (Mirbeau dossier BA/1190, item 49, B.A.M.P.P.). The coalition's manifesto was published in most of the left-wing newspapers, including *Le Père Peinard*, 23 October 1898. As well as Mirbeau, the signatories included the anarchists Sébastien Faure, Charles Malato and Emile Pouget. Items 53 and 63 in the same police file are reports of the meetings of this revolutionary group. Item 78 is a report suggesting that Mirbeau was subsidising *Les Temps Nouveaux*. Dossier EA/52, item 40, gives an account of Mirbeau's active support in October 1898 for the anarchist-inspired Bourses du Travail (labour exchanges intended to compete with the employer-oriented *bureaux de placement*). These and many more documents show how Mirbeau's anarchism and dreyfusism co-existed and drew their inspiration from the same source of vehement idealism.
8 *Cf.* Lazare's obituary in *T.N.*, No. 19 (5 September 1903).
9 Maitron, *op. cit.*, p. 315.
10 Mirbeau dossier BA/1190, item 68 (B.A.M.P.P.).
11 *Le Journal du Peuple*, 3 May 1899.
12 The most violent of all Mirbeau's verbal attacks on Méline is 'Une Face de Méline', *ibid.*, 1 March 1899.
13 Mirbeau apologised publicly to Reinach for the harsh things he had once said of him. 'Palinodies', *L'Aurore*, 15 November 1898.
14 *Les Grimaces*, No. 5 (18 August 1883). This article was quoted *in extenso* by Paul Mathiex in an article in the right-wing press: 'Un Républicain de vieille date', *Le Jour*, 14 November 1898.
15 Mirbeau's anti-bourgeois attitude at least had remained constant during his swing from Right to Left. Mathiex's campaign against Mirbeau, conducted in *La Patrie* and *Le Jour* from September to December 1898, was supported by *L'Intransigeant* (24 October 1898) and *La Libre Parole* (21 December 1898), which also reprinted old articles from *Les Grimaces*. *Cf.* also *La Patrie*, 17 September 1898. Mirbeau's replies to these criticisms show that he was genuinely sorry that he had ever expressed such reactionary opinions. *Cf.* 'Palinodies', *op. cit.*, and 'Un Mot personnel', *L'Aurore*, 21 December 1898.
16 T. Gribelin, 'Octave Mirbeau. Son amitié littéraire et politique avec Emile Zola' (unpublished *D.E.S.* dissertation, University of Besançon, 1965) is a short but on the whole excellent study which provides much valuable documentation on the Mirbeau–Zola relationship. Mlle Gribelin does not, however, give much interpretation of the various ups and downs in the friendship, and fails to stress the role of catalyst that Dreyfus played in the revival and intensification of their association in the 1890s.
17 See the letter of 19 April 1886, reproduced in *ibid.*, pp. 58–9.
18 A. Antoine, *Le Théâtre* (Paris: Editions de France, 1932), pp. 202–5. Mirbeau's

article was entitled 'Le Public et le théâtre', *Le Gaulois*, 21 April 1887.
19 Though he had written *Germinal* (1885), and though the words of his fictional anarchist Souvarine were often quoted in support of anarchist doctrine, Zola was not regarded by the anarchists as a kindred spirit. Indeed, in the 1880s and early 1890s, Zola tried to dissociate himself from the anarchism of so many of his young literary contemporaries (*cf.* Ternois, *op. cit.*, pp. 326–7). Zola's questionable behaviour in the affair of the Société des Gens de Lettres (1891), and his refusal to sign the petition for Jean Grave (1894), only served to convince Mirbeau that his anarchist friends were right about Zola's cowardly and mercenary mentality. Two typical anti-Zola articles written in anarchist milieux were: Y. Rambosson, 'Un Crapaud', *La Plume*, No. 212 (15 February 1898), and E. Pouget, 'La Question Dreyfus', *Le Père Peinard*, 16 January 1898.
20 Zola was aware of Mirbeau's diminishing sympathy; but in 1888 he wrote to Mirbeau in prophetic vein: 'Vous êtes un croyant, facile aux conversions, et si jamais la vérité se refait en vous sur mon compte, je vous connais d'une assez grande bonne foi pour la confesser.' Letter of 9 August 1888, quoted from Gribelin, *op. cit.*, p. 130. Zola proved to be right, but his own change of attitude had much to do with the subsequent revival of their friendship.
21 *Servitude et grandeur littéraires*, pp. 134–5.
22 A letter from Zola to Rosny (collection of M Robert Borel-Rosny) shows how abrupt and indifferent Zola could be, for he refused to read Rosny's first novel, and would not help the young writer in any way.
23 Letter in the collection of M Robert Borel-Rosny.
24 See Mirbeau's article 'Chez l'illustre écrivain', *Le Journal*, 28 November 1897.
25 *Cf.* Gribelin, *op. cit.*, p. 39. It seems likely that Zola's brave article 'Pour les Juifs', *Le Figaro*, 16 May 1896, had more than a little to do with this initial reconciliation.
26 *Le Figaro*, 25 November 1897.
27 Letter of 26 November 1897, quoted from Gribelin, *op. cit.*, p. 67.
28 Gohier, an anarchist sympathiser, was tried and acquitted in March 1899 on a charge of defamation of the army in his book *L'Armée contre la nation* (Paris: Editions de la *Revue Blanche*, 1898). Mirbeau was a witness for Gohier at the trial, and gave a speech at the banquet to celebrate his acquittal. See *L'Aurore*, 7 April 1899. Henri Leyret was, like Mirbeau, a member of the Coalition révolutionnaire (see note 7 above), and was responsible, in 1894, for the petition against Grave's imprisonment.
29 L. Daudet, *La Vie orageuse de Clemenceau* (Rio de Janeiro: Chantecler, 1943), pp. 118–9.
30 *Servitude et grandeur littéraires*, p. 135.
31 L. Daudet, *Souvenirs*, vol. 2 (Paris: Nouvelle Librairie Nationale, 1926), p. 46.
32 On the anarchism of *La Revue Blanche*, and its important role as a centre of dreyfusard activity, see A. B. Jackson, *La Revue Blanche, 1889–1903* (Paris: Minard, 1960), pp. 23, 45–6, 57, 95–6 and 100–9.
33 'Protestation', *La Revue Blanche*, tom. XV (1898), pp. 161–2.
34 *Cf.* Jackson, *op. cit.*, pp. 106, 110–15, and 123–5; also Blum, *op. cit.*, pp. 546–7.
35 *Cf.* 'La Loi du meurtre', *L'Echo de Paris*, 24 May 1892, and 'Divagations sur le meurtre', *Le Journal*, 31 May 1896.
36 For example 'La Loi du meurtre', *op. cit.*, forms part of the preface in the published version of *Le Jardin des supplices*; 'Profil d'explorateur', *Le Journal*, 15 July 1894, forms part of Part One of the book *(En mission)*; and 'Un Bagne chinois', *ibid.*, 14 and 21 February 1897, was incorporated into Part Two.
37 'La Loi du meurtre', *op. cit.*
38 The publishers of the most recent English translation of *Le Jardin des supplices* (The

Garden of Tortures. London: Tandem, 1969), possibly interested in the pornographic appeal of the novel, have entirely omitted Mirbeau's lengthy preface, thus leaving the unsuspecting English reader without the key to the book.
39 This is how Mario Praz (mis)understands the novel. *The Romantic Agony*, *passim*.
40 Writing in *Le Journal du Peuple*, 11 September 1899, Mirbeau's anarchist friend Sébastien Faure explained the motivation for Mirbeau's deliberate sadism: 'Il était jeté dans une lutte âpre, sans merci, qui paraissait sans espoir. Il souffrait dans sa chair, son coeur, et sa pensée de toutes les douleurs subies par un autre. On peur croire aussi qu'il a voulu gagner les générations futures à de fraternelles douceurs par l'atroce peinture des cruautés d'hier, d'aujourd'hui.' 'En passant. *Le Jardin des Supplices*', *Le Journal du Peuple*, 11 September 1899.
41 *Ibid*.
42 It is worth noting that Kafka's *In der Strafkolonie*, regarded by many as one of the most disturbing books of modern literature, was directly inspired by *Le Jardin des supplices*. *Cf.* W. Burns, '*In the Penal Colony*: variations on a theme by Octave Mirbeau', *Accent*, No. 17 (winter 1957), pp. 45–51.
43 *Le Jardin des supplices* (Paris: Fasquelle, 1913 edition), pp. 112–13.
44 *Ibid*., pp. 293–4.

Chapter VII
The theatre of ideas (1897–1908)

> Peu d'écrivains ont aussi librement projeté qu'Octave Mirbeau leur caractère et leurs convictions dans leur oeuvre.
>
> (Gérard Bauër)

The difficulties Mirbeau experienced with his fourth novel made him look to the drama as a possible outlet for the polemical talents which had made him famous as a journalist but which, by their very nature, were hindering the advancement of his reputation as a novelist. Mirbeau was no poet,[1] and he still had many things of consequence to say, so an attempt at the drama seemed a likely solution. He had after all been theatre critic on *L'Ordre de Paris*; he had written many articles in other papers on the leading playwrights of the day; he had always been a regular theatregoer, and was the friend and defender of actor–managers like Antoine and Lugné-Poë as well as established dramatists like Maeterlinck, Sardou and Becque; he had even tried his hand at short dramatic sketches, and several of them had been published successfully as newpaper articles.[2] His talent for dialogue, his gift for rendering lifelike the conversations of his fictional characters, was evident, and not even his critics denied him that. The recent vogue also towards more socially-conscious drama, particularly in the Théâtre Libre and the Théâtre de l'Oeuvre, which Mirbeau supported and frequented from their foundation,[3] had been a parallel development to Mirbeau's own intellectual evolution, and it is no coincidence that he should begin to write his first full-length drama at the time when he was most deeply involved with the anarchists, and that this drama should be, to quote his own words to Grave, 'une pièce sociale, et anarchiste, mais sans prêche, sans tirades'.[4]

It was Mirbeau's anarchism which led him ultimately to the drama, for he sensed that here, far more than in the novel, was the easiest and the most appropriate place for him to talk freely about the social realities which occupied so much of his attention. Like many of his contemporaries Mirbeau considered that the theatre, more than any other artistic medium, had a social and didactic role to play, 'par la force seule, par la force éducatrice et civilisatrice de la beauté . . . .'.[5]

Hence his support for Antoine's Théâtre Libre, which had brought the theatre back to 'plus de logique, à plus d'humanité, au pittoresque de la réalité, à l'emotion—la seule poignante—de la vie', and had inculcated in theatre audiences 'un peu plus de goût pour la vérité!'[6] In one of his rare moments of praise for popular taste, Mirbeau even said once, in reply to an *enquête* by Georges Bourdon of the *Revue d'Art Dramatique*, that he thought that the working-class audience actually preferred social dramas to the kind of frivolous entertainment associated with middle-class theatres:

> Donnez-lui à choisir entre une pièce d'amour et une oeuvre sociale, où s'agiteront toutes les choses mystérieuses qui travaillent la société et d'où sortira l'avenir, vous verrez avec quelle passion ardente et enthousiaste il portera et acclamera l'oeuvre sociale![7]

There were thus several factors which prompted Mirbeau to make his debut in the world of drama. His close communion with the contemporary movement of the literary tide, his increasing difficulties with the form of his novels, and perhaps also a certain amount of literary vanity, were all responsible in some measure for this excursion into a new *genre*. But the fact that all of Mirbeau's dramatic productions turned out to be works of intense social criticism, and particularly that his first play, *Les Mauvais Bergers*, should be the tragic tale of a sympathetically portrayed anarchist in his fight against the capitalist machine, clearly showed that Mirbeau's theatre, described by Henry Bauër as 'antisocial',[8] owed much of its existence to Mirbeau's long-standing contact with the antisocial theories of anarchism and the consequent effect these theories had upon his social consciousness.

The immediate link between Mirbeau's association with the anarchists and his first full-length play *Les Mauvais Bergers* was more evident to Mirbeau's contemporaries than it would be to a modern audience. Emile de Saint-Auban, who had conducted Jean Grave's defence in 1894, laid his finger on the source of inspiration of Mirbeau's play, and particularly of its main character the anarchist Jean Roule, when he wrote:

> M. Mirbeau le connaît bien, ce frère de sa fantaisie; dans des procès fameux, il lui porta son témoignage; jadis, il fit et refit son portrait en des articles frémissants ... ces articles, leur verbe haut, leur psychologie dramatique, je les retrouve dans le passion nerveuse, la vibration sonore des *Mauvais Bergers*. Lorsque je défendais Jean Grave, M. Mirbeau créait Jean Roule ...[9]

Jean Roule is a militant anarchist who is trying to awaken his fellow-workers to the iniquities of the capitalist system which is depriving them of their rights and maintaining them at subsistence level. Jean's criticisms of the wealthy factory-owner Hargand, and especially Jean's exalted speeches during the workers' meeting in the forest in Act 4, are based directly on the writings of Grave with which Mirbeau was so familiar, and also on the often more violent ideas of other anarchists, which Mirbeau had encountered in the anarchist press. Many of Mirbeau's critics reproached him for a lack of originality in this dramatisation of the clash between capitalism and the demands of the proletariat. But while it is true that Mirbeau did 'borrow' the basic theme of his play from Becque, Hauptmann and Curel, as well as more specific ideas from Zola, the importance and the originality of the character of Jean Roule ultimately outweighs these considerations, and endows Les Mauvais Bergers with a flavour all of its own.[10] Though no longer performed, it still stands both as a valuable socio-historical documentary and as a highly-personalised analysis of a continuing human dilemma.

Mirbeau tried to avoid at all costs in his play any degeneration into vulgar pamphleteering. Jean Grave himself, by a strange touch of irony, had warned Mirbeau of the dangers with just such a subject, for he wrote to Mirbeau in July 1893:

> La portée de votre pièce sera bien plus grande si la morale découle de l'action elle-même. Les tirades sont bonnes pour le livre de discussion, mais pour le roman, et le théâtre surtout, une situation bien décrite, une opposition de scènes bien dessinées, sont bien meilleures à mon avis.[11]

Mirbeau hardly needed the advice of a self-educated cobbler when it came to writing literature; but as it happened it was good advice, and Mirbeau was careful in Les Mauvais Bergers not to overload the dialogue with didactic ideology. He achieved this in a number of ways, each of which bolstered up the feasibility of Jean Roule as a real-life character and added meaning to the criticisms he was allowed to level at the society around him. To begin with, there was the well-conceived plot and the skilful juxtaposition of scenes which Grave had recommended. Mirbeau's exposition of the situation, the workers' plight, the threatened strike, the role of Jean Roule, and his handling of the scenes throughout the play, seem like the skilful products of a veteran dramatist rather than of a raw beginner. Only perhaps Act 5, with its 'third party' accounts of the bloody battle between the strikers and the army, and its multiplication of dead and dying bodies, was a weak link in an otherwise technically sound drama—and even

Shakespeare never resolved that particular problem (witness *Julius Caesar* and *Macbeth*).

The sectarian anarchism of Jean Roule is made more dramatically acceptable also by the love-affair between him and the heroic Madeleine Thieux (first played on stage by Mme Sarah Bernhardt). Jean's deep-seated affection for this remarkable girl, and beyond her, for her unfortunate family, provides the anarchist with humanitarian motives for his desire to improve the workers' lot, and Madeleine's pious devotion to Jean helps Mirbeau to play down the fanaticism in the anarchist which might otherwise have invalidated his arguments in the eyes of the reader or of the theatre audience. This is clearly Madeleine's role within the play itself, for in the forest scene in Act 4, she is the one who persuades the ugly mob to renew its confidence in Jean. By emotion, therefore, rather than by the dryness of political tirade, Mirbeau is able to bring about the tragic clash which results in the bloodshed of Act 5 and the final, ironic words of the old Louis Thieux, Madeleine's demented father: 'C'est la paye!'

Mirbeau's portrayal of the most extreme proletarian propaganda is helped also by the reasonable and honest character of the main protagonist on the capitalist side of the fence: the owner of the factory himself, M Hargand. For once Mirbeau realised that to make this man the repository of all the foibles and vices of the ruling classes would be to destroy the validity of his proletarian opponent; and the balance which Mirbeau achieves as a result of his sympathetic portrayal of Hargand is quite remarkable and almost, sad to say, unique in Mirbeau's writings. Mirbeau created many more memorable characters than M Hargand, but never did he again achieve such success through moderation as he did with the industrialist in *Les Mauvais Bergers*. Hargand's associates, who figure with him mainly in Act 2, are lifeless and almost meaningless caricatures in comparison with him. Mirbeau is thus able to avoid laying the blame for the tragic denouement at the capitalist's door, and the impartiality thus gained adds to the importance of the play as a statement of a serious and lasting problem of industrial society.

Mirbeau's exposition of the conflict between labour and capital was inevitably misunderstood by many of his contemporaries who did not appreciate Mirbeau's own position. The established right-wing critics like Sarcey and Lemaître, in the *Figaro* and the *Revue des Deux Mondes*, almost automatically assumed that Mirbeau was a violent pessimist who concluded in favour of the sterility of armed revolt. Rochefort, the celebrated pamphleteer of *La Lanterne*, saw the play as a poorly-conceived attack on parliamentarian socialism. Others, like the ironic Jules Renard in his *Journal*, dismissed the whole thing as an example of worthless dilettantism. The critics were not just divided, they were spreadeagled by Mirbeau's play. *Les Mauvais Bergers* had been awaited with such bated breath for so long,[12] that when it was finally performed (14 December 1897) most of the critics seemed to overshoot the mark and give their opinion of Mirbeau's own social philosophy rather than an account of the play itself; and as Mirbeau noted after this critical barrage, this resulted in a proliferation of interpretations which he felt obliged to correct. Thus, in reply to Rochefort, Mirbeau explained the significance of the title *Les Mauvais Bergers*: all those who try to lead other men on, including even Jean Roule himself, were included within the scope of the reproach contained in the phrase.[13] This is a clear indication of the depths of Mirbeau's anarchism, for he regarded any authority, whatever the source, as a potential evil, and his play stands as a monument to his individualism. The anarchists realised what Mirbeau was trying to do, and agreed that Mirbeau had been successful. Grave and Chaughi in *Les Temps Nouveaux*, and Faure in *Le Libertaire*, appreciated that Mirbeau's own anarchism was not centred in any one particular character or in any one particular tirade, and that not even Jean Roule was a typical anarchist, but that Mirbeau's anarchism was reflected in various qualities and in various remarks of different characters in the play. Sébastien Faure pointed out in particular that a true anarchist would not act as a strike-delegate or give the kind of commands uttered by Jean Roule,[14] and Mirbeau, in his reply to Rochefort, showed that he was aware of this.[15]

The critics who had no real appreciation of anarchist philosophy also reproached Mirbeau for not coming to any conclusions, or rather, for concluding on a question mark, as if allowing Jean Roule or Hargand to win would provide a satisfactory solution to the problem. The pessimistic denouement was in fact indicative of Mirbeau's personal viewpoint, as he said in reply to his critics: 'Si je l'avais, cette solution, croyez que ce n'est point au théâtre que je l'eusse portée, c'est dans la vie!'[16]

If anarchism was utopian in its hopes for the future, it was nevertheless realistic and pessimistic about the present—this is the duality of revolt which Mirbeau shared with the anarchists—and the anarchists themselves clearly recognised that *Les Mauvais Bergers* was a realistic and pessimistic statement of the impasse which had been reached in their struggle to change the *status quo*. They accepted the blackness of the denouement, and like Mirbeau in his brighter moments hoped that one day life might reappear out of the ruins of death. The anarchist Charles Albert welcomed Mirbeau's play, denouement and all, as part of 'ce théâtre d'éducation et de révolte si naturel à notre époque',[17] while the anarchist René Chaughi particularly endorsed the scene where Jean Roule presents the minimum demands of the strikers, and wrote of the final scenes of carnage: 'C'est toujours ainsi que la bourgeoisie a répondu aux réclamations ouvrières.'[18] And Sébastien Faure confirmed the pervading anarchism of Mirbeau's play by analysing the economic implications of the plot:

> Cette lutte séculaire et irréductible entre riches et pauvres, cette stérilité de toute prétendue d'amélioration, cette radicale impuissance de toute soi-disant réforme, n'est-ce pas l'observation constante sur laquelle travaille l'effort anarchiste et de laquelle il tire ses conclusions contre la propriété privée?

Politically too *Les Mauvais Bergers* was accepted by the anarchists as an adequate representation of some of their major principles, and particularly of anti-parliamentarianism. Commenting in the same article on Jean Roule's rejection of the offer of help from the socialist *députés* in Act 4, Faure praised the way in which Mirbeau denounced and stigmatised 'l'influence néfaste des politiciens, si radicaux, si socialistes soient-ils, l'inanité du suffrage universel, le mensonge de tous les programmes . . . l'étouffement de l'Esprit révolutionnaire par les endormeurs du Parlement'.[19] If we compare Faure's interpretation of Jean Roule's action—so misunderstood by all but the anarchist critics—with what Mirbeau himself said by way of clarification, then we can only conclude that the anarchist interpretation was right, for Mirbeau wrote shortly after the first performance of his play:

> J'ai fait parler l'anarchiste comme il convient qu'il parle, et rien de plus.
> Est-ce à dire que ces paroles me soient antipathiques? . . . Je mentirais si je disais oui! Comme lui, j'éprouve une haine violente contre ce qu'on appelle le groupe collectiviste de la Chambre . . . contre des politiciens que je juge être les ennemis—les pires ennemis—de toute liberté, de toute beauté, de toute justice sociale. Comme les fusils Lebel, ces paroles sont parties toutes seules.[20]

The excessive reactions of the right-wing critics, divided in their interpretations through ignorance of Mirbeau's intentions but united in their disapproval, and the favourable comments of the anarchist writers, which tied in closely with Mirbeau's own remarks about his play, leave little doubt that *Les Mauvais Bergers* was indeed the 'pièce sociale et anarchiste' which Mirbeau had promised to Jean Grave over four years before it was performed.

Les Mauvais Bergers, in spite of its surprising qualities for a first play, and although it was one of the best of the many social dramas of the contemporary trend, was not a great critical or box-office success, perhaps because in spite of Mirbeau's striving for impartiality the play was inevitably too partisan to receive widespread acclaim from a predominantly bourgeois theatregoing public. Six years later however Mirbeau had his revenge when, through the friendship of Jules Claretie, Director of the Comédie-Française, he saw what proved to be his most lasting work, *Les Affaires sont les affaires*, performed in the sanctum of French drama, and experienced the personal satisfaction of having his play acclaimed on all sides as a masterpiece and a classic in the grand style.[21]

The reason for the success of Mirbeau's second full-length play and the comparative failure of his first lies in the relative dilution in the second of Mirbeau's polemical argumentation. Referring to *Les Affaires sont les affaires*, Martin Schwarz rightly comments: 'Il y a peu de polémique dans la pièce et l'art y gagne énormément.'[22]

It is clear that from the failure of *Les Mauvais Bergers* Mirbeau had realised the need to water down the virulence of his anarchistic temperament, to make his social criticism more general, less intense, and above all, more self-evident. *Les Affaires sont les affaires* is the only play in which he achieved this and displayed the great art of which he was capable. For this reason, however, this story of Isidore Lechat, the unscrupulous businessman who uses people like pieces on a chessboard, is of less interest for the purpose of this study than an inferior work like *Les Mauvais Bergers*, simply because it reveals less of Mirbeau's anarchistic convictions. This is not to say that the play is quite without polemics, for Mirbeau would have been incapable of writing such a work. In fact the play is all the more philosophically valid for the superior literary manner in which Mirbeau's social criticisms are expressed.

It is important first to realise that the central character and his obnoxious qualities had already made an appearance in Mirbeau's published writings, in the short story 'Agronomie' (in the *Lettres de ma chaumière*). The Lechat of *Les Affaires sont les affaires* appeared in this short story almost exactly as he reappeared over seventeen years later in the play—even the surname was unchanged. Mme Lechat also made the transition from prose to drama with very few changes or additions to her character. The social criticism implied therefore by the characters of the Lechat couple remained on the same level as that of the *Lettres de ma chaumière* of 1885–6, which were written at a time when Mirbeau's anarchism had not reached its fullest intensity. The most important character after Lechat himself in *Les Affaires sont les affaires* is Lechat's daughter Germaine, who did not appear in

'Agronomie'. She was created much later, and quite clearly reflects the more intense, socially-critical attitudes which Mirbeau developed through his contact with the anarchists. It is in the words of Germaine Lechat, with her idealism and her violent hostility to her corrupt family, and in the words of her more reasonable lover Lucien Garraud (who for the purposes of the drama acts as her confidant), that Mirbeau expresses most overtly the anarchistic comments which, if overdone, might have upset the balance and the appeal of the play as a whole.

Germaine represents the hostile and active will which opposes Lechat and refuses to be steam-rollered like everybody else in the play. As the necessary counterbalance to Lechat's dominance, her (Mirbeau's) comments on Lechat's methods are dramatically motivated and therefore aesthetically acceptable. When for example Germaine refuses to be part of her father's deal with the Marquis of Porcellet (Lechat wants her to marry the Marquis' son Robert), her confession that she has taken a lover of her own choice, and her marked insistence throughout the play upon the principle of free love, seem to arise naturally in opposition to her father's demagogic and mercenary views. Germaine's detailed account of her father's financial amorality is similarly built into the fabric of the plot, for in order to overcome the scruples of her lover, who owes her father a great deal for his position as scientific adviser, she must justify her revolt and is therefore given plenty of opportunity for highlighting her father's misdeeds. There is a scene also (in Act 1) where Germaine takes the side of the unfortunate gardener, whose dismissal from the Lechat home owing to the pregnancy of his wife (a familiar theme in Mirbeau's work) is a practical example of the callousness of this capitalist overlord. This early scene serves to focus attention from the very beginning on the conflict between Lechat and his refractory daughter, for the gardener, recognising in her a sympathetic spirit, presages the outcome of the play with the words: 'Quand on a un coeur comme le vôtre . . . on ne peut pas être heureux ici . . .'[23]

The success of Mirbeau's play lies in the fact that Germaine Lechat's role as counterbalance to and critic of her otherwise all-powerful father is as technically well-executed as it is dramatically necessary, and Mirbeau is free to use her within that role as his own mouthpiece whenever he so desires. One of Germaine's lines in particular is a valuable commentary on the vehemence of Mirbeau's own social criticism: '. . . c'est parce que j'ai le coeur plein de pitié que j'ai aussi le coeur plein de haine . . .'[24] The fact that Mirbeau provided himself with a mouthpiece in this way, and in a play which was so deliberately non-polemical and in which for once he kept frank expression of his views in the background, shows to what extent Mirbeau's literature, good or bad, was always an expression of his deepest convictions.

The subject of the play itself—the iniquitous social abuses perpetrated by unscrupulous financiers under a capitalist regime—was not a new one by any means. Becque, Zola and Dumas *fils* had used it in the recent past, like Balzac and Lesage before them. But Mirbeau's creation of the monstrous financier Isidore Lechat, who eats, drinks and sleeps money and profit, and who even in the depths of his grief at the death of his son can successfully conclude a tricky business deal almost by instinct, ranks with the best creations in this field. Mirbeau himself had walked the corridors of financial intrigue; but it was not until many years after his experience on the Bourse that he felt the personal need to communicate his reflections on the lust for gold. By 1890, when he told Edmond de Goncourt of his desire to write a novel on money,[25] Mirbeau had come into contact with anarchist thinking, and there is no doubt that the forceful reasoning of Kropotkin against the iniquities of capitalism would considerably sharpen Mirbeau's own critical view of a system which he had seen at close quarters.

Instead of the novel in 1890 there was the play *Les Affaires sont les affaires* in 1903; and perhaps Mirbeau's treatment of the subject gained in vitality on stage more than it might have gained in depth in novel form. *Les Affaires sont les affaires* was regarded by all, even by the most reactionary critics, as a critique of materialistic capitalism; but it was able to impose itself upon a middle-class and wealthy audience by the qualities of its style, its humour, its dramatic realism and its technical brilliance. The theatre critic of *La Plume* found it fascinating to watch an audience made up mainly of businessmen, bankers and the last representatives of the old aristocracy shouting 'Encore' as they were being whipped and lashed for three solid hours by the 'main vengeresse de M. Octave Mirbeau'.[26] The absurd prejudices of the middle class, the roguery of financiers, the decadence of the nobility, the stupidity and hypocrisy of politics, the venality and corruption of the press, all these are included in this great play, which the same critic describes as 'l'oeuvre synthèse de l'époque'.[27]

It is important to note in passing just what the performance and, more important, the acclamation of a writer like Mirbeau in the Théâtre-Français really meant at that time. At the risk of oversimplification, much of the French literary *avant-garde* regarded this success of an anti-academic writer like Mirbeau as a victory for liberal, some would say revolutionary, ideas. Though he was not accepted by the literary scholars like Brunetière and Faguet, Mirbeau had a great following amongst his fellow writers, and outside France Tolstoy considered Mirbeau as 'celui qui représente le mieux le génie séculaire de la France'.[28] The tangible evidence of this feeling of triumph amongst the non-established writers was a literary banquet organised by *La Plume* in Mirbeau's honour on 6 June 1903, when *Les Affaires sont les affaires* had already been running for six weeks with full houses every night. The speeches by Karl Boès, Mécislas Golberg and the Armenian Archag Tchobanian deliberately stressed their satisfaction that the bold and courageous ideas expressed by Mirbeau were now being heard where it really mattered. This too was the reaction of Mirbeau's anarchist friend Jean Grave, for he saw the success of the play as 'une des meilleures preuves que l'idée poursuit tout doucement son chemin, et s'implante partout'.[29]

In *Les Affaires sont les affaires* Mirbeau achieved his greatest and most durable success by the moderation of his polemical outbursts; but it was something he proved incapable of repeating. With *Le Foyer*, his third and last full-length play, written in collaboration with Thadée Natanson and finally performed in December 1908, Mirbeau evidently thought he had produced the magical formula once again,[30] but he was sadly mistaken. Critics as different as Adolphe Brisson in *Le Temps*, and Henry Bordeaux in *La Revue Hebdomadaire*, were agreed that *Le Foyer* was much inferior to *Les Affaires sont les affaires*. The critics were almost unanimous too on the source of the new play's inferiority; for though Jacques Copeau tried to argue that *Le Foyer* was not a *pièce à thèse*,[31] he was outnumbered by the critics who thought it was, and who insisted that this was why the play had not lived up to expectations.

The thesis of the play was explained quite openly by Mirbeau's collaborator Thadée Natanson, former editor of *La Revue Blanche*, when he said of their intention in *Le Foyer*: 'Nous avons voulu dévoiler les abus de la fausse philanthropie et plaider en faveur de la justice contre l'hypocrite charité.'[32] It was because this thesis was too apparent in this story of baron Courtin's dubiously charitable home for young ladies, because the characters were subordinated to the moral of the play as a whole, and also because of the very nature of the social satire involved, that the critics, while praising certain qualities of Mirbeau's style, dismissed the play and soon forgot it. Many of the critics spoke of the excesses forced on the play by Mirbeau's polemical purpose: the way in which the 'Foyer' itself is portrayed like a prison; the over-exaggeration of the weaknesses of the characters, and particularly of Courtin; and, we might add, the rather contrived way in which Mme Courtin's lover d'Auberval 'happens' to express very radical and socialistic opinions which draw out farcically reactionary replies from the baron—all these things detract from the theatrical success of *Le Foyer*. As Pierre Brisson puts it:

> ... tous ces excès ... brouillaient les nuances auxquelles Mirbeau s'était attaché d'autre part. Il eût suffi de maintenir les caractères et de dégrossir les circonstances pour que la sonorité de la pièce ... fût devenue autrement forte et profonde.[33]

There was more to the unfavourable reception of the play however than such critical comments on the all-important question of its artistic imbalance. *Le Foyer* was also a cause of scandal, both before and after its opening performance in 1908—a scandal caused not by aesthetic considerations but by the very nature of the subject-matter of the play. To attack private and public philanthropy in such a way—for Courtin not only dips his hands into the funds of the institution but also leaves the running of it to a woman whose brutality results in the death of one girl and the injury of another—was a deliberate insult to a very large section of French society; and to do it in the home of French theatre was a deliberate act of aggression against a principle which was dear to the upper and middle classes.[34] Jules Claretie was clearly afraid of the consequences when, after having first accepted the play in 1906, he vacillated and put off its performance, finally, even after he had successfully negotiated the suppression of a whole act, refused to stage the play at all.[35]

Claretie, it seems, when he read the play, was 'effarouché par son extrême violence';[36] and his insistence upon certain changes in the play—including what seemed to him the cardinal point of demoting Mirbeau's baron from the Académie Française where Mirbeau had put him—when it met with the authors' refusal, emboldened him to risk a scandal by refusing to perform a play he had already accepted. This academician, whose praises had been sung by the young radical writers for his courage in staging *Les Affaires sont les affaires*, was unwilling to let its more polemical, controversial and violent successor pass.

The reactionary press was of course solidly behind Claretie, and *L'Intransigeant*'s Léon Bailby was typical of many of his journalistic colleagues when he wrote of Mirbeau's attempts to have *Le Foyer* staged at the Théâtre-Français:

> On veut nous montrer que le Temple-Richelieu est fait expressément pour ces oeuvres de satire anarchique, et que l'Etat paye une subvention à ses comédiens afin de donner l'estampille officielle au théâtre révolutionnaire.[37]

On the opposite side of the fence were young writers like Paul Léautaud, who wrote in his diary on 30 April 1908:

> Pour une fois, on voit un auteur qui résiste aux exigences de la Comédie-Française, qui ne se soumet pas comme les autres, qui ne se prête pas aux tripatouillages, aux adoucissements, à tout ce qu'on lui demande, pour réussir à être joué. On doit être avec lui absolument, entièrement.[38]

Mirbeau and Natanson felt so strongly about the rejection of their play that in consultation with Henry Bréal and Henry Robert, acting solicitors—the latter had, like Mirbeau, been a collaborator on *L'Humanité* from its foundation in 1904—they filed an injunction against Clartie, and pursued the affair into the law courts when he refused to remedy the situation. For many weeks the press was full of the *Affaire du Foyer*, and the police kept a close watch, dutifully filing reports and press-clippings into Mirbeau's ever-fattening dossiers.[39]

For once however the law was on Mirbeau's side, and on 20 May 1908 the court ruled that the rehearsals which had been interrupted in March be resumed, and that the play be performed at the earliest opportunity. Claretie's cold feet had come too late to prevent this controversial play from reaching the stage, and he found himself obliged by law to put *Le Foyer* on. He had his revenge though, when, after full houses for several weeks—no doubt the effect of all the scandal and publicity—the hostile reception and the dwindling audiences finally enabled him after only forty-three performances to take the play off. It was never to be performed again at the Comédie-Française.

The extreme Right also had its revenge on *Le Foyer*. On the second night of the play's opening week, the performance was violently interrupted by the boisterous protest of a group of men —twelve of whom were detained and charged with causing an affray—who had come especially to stop the performances, as they told reporters: 'Nous ne sommes pas venus pour nous amuser, mais pour interdire le Théâtre Français à M. Mirbeau, comme nous avons interdit l'Odéon à Zola.'[40] The signal for the disturbance to begin was the line spoken by Courtin's secretary Dufrère in Act 2 Scene 6: 'L'abbé Leroze s'est donc décidé à violer le secret de la confession?' Mirbeau was never very tender towards the Catholics, and his portrait of the scheming Abbé Leroze, implicated in the scandals of the 'Foyer', was calculated to shock and offend. But this illegal interruption of Mirbeau's play was symptomatic of the moral indignation of conservative and reactionary opinion about *Le Foyer*; and whilst the play enjoyed a limited amount of success in the provinces at Saint-Etienne, Roanne, Grasse, Le Puy, Bourges and Nice, it was banned by the municipal authorities in as many places as it was played, and Mirbeau did not make many friends, or much money for that matter, out of the whole affair.[41]

The reactionary paper *L'Intransigeant* referred to *Le Foyer* as a work of 'anarchistic satire'; and it was precisely because Mirbeau allowed his anarchism (and no doubt also the anarchism of his collaborator Thadée Natanson) to dominate his literary talents that the play failed to reach the standard of *Les Affaires sont les affaires*.[42] The characters and the plot are overshadowed by Mirbeau's patently obvious desire to speak his mind about the hypocrisy of upper-class philanthropy. It was a subject on which Mirbeau had long had strong feelings, and much that he wrote from 1885 onwards prefigured the main theme of *Le Foyer*.

The original stimulus for *Le Foyer* may well have been the series of articles which Maxime Du Camp had written on the wonderful work performed by public and private charities. The articles appeared in *La Revue des Deux Mondes* between 1883 and 1890; and in 1885 Mirbeau wrote an ironical article about the report which Du Camp had just presented to the Academy on the *prix de vertu*. This article, 'L'Envers de la vie',[43] attacking the Academy and undermining the value of such public charity, is a clear foretaste of *Le Foyer*, in which Courtin, academician in spite of Claretie's efforts, successfully extricates himself from a compromising financial situation and prepares himself for an Adriatic cruise during which, in company with his wife and her lover, he intends to draw up his report for the Academy on the *prix de vertu*.

But as with so much of Mirbeau's criticism of society, his opposition to public charity was intensified and made articulate by his contact with anarchist ideas on this same subject. The anarchists believed that charity was basically conscience-money given to the less fortunate both to justify riches and to purchase gratitude and dependence; they believed also that it was often used as a political tool, a kind of mock-reform which preserved the *status quo*.[44] It was clearly in the light of these ideas that Mirbeau's young hero Sébastien Roch expressed Mirbeau's own anarchistic views when he said:

> Oh! la charité que j'ai tant aimée, la charité qui me semblait plus qu'une vertu humaine, la directe et rayonnante émanation de l'immense amour de Dieu, la charité, voilà le secret de l'avilissement des hommes! Par elle, le gouvernant et le prêtre perpétuent la misère au lieu de la soulager, démoralisent le coeur du misérable au lieu de l'élever. Les imbéciles, ils se croient liés à leurs souffrances par ce bienfait menteur, qui de tous les crimes sociaux est le plus grand et le plus monstrueux, le plus indéracinable aussi. Je leur ai dit: 'N'acceptez pas l'aumône, repoussez la charité, et prenez, prenez, car tout vous appartient.'[45]

As the years passed, Mirbeau became still more outspoken on this subject, and in 1892, in an article in which he used the words of Jean Grave concerning the atrocious conditions in police jails to undermine the claims made by that great philanthropist Jules Simon, Mirbeau waded into public charities in no uncertain manner:

> ... je me méfie, d'instinct, de toutes les sociétés de philanthropie de ce temps. J'en connais quelques-unes, et elles ne me rassurent pas sur les autres que j'ignore, car je vois qu'elles ne profitent, en général, qu'à ceux qui les fondent. Ou bien, c'est une distraction à l'oisiveté des femmes . . . ou bien c'est une affaire, un commerce comme un autre, une exploitation en règle . . .[46]

This article was reprinted by the anarchists, as were several of Mirbeau's pronouncements on this matter of philanthropy, on which he had a wholly anarchistic outlook.[47] It was in this spirit that *Le Foyer* was written; and it was because of the nature of Mirbeau's feelings on this subject that he was unable, or unwilling, to moderate them. *Le Foyer* stands as a valuable reflection of an extremist, minority viewpoint on a particular minor issue of pre-1914 France, and it is an interesting portrait of the manners of the *Belle Epoque*; but its failure to rise above the polemical, its lack of more general significance, and above all, its failure to find the artistic balance of which Mirbeau was so rarely capable, have made it fail the test of time. It is also a good example of how Mirbeau's temperament was not only the main ingredient of the writer's originality but also the artist's own worst enemy.

Far more suited to the intense social criticism which deformed so many of Mirbeau's lengthier literary productions were the short, pithy, one-act playlets which he interspersed amongst the plays and novels of this, the period of his greatest notoriety. These anecdotal plays—there were six of them in all—are very reminiscent of Chekhov. They were in fact dramatised adaptations of newspaper articles and short stories from *Le Journal*. Mirbeau's satirical temperament was most at home in these short pieces, and his unrivalled gift for dialogue enabled him to turn them into highly entertaining one-act plays. The fact that they have been performed more often and more recently even than *Les Affaires sont les affaires* is evidence of their abiding worth, and they were certainly very popular during Mirbeau's lifetime.[48] A brief examination of them helps to illustrate how the limitations of form and length worked in Mirbeau's favour, demanding as they did an intensity of action, characterisation and dialogue which he could easily supply, and affording a more appropriate and acceptable opportunity for social and moral didacticism.

The first and longest of these playlets, *L'Epidémie*, was built around a short story which first appeared in *Le Journal* on 3 February 1895: 'Monsieur Quart'. M Quart, who becomes plain Joseph in *L'Epidémie*, is the ultimate embodiment of all the most ridiculous traits of the bourgeoisie that Mirbeau's antipathy towards the middle class could dredge up. His mediocrity, his conformity, his regularity, his reliability, his docility and all the other traits which Mirbeau can compress into the space of one character must make him a leading candidate for the most 'typical' bourgeois of any literature. In *L'Epidémie*, the lyrical panegyric pronounced by the local mayor at M Quart's death becomes an important turning-point in a council meeting where the council is discussing the typhoid epidemic in the local barracks. The honest councillors propose to take no action either to help the beleaguered soldiers or to prosecute the butcher responsible for supplying the infected meat ('cet incident—purement commercial' and 'les soldats sont faits pour mourir'). When, however, the news is brought of Joseph's (M Quart's) death—the first bourgeois to die from the dreaded disease—they immediately condemn the butcher ('Barbaroux est un misérable . . . un empoisonneur . . . un assassin . . . un socialiste . . .'), and feverishly prepare to take firm and drastic measures to protect the townspeople ('Guerre aux microbes! . . . Vengeons Joseph!').

First performed at the Théâtre Antoine on 29 April 1898, *L'Epidémie*, with Antoine in the leading role of the mayor, confirmed Mirbeau's theatrical talent—it was only his second play to be performed, and no doubt because it was of a different type to *Les Mauvais Bergers* it received rather better notices from the critics. Yet, surprisingly, many of them objected to the overexaggeration of the characters, not appreciating that in this shorter type of play this technique adds the touch of farce which lightens and sweetens the otherwise sombre and bitter satire. The anarchists especially felt that they could recommend this type of theatre. Perhaps they felt that Mirbeau had given a successful literary rendering of their own anti-bourgeois attitude. The anarchist Charles Albert certainly understood and appreciated Mirbeau's technique when he wrote in the literary supplement of *Les Temps Nouveaux*: 'C'est par la charge, par l'exagération caricaturale du trait que l'auteur obtient le rire. Ce procédé, ici comme en certaines de ses chroniques, Mirbeau le manie en maître.'[49] Mirbeau had undoubtedly hit on a successful way of expressing his social criticism, and it was one which was made easy for him by his innate tendency towards exaggeration and caricature.

Les Amants, described by Mirbeau as a *saynète*, and first performed at the Grand-Guignol theatre in July 1901, was based on the short sketch of the same title which appeared in *Le Journal* on 11 July 1897. Set around a park bench on a balmy summer's evening, this very short and sickly love-scene was Mirbeau's tongue-in-cheek contribution to the nauseating vogue of the sentimental theatre. Mirbeau had expressed himself often and vehemently enough on this type of literature and the social decadence it implied for us to see this playlet as an ironical gesture by Mirbeau and a deliberate demonstration by him of the ease with which such drama could be created, light, frivolous and above all, meaningless.

Vieux Ménage, performed in October of 1901, again on the stage of the Grand-Guignol theatre, was also based on an article previously published in *Le Journal* (29 July 1894), where it appeared under a slightly different title: 'Les Vieux Ménages'. It was a return to the social satire of *L'Epidémie*. The brilliantly constructed dialogue between a retired middle-class couple, whose selfishness is as great as their hypocrisy in their dealings with each other, is an entertaining but none the less scathing attack on the manners, habits and outlook of a large section of society which was now becoming Mirbeau's *bête noire*. The catholic former magistrate who had also dabbled in politics might be able to hoodwink his neighbours about his private morality, but he could not hide it from his wife:

> La moralité . . . la pudeur . . . la vertu . . . voilà d'étranges paroles dans ta bouche . ... Invoque-les devant les autres, si tu veux . . . Mais entre nous? . . . Ah! non . . . tu devrais t'éviter ce ridicule de les prononcer . . . Il y a longtemps que tes sales vices les ont abolies en moi . . .[50]

The wedge of cynicism driven between these two is used by Mirbeau to allow each partner to speak the truth about the other, and the result is a harmonious and meaningful play.

In *Le Portefeuille*, performed in February 1902 at the Théâtre de la Renaissance, Mirbeau's target is considerably reduced while the intensity of the satire is stepped up. While the press, and the state of French literature, were attacked as decadent,[51] the main butt of Mirbeau's criticism was his regular watchdog, the police. The brutal stupidity of the police is always an accepted fact in extreme left-wing circles, and Mirbeau's *commissaire* in *Le Portefeuille* is a classic character with all the foibles traditionally attributed to the preservers of law and order.

The anecdote which forms the basis of the plot of *Le Portefeuille* —the maltreatment of an honest tramp who finds a wallet full of money and hands it in at the police station—was based on an incident which Mirbeau had read of in the papers.[52] His first version of the story appeared in *Le Journal* on 23 June 1901, and his one-act play was a dramatised extension of it.⁵³ The farcical, almost slapstick, presentation of the *commissaire de police*, whose secret meetings with his mistress are hidden behind a pretence of interrogating her on suspicion of streetwalking, contrasts so successfully with the serious implications behind his shameful treatment of the honest Jean Guenille, that it is not surprising that *Le Portefeuille* was warmly applauded when it was first performed in 1902.⁵⁴ The variations of mood are executed with all the skill of a brilliant playwright such as Anouilh, while the poignancy of the social satire aimed at a society which favours the rich ('N'attaquez jamais les millionaires, mon brave homme . . . Ils sont indispensables au mécanisme social . . .'), and the clever ('Il ne s'agit pas d'être honnête . . . Il s'agit, seulement, de respecter la loi . . . ou de la tourner . . . ce qui est la même chose . . .'), at the expense of the poor and homeless ('Ah! vous eussiez mieux fait, je vous assure, de trouver un domicile . . . plutôt que ce portefeuille!'), places the play on the same level as the best of Anatole France and Bernard Shaw.⁵⁵

The same cannot be said of Mirbeau's fifth one-act play, *Scrupules*,⁵⁶ mainly perhaps because the social criticism in the play is restricted to a discussion of the rights and wrongs of theft, and there is no opportunity for Mirbeau to inject poignancy or near-tragedy into the play and thus to give it a more far-reaching appeal. An elegant burglar who is disturbed at work by a broad-minded householder and who sits down to explain why he has turned to crime is hardly a match for the pathetic figure of Jean Guenille when it comes to an emotional response to social criticism; and yet within the limitations of the plot, *Scrupules* is an entertaining presentation of a serious theme, and one which sheds light on a further ideological link between Mirbeau and the anarchists.

The possible sources for the character of Arthur Lebeau,⁵⁷ the parisian 'clubman' who carries his dandified manners into the execution of his nocturnal raids, are fascinating to reconstruct, for Lebeau is part of a literary tradition of the elegant burglar.⁵⁸ The concept of the intellectually-motivated thief, of course, goes back a very long way, perhaps even as far as Robin Hood himself; but the declarations made by Arthur Lebeau to his patient 'victim' tie him in firmly with those anarchists who, in the late nineteenth and early twentieth centuries, practised what they referred to as *la reprise individuelle*, and who, more important still, made sure of having sound philosophical motives to explain away their crimes. Lebeau was clearly a compound of anarchists like Duval, Pini, Ortiz and Marius Jacob.⁵⁹ Any one of these anarchist burglars could have spoken, as Lebeau does, of 'une société mal faite, où tout vous blesse, et qui ne vit que de mensonges';

they all believed as Lebeau does that theft is 'l'unique préoccupation de l'homme',⁶⁰ and that in a capitalist society the most honest and least hypocritical profession was that of a burglar. With the serene egotism which so many anarchists displayed when they were brought to trial, Lebeau explains to the man whose house he is in the process of burgling: '. . . de tous les êtres que j'ai connus, je suis le seul qui ait courageusement conformé ses actes à ses idées et adaptée hermétiquement sa nature à la vraie signification de la vie . . .'⁶¹

The last of Mirbeau's playlets, *Interview,* first performed at the Grand-Guignol on 1 February 1904, was an amalgam of Mirbeau's opinions on two topics which had received particular notice during the years of anarchist terrorism in the 1890s. The first was the role which the press played in providing information to the police and informing public opinion, and the second was the theory of criminality advanced by the Italian Cesare Lombroso, who explained both anarchist terrorism and poverty as the products of physiologically-based neuroses.⁶² Mirbeau's vociferous criticisms of the venality and corruption of the French press had appeared often enough over a period of many years for the French reading public to know what a low opinion of it Mirbeau had. The short story 'Interview'—the prose version of the play (*Le Journal,* 19 January 1896)—was the direct result of Mirbeau's reflections on the way in which the French press had aided, abetted and often even goaded the police in the repression of the anarchists. When 'Interview' appeared, in 1896, this aspect of the role of the press had been hotly discussed for some time, and Mirbeau's short story was a literary rendering of this point of polemical discussion.⁶³ Mirbeau himself had written at the height of the anarchist terrorism that the press had forgotten its rightful role—to maintain the balance between the abuses of authority and the rights of human freedom—and had been transformed 'en police qui traque, en tribunal qui condamne, en bourreau qui exécute';⁶⁴ and expanding on the significance of 'Interview' two days after the publication of the short story, he wrote that the press had become 'quelque chose comme la succursale de la préfecture de police, et l'antichambre du cabinet du juge d'instruction'.⁶⁵

The maleficent press is represented in *Interview* by the farcical, yet rather disturbing figure of the senior reporter from *Le Mouvement*:

Je suis la Presse, moi . . . Douze millions de lecteurs . . . La Presse est la grande force moderne . . . la grande éducation . . . moderne . . . la conscience universelle . . . Elle dénonce . . . juge et condamne . . . La Presse est tout . . . Tâchez de ne pas l'oublier . . .⁶⁶

His mission is to interview a certain Chapuzot of Montrouge who has assaulted his wife with a bottle; but by mistake he has come to Montmartre and has found a Chapuzot who is unmarried. This Chapuzot, a bar-owner, is subjected to a fierce cross-examination at his own bar, and is threatened with all sorts of reprisals if he will not admit that he has assaulted a wife he does not have: 'Je dirai que votre établissement est un repaire d'anarchistes.'[67]

Worked into the fabric of this satire of the press's abuse of its power was an anecdote which Mirbeau had previously published in *Les Vingt et un jours d'un neurasthénique*. Dr Triceps' faithful exposition of Cesare Lombroso's theories of genius, criminality and poverty in *Les Vingt et un jours*[68] forms the basis of what the reporter tells the bewildered Chapuzot, to reassure him that he will receive expert medical treatment if he admits his crime! Like the anarchists themselves, Mirbeau objected to Lombroso's primitive psychiatry because it encouraged the conservative mind to think of anarchists as sick, and worse still, it diverted the responsibility for social unrest and economic inequality from the middle-class capitalist state to the individual, who was conveniently classed as abnormal. Lombroso's view was an essentially reactionary one, and Mirbeau did all he could to pour ridicule on it.[69]

Though the effects in *Interview* are overdone—Mirbeau admitted to Renard: 'C'est grossier d'un bout à l'autre'[70]—and though more than any of the other one-act plays, it is more obviously a vehicle for the expressions of Mirbeau's 'pet hates', it is an amusing farce, and it serves to show how much, even in 1904, Mirbeau was still preoccupied with the same social phenomena as those which had led him to sympathise with anarchism and the extreme Left over a decade before.

The same applies also to the bulk of Mirbeau's literary output. These six short playlets, published together in 1904 as *Farces et moralités*, were, as the title suggests, intended to amuse; but they were also intended to instruct and to make it clear what Mirbeau thought on certain important issues.[71] Different issues, but of similar social and philosophical nature were the motivating forces behind *Le Foyer*, *Les Affaires*. *Les Mauvais Bergers sont les affaires* and each of these, and some more successfully than others, was a literary expression of Mirbeau's libertarian temperament. The fact that Mirbeau was successful with the relatively unpolemical three-act play *Les Affaires sont les affaires* (in which he came very close to the great art he so coveted), as well as with the piecemeal one-act plays (whose pithy and caricatural scripts were carried over almost entirely from Mirbeau's journalism), highlights one of Mirbeau's greatest dilemmas: how to effect a division between the artist and the journalist. It was probably because Mirbeau never succeeded in making that divison that, in spite of his contemporary success, his art was generally too polemical to stand the test of time, and his journalism was too polemical and often too aesthetically contrived to build for him a solid reputation as a social commentator worthy of note for later generations. The dilemma was itself an integral part of Mirbeau's temperament: he was unable to choose, because the artist and the journalist in him were inextricably intertwined, and notwithstanding the occasional successful exceptions in one direction or the other, none of his works was ever entirely the product of one aspect of his conflicting talents.

Notes

1 Mirbeau once told Apollinaire he found it ridiculous that anyone should write in verse! G. Apollinaire, 'Revue de la quinzaine', *Le Mercure de France*, 1 November 1918, p. 178.
2 The posthumous volume *La Vache tachetée* contains several such playlets dating from the late 1880s and early 1890s, including 'Le Poitrinaire' and 'En route'.
3 This vogue has been described as 'le drame anarcho-humanitaire'. *Cf*. Knowles, *op. cit.*, pp. 408–11. See also R. Rolland, 'Le Théâtre du peuple', *Les Cahiers de la Quinzaine*, 5e série, No. 4 (1903), pp. 83–98, and H. Poulaille, *Nouvel Age littéraire* (Paris: Valois, 1930), chapter on 'Le Théâtre et le peuple'. On Mirbeau's admiration for Antoine's Théâtre Libre, see his article 'Chemin de croix', *Le Journal*, 21 January 1900. On his early interest in Lugné-Poë's Théâtre de l'Oeuvre, see Mauclair, *op. cit.*, p. 103.
4 Letter of July(?) 1893 (I.F.H.S.).
5 'Le Théâtre populaire', *Le Journal*, 9 February 1902.
6 'Chemin de croix', *op. cit.*
7 G. Bourdon, 'Le Théâtre du Peuple. Opinions', *La Revue Bleue*, 25 January 1902, p. 480.
8 H. Bauër, '*Les Mauvais Bergers* d'Octave Mirbeau', *L'Echo de Paris*, 15 December 1897. Mirbeau evidently agreed with Bauër's interpretation of the play, for he wrote to thank Bauër in these terms: 'C'est que, en vous lisant, j'ai senti battre mon âme dans la vôtre.' Quoted from G. Bauër, 'Octave Mirbeau, héros de son théâtre', *Les Annales*, No. 106 (August 1959).
9 *L'Idée sociale au théâtre* (Paris: Stock, 1901), p. 103.
10 Becque's *Michel Pauper* (1871), Hauptmann's *Die Weber* (first performed in France as *Les Tisserands* in 1893), and Curel's *Le Repas du lion* (1897) all brought the question of industrial economy on to the stage. The strike, and particularly the night meeting of the workers in the forest, are very reminiscent of Zola's *Germinal*, which Mirbeau admired greatly.
11 Letter from Grave to Mirbeau, dated 9 July 1893 (J.R.U.L.M.).
12 Mirbeau's first play was, as Fernand Vandérem put it, 'très guettée'. *Op. cit.*, p. 137.
13 'Un Mot personnel', *Le Journal*, 19 December 1897.
14 '*Les Mauvais Bergers*', *Le Libertaire*, 25 December 1897.
15 'Et quand Philippe Hurteaux . . . crie: « Et toi aussi, Jean Roule, tu parles comme un député! » cela ne peut tromper personne et équivaut à dire: « Toi aussi, tu es un mauvais berger ».' 'Un Mot personnel', *op. cit.*

16 *Ibid.*
17 'La Clairière', *T.N.(S.L.)*, No. 51 (April 1900).
18 *'Les Mauvais Bergers'*, *ibid.*, No. 35 (December 1897).
19 *'Les Mauvais Bergers'*, *op. cit.*
20 'Un Mot personnel', *op. cit.* On Mirbeau's mistrust of socialist collectivism, see his criticism of Jaurès in 'Questions sociales', *Le Journal*, 20 December 1896. Reproduced in *Les Ecrivains*, vol. II.
21 *Les Affaires sont les affaires* still forms part of the repertory of the Comédie Française.
22 Schwarz, *Octave Mirbeau*, p. 137.
23 *Les Affaires sont les affaires* (Paris: Fayard, illustrated edition 1911), p. 14.
24 *Ibid.*, p. 49.
25 Goncourt, *op. cit.*, vol. 17, p. 35.
26 Maurice Beaubourg, *'Les Affaires sont les affaires'*, *La Plume*, 15 May 1903, p. 591.
27 *Ibid.*, p. 592.
28 E. Sémenoff, 'Revue du mois', *Le Mercure de France*, 16 September 1903, p. 808.
29 *'Les Affaires sont les Affaires'*, *T.N.(S.L.)*, No. 2 (May 1903).
30 '. . . je suis sûr que le public accueillera *Le Foyer* avec encore plus de faveur que *Les Affaires sont les affaires*. Car ma dernière pièce surpasse la précédente autant que celle-ci surpassait *Les Mauvais Bergers* . . .'. P. Gsell, 'Octave Mirbeau', *La Revue*, 15 March 1907, p. 219.
31 In his article *'Le Foyer'*, *La Grande Revue*, 25 December 1908.
32 Quoted from *ibid.*
33 *Le Théâtre des années folles* (Genève: Editions du Milieu du Monde, 1943), p. 21.
34 *L'Action Française* was not the only right-wing newspaper to express the indignation of its readers at the implications of *Le Foyer*. See J. Renard, *Journal* (Paris: Gallimard, 1935), entry for 27 January 1909.
35 *Cf.* Paul Léautaud, *Journal littéraire*, vol. 2 (Paris: Mercure de France, 1955), pp. 147–8. The act of *Le Foyer* which was dropped is set in the 'Foyer' itself, and is a vivid portrayal of the atrocious conditions inside this so-called charitable institution. It is included in most of the published versions of the play.
36 A. Brisson, *Le Théâtre*, 4e série (Paris: Librairie des Annales Politiques et Littéraires, 1909), p. 221.
37 *'Le Foyer'*, *L'Intransigeant*, 10 March 1908.
38 *Journal littéraire*, vol. 2, p. 187.
39 Not the least of the ironies in the *Affaire du Foyer* was that Claretie's defence was conducted by Maître Du Buit, who had been prosecuting attorney in several of the anarchist trials of the 1890s. In 1901, Mirbeau published an anecdotal caricature of Du Buit in *Les Vingt et un jours*, pp. 76–9.
40 'Grave tumulte au Théâtre-Français', *Le Matin*, 9 December 1908.
41 *Cf.* *'Le Foyer* interdit', *Paris-Journal*, 1 February 1909.
42 Natanson's influence on the anarchistic ambiance of the *Revue Blanche* is discussed in Jackson, *op. cit.*, p. 30.
43 *Le Matin*, 4 December 1885.
44 *Cf.* Kropotkin, *Paroles d'un révolté*, p. 342.
45 *Sébastien Roch*, pp. 103–4.
46 'Les Petits Martyrs', *L'Echo de Paris*, 3 May 1892.
47 'Les Petits Martyrs' was reprinted in *La Révolte (S.L.)*, No. 35 (28 May 1892). *Cf.* also Mirbeau's article 'Dépopulation', *Le Journal*, 2 December 1900 —reprinted in *T.N.(S.L.)*, No. 6 (June 1901)—in which Mirbeau criticised philanthropists like Simon and Piot. The idea of 'unmasking' a particular institution, as in *Le Foyer*, may well have come to Mirbeau from an article in *Le Libertaire*—Gustus, 'Exploita-

tion philanthropique', *Le Libertaire*, No. 21 (4 April 1896)—in which the abuses being perpetrated at an orphanage in Thonon-les-Bains were exposed.
48 *Le Portefeuille*, perhaps the most popular of Mirbeau's one-act plays, was revived in 1951 and staged along with Shaw's *Androcles*, at the Gaîté-Montparnasse, Paris.
49 '*L'Epidémie*', *T.N.(S.L.)*, No. 5 (May 1898).
50 *Vieux Ménage* (Paris: Les Belles Lectures, 1950), p. 24.
51 Jérôme Maltenu's serious article on the Patagonian police force is not frivolous enough to be accepted by any newspaper! As for the literary scene, the following words from the police commissioner are intended by Mirbeau to be ironic: 'Je trouve que le théâtre se traîne, Monsieur Jérôme Maltenu, dans des redites fatigantes . . . dans des banalités . . . oiseuses . . . On n'y attaque pas assez de front la question sociale . . . Du sentiment . . . des couchages . . . de l'adultère . . . je t'adore . . . prends-moi . . . donne-moi tes lèvres . . . tant qu'on veut . . . Des réformes . . . des idées . . . jamais . . .'. *Le Portefeuille* (Paris: Fasquelle, 1902), pp. 2–3. Shortly after this, the commissioner begins to speak to his mistress in these very terms!
52 *Cf.* Schwarz, *Octave Mirbeau*, p. 133.
53 The short story 'Le Portefeuille' was incorporated into *Les Vingt et un jours*, pp. 301–8.
54 Antoine, *op. cit.*, p. 432. *Cf.* also M. Beaubourg, '*Le Portefeuille*', *La Plume*, 15 March 1902. The play was popular with the anarchists, who performed it within their own groups; *cf.* J. Grave, '*Le Portefeuille*', *T.N.(S.L.)*, No. 44 (March 1902).
55 Edmund Wilson regarded Mirbeau as the French equivalent of Shaw. See his *Classics and Commercials* (New York: Farrar, Strauss & Co., 1950), p. 477.
56 First performed May 1902 at the Grand-Guignol.
57 In the stage version as well as in the original short story ('Scrupules', *Le Journal*, 26 January 1896), the burglar is simply referred to as 'le voleur'; but in *Les Vingt et un jours* where the anecdote reappears (pp. 271–9), he is given the name Arthur Lebeau.
58 Mirbeau may well have been the first writer to introduce the elegant anarchist burglar into literature. The 1896 version of 'Scrupules' preceded by two years Darien's anarchist-inspired novel *Le Voleur*. Zola's *Paris* (1898) also features a band of anarchist burglars. The 1967 film version of Darien's novel stars Jean-Paul Belmondo in a role remarkably similar to that of Mirbeau's Arthur Lebeau.
59 Duval was brought to trial in 1886 for robberies which included a break-in at the home of the fashionable Madeleine Lemaire; Pini, at his trial in 1889, accussed capitalism of being the real robber; Ortiz was something of a dandy and was convicted of theft at the Procès des Trente (1894); and Jacob, like Ortiz, was the leader of a professional group of anarchist burglars operating between 1900 and 1905 (*Scrupules* was staged in 1902). Mirbeau's 'voleur' was so much in line with these anarchists that Jacob's declaration at his trial in 1905 reads like an echo of Lebeau's fictional lines. *Cf.* M. Jacob, 'Pourquoi j'ai cambriolé', *Le Balai Social*, No. 9 (15 April 1905); see also A. Sergent, *Un Anarchiste de la belle époque: M. Jacob* (Paris: Seuil, 1950).
60 Proudhon's celebrated phrase 'La propriété c'est le vol' was the philosophical basis of the anarchist *reprise individuelle*: 'Les bourgeois sont donc mal venus de crier au vol lorsqu'on veut les forcer à restituer, car leur propriété n'est, elle-même, que le fruit d'un vol.' Grave, *La Société mourante*, p. 64.
61 *Scrupules*, in *Farces et moralités* (Paris: Fasquelle, 1904), p. 224. Shortly after its first performance in 1902, *Scrupules* appeared in the ephemeral libertarian journal *Les Annales de la Jeunesse Laïque*, No. 2 (July 1902).
62 *Cf.* for example *Gli anarchici* (1894), translated into French in 1897.

63 The story was immediately popular in anarchist circles; see *T.N.*, No. 39 (25 January 1896).
64 'Rêverie', *Le Journal*, 11 March 1894.
65 'La Police et la presse', *Le Gaulois*, 21 January 1896. Recommended by the anarchists in *T.N.*, No. 39 (25 January 1896), and reprinted later in *T.N.(S.L.)*, No. 51 (May 1904). Mirbeau's sentiments tallied exactly with the anarchists on this subject; cf. 'Un Valet de bourreau', *Le Libertaire*, No. 62 (15 January 1897).
66 *Interview*, in *Farces et moralités*, pp. 254–5.
67 *Ibid.*, p. 282.
68 *Op. cit.*, pp. 315–9.
69 *Cf.* 'Scientismes', *Le Journal*, 30 June 1895.
70 Renard, *op. cit.*, p. 600.
71 Victor Méric, who was closely associated with the militant anarchist movement in Italy, thought so highly of Mirbeau's one-act plays that he published translations of them in Italian: *Farse e moralità* (Milano: Sonzogno, 1930). He also published and prefaced a translation of *Les Mauvais Bergers*: *I Cattivi Pastori* (Milano: Zerboni, 1911).

Chapter VIII
The social conscience of the *Belle Epoque* (1900–7)

... ce n'est qu'à force de dire et de redire les choses qu'on parvient à les faire entrer dans la cervelle des gens.

(Mirbeau, in 1902)

The three novels which Mirbeau published between 1900 and 1907 at the height of his fame were, ironically, inferior in literary quality to most of his previous work. His individualism, his frustrated idealism and his exasperation with the *status quo* had soured his outlook to such an extent that he was obliged by his temperament to construct these three novels from short polemical pieces which spanned the whole range of social activities, from the problems of prostitution and alcoholism to the need for international cooperation between countries and the protection of human civil rights. *Le Journal d'une femme de chambre* (1900), *Les Vingt et un jours d'un neurasthénique* (1901) and *La 628–E8* (1907) read more or less like what they are, collections of newspaper articles strung together, with varying degrees of success, on a slender fictional thread. As works of literature they have not stood the test of time, in spite of what Paul Léautaud thought about 'le roman pamphlet' and its durability;[1] but as one man's view of the problems of an important and exciting era they are extremely interesting. They are rendered all the more fascinating because that man, though his sincerity was never in doubt, was capable of exaggerating the facts beyond the point where even truth itself dissolves into farce. It was in these short polemical pieces that Mirbeau's highly subjective view of contemporary issues flourished most successfully.

It is essentially to Mirbeau's anarchism that we owe these highly original portraits of the foibles and the preoccupations of the *Belle Epoque*. His opposition to society, sharpened in the closing decade of the nineteenth century by his contact with anarchist ideology, had caused him to develop a satirical and virulent style all of his own, and there were many who regarded him as the 'Ravachol de la littérature'.[2] His later novels increasingly reflected the radical opinions which caused the middle-class reading public and the conservative critics to regard him as a misanthropic malcontent or as a publicity-seeking scandalmonger. It was in the spirit of combativity which Mirbeau had developed particularly from rubbing shoulders with the anarchists that he continued well into the twentieth century as the quixotic individualist who would not allow French society to settle on its lees.

If, during the *Belle Epoque*, Mirbeau's contact with the anarchist movement was not as direct as it had been in the early 1890s, this was due in part to the break-up of the movement after 1894 as a result of the fierce repression, and the desire on the part of the militants to seek new and varied ways of spreading anarchist ideas. Yet Mirbeau kept in touch with some of the leaders of the movement, especially Sébastien Faure, and to a lesser degree Malato and Grave. Their paths crossed frequently: Dreyfus, the Bourses du Travail, the popular universities,[3] the Coalition Révolutionnaire,[4] the Tailhade trial in 1901,[5] the anti-czarist movement of 1905,[6] and many other affairs and incidents saw Mirbeau working shoulder to shoulder with anarchists in a common desire to stem the tide of reaction and establish freedom as the basis of the life of society. Throughout this period too, the anarchist newspapers continued to reprint Mirbeau's writings for propaganda purposes, and the columns of *Les Temps Nouveaux* are full of references to him and his works. The fact that in 1905, immediately after the bomb attack on the visiting Spanish king Alfonso in the rue de Rohan (31 May 1905), the houses of Malato and Mirbeau were searched (Malato was later tried and acquitted of complicity) also shows quite clearly how, even over a decade after the Procès des Trente, the authorities associated Mirbeau with the anarchists, and thought him dangerous enough to be watched.[7]

Quite apart from these direct links with the anarchists, Mirbeau shared a common fund of ideas with them, and these ideas found their way into his novels as well as motivating certain important actions in his daily life. His belief that society was in need of regeneration, for example, not only inspired the gloomy picture which he painted of humanity in *Les Vingt et un jours*, but also caused him to look for the antidote in humanitarian reform. His conviction that the decadence of society was illustrated in the decadence of its literature and its art not only inspired his scathing criticisms, in *Le Journal d'une femme de chambre* and *La 628–E8*, of the Paul Bourget type of literature, but also made him search for the remedy in the rediscovery of authentic values. This was how he envisaged his role as a member of the Académie Goncourt; and on more than one occasion he was close to resigning because he could not secure recognition for artists whose talents he admired. Anti-clericalism, anti-militarism, anti-parliamentarianism, the abolition of the death-penalty, internationalism, pacifism, the secularisation of education, the reduction of State interference in individual enterprise, anti-patriotism, anti-capitalism—Mirbeau expressed himself on all these subjects in these three novels, and did what he could in daily life to reinforce what he wrote and thus bring about a better world.

Le Journal d'une femme de chambre, perhaps the most famous of Mirbeau's novels owing to the two motion pictures that have been made of it (by Jean Renoir and Luis Buñuel), is conveniently summed up by the publisher of the latest paperback edition as a 'satire virulente des moeurs parisiennes ou provinciales de la Belle Epoque vue du côté de l'office'.[8] It is the best of this group of Mirbeau's novels, largely because the fictional thread which binds the work together is more successful in this novel than in the others. The diary of Célestine, the chambermaid who narrates her experiences in service both in Paris and the provinces, was not a new idea in literature, but it was a convention which was especially suited to Mirbeau, and he made full use of the opportunity it afforded him of giving a frank and authentic inside view of the society he sought to condemn. If, as André Beaunier says in criticism of Mirbeau's excesses in *Le Journal d'une femme de chambre*, Mirbeau 'a cru que le service de la vérité voulait qu'il traînât l'univers dans la boue',[9] the fact still remains that the experiences of Célestine, in their picaresque variety, enable Mirbeau to speak with impunity and with a certain ring of truth about the dirty linen of the *Belle Epoque*.

Beneath the surface-level of the tale of the peregrinations of Célestine from house to house and her account of the characters and manners of her various employers and acquaintances, the book is held together by a number of important themes which give Célestine's rather scabrous autobiography a more serious significance. One point which is made clear time and again throughout the story—and this is something of which Célestine herself is painfully aware—is that no matter how much she may criticise or dislike her employers, like all the servants we encounter in the book she gradually begins to adopt their foibles and imitate their vices: 'C'est un fait reconnu que notre esprit se modèle sur celui de nos maîtres, et ce qui se dit au salon se dit également à l'office'.[10]

This corruption of the working class by its employers was a cause of concern to Mirbeau who, in his opposition to the middle class, dreaded the thought of the perpetuation of those bourgeois faults he hoped would disappear. In his attempt to forestall the nefarious influence of this master–servant relationship, Mirbeau shows in *Le Journal d'une femme de chambre* how a kind and potentially sincere girl like Célestine becomes as hard and hypocritical as her employers through continued contact with a degenerate class. Her admiration for the rich and famous, her preference for the obsequious and snobbish valets she meets, her unhealthy fascination for the anti-semitic child-murderer Joseph, and her ultimate marriage to him, followed by her elevation to the rank of employer as a result of the purchase of a café with the silver Joseph has stolen from his former employers, all these things show how badly corrupted a 'child of the people' can become. The words which Célestine herself uses to explain the corruption of a servant apply ironically to her also:

> Un domestique, ce n'est pas un être normal . . . Du peuple qu'il a renié, il a perdu le sang généreux et la force naïve . . . De la bourgeoisie, il a gagné les vices honteux . . . et les sentiments vils, les lâches peurs, les criminels appétits . . .[11]

It is this regrettable process, which Mirbeau deplored out of social considerations, that forms one of the most interesting developments in the book. One of Mirbeau's colleagues on *La Revue Blanche*—where *Le Journal d'une femme de chambre* first appeared in serialised form—highlighted this aspect of the book as its most important contribution to social progress and reform:

> Or, le *Journal d'une Femme de chambre* expose en toute évidence l'ignominie de la *domesticité*. Une civilisation supérieure doit abolir celle-ci comme fut aboli l'esclavage dont elle n'est que l'insuffisante atténuation.[12]

The other important theme which Mirbeau is trying to stress in the novel arises from the large number of abnormal and perverted people Célestine meets in the course of her travels. Many critics dismissed this as unrealistic exaggeration; but what they failed to see was that this over-populating with 'monsters' was Mirbeau's way of saying that normality and abnormality had been reversed in a world full of iniquity behind hypocrisy. Mirbeau believed that society was corrupt and had its values wrong; he therefore portrayed abnormality as the socially-acceptable norm. From the boot-kissing mania of M Rabour in the opening chapter through to the militant anti-semitism of the man Célestine finally marries, Mirbeau is showing us a nightmare world, a moral garden of tortures, in which the principles he values are rarely glimpsed, where right is wrong, and where wrong is rewarded.

It is hardly surprising therefore that the name of Dreyfus should be evil-spoken of in the world with which Célestine is familiar. 'Si le traître est coupable, qu'on le rembarque . . . S'il est innocent, qu'on le fusille . . .', cries Joseph to Célestine's delight.[13] Célestine, who has no particular reason to believe Dreyfus guilty, is like so many millions of French people whose spirit of conformity led them to swallow all the lies of the army's high command and shout for the blood of an innocent man.

Many of the episodes in the novel consist of separate articles on topics which had already excited Mirbeau's anger or evoked his outspoken opinion during his period of revolutionary journalism on *Le Journal* (though this is even more true of *Les Vingt et un jours* which hardly contains any original material at all). The iniquity of the *bureaux de placement* and of convents, the soporific effect of religion, the hypocrisy of public charity, the oppression of the poor, the inanity of the literature of the salons and of the decadent aesthetes, the denial of human rights, the pettiness of the middle-class mind and the indifference of the law to a poor man's complaint against a rich one—all these were subjects on which Mirbeau had expressed his opinion in *Le Journal* between 1894 and 1898, and they give *Le Journal d'une femme de chambre* a polemical flavour which stamps it as the work of a violent critic of society who could not wholly hide his journalism in his art. Small wonder then that the extreme Left, and particularly the anarchists, greeted the book as 'le plus rude pamphlet qui ait jamais contraint notre bourgeoisie à sa nudité'.[14] Jean Grave was not the only reader to declare, on laying down the book with a shudder: 'Ce qu'il y a, en effet, de saleté et de pourriture sous le beau décor de notre état social.'[15]

Yet if *Le Journal d'une femme de chambre* stretched the limits of realism to breaking-point, *Les Vingt et un jours d'un neurasthénique* abandoned all but the pretence of a credible fictional plot. Rachilde, who described the book as 'le carnet d'un reporter, le fond de tiroir d'un journaliste',[16] realised, like most of Mirbeau's readers, that the narrator in *Les Vingt et un jours* is Mirbeau himself, and that the interminable succession of anecdotes about people he meets while on a rest-cure in the Pyrenees is a revival and a recasting of previously published pieces, linked together only by the character of the man who wrote them and the random meetings of his narrator. For the first time in what purports to be a novel—'On chercherait en vain, dans notre littérature, un livre comparable aux *Vingt et un Jours*', wrote Roland Dorgelès[17] —Mirbeau abandons his fictional narrator and steps down, thinly disguised as a middle-class spa-worshipper, into his own tale.

The idea for this thinnest of plots came from a rest-cure which Mirbeau undertook at Bagnères-de-Luchon, 'reine des Pyrénées', in the summer of 1897.[18] While he was there trying to rid himself of a troublesome catarrh, he continued to send his weekly articles to *Le Journal*, and wrote a series describing some of his experiences. It was this series, entitled 'En traitement' (*Le Journal*, August–September 1897) which was to form the basis of *Les Vingt et un jours* four years later.

The book is a gallery of satirical portraits, a collection of amusing anecdotes, and a succession of polemical pamphlets which could have been extended indefinitely. It is only the narrator's return to Paris at the end of his rest-cure that releases both him and the reader from the depressing claustrophobia of this fashionable health resort. The place is populated, through Mirbeau's grotesque imagination, with hordes of narrow-minded, self-centred, pleasure-seeking, money-loving and hypocritical creatures, many of whom, like Mirbeau's arch-enemies Georges Leygues and Maître Du Buit, are mentioned by name.[19] Under Mirbeau's pen, Luchon becomes something approaching a madhouse, while through the paper-thin walls of his custom-built hotel, supplemented by all the confessions of those he meets in the nearby Casino, Mirbeau is able to build up a morbid and horrifying picture of the ugliness of contemporary upper and middle-class life.

André Gide was undoubtedly right when he suggested that monsters were absolutely indispensable to Mirbeau, and that Mirbeau motivated his satirical posture by heaping ignominious faults upon his characters' heads.[20] This was part and parcel of Mirbeau's original and personal caricatural style, and no critic ever understood this better than Roland Dorgelès, who wrote: 'L'esprit créateur de Mirbeau m'est toujours apparu comme une étrange machine à transformer le réel.'[21]

The monstrous egotism of Robert Haguemann in chapter 1; the unbelievable obscurantism of Dr Triceps in chapter 3; the excessive moral and physical degeneracy of the Tarabustin family in chapter 5; the incredible hypocrisy of Emile Ollivier—mentioned by name[22]—in chapter 8; the intense anti-dreyfusism of Colonel Présalé in chapter 9; the imperialist brutality of General Archinard—also mentioned by name—in chapter 9;[23] the inordinate decadence of the rich American aesthete Dickson-Barnell in chapter 12; the heartless cruelty of the Russian Prince Karaguine in chapter 13; the thorough dishonesty of the royalist politician Portpierre in chapter 17; the over-enthusiastic bureaucracy of the mayor of Le Kernac in chapter 20 . . . the list of people satirised by Mirbeau is very long indeed.

The butts of Mirbeau's ridicule are hardly recognisable as real people when Mirbeau has finished with them in *Les Vingt et un jours*. Where many critics went wrong was in trying to judge the novel on the basis of realism. Even recently, one critic has taxed Mirbeau with indifference to the beauties of nature because he represents Luchon as a claustrophobic town when everyone else says how pleasant it is.[24] As if *Les Vingt et un jours* were some kind of tourist guide! The basis of the novel was Mirbeau's temperamental aversion to the middle class and his philosophical conviction that their society was evil; Mirbeau was not primarily concerned with realism. Small wonder then that he complained sadly to Geffroy on one occasion: 'Je suis un caricaturiste, et l'on n'aime pas la caricature.[25]

Happily, there were many who appreciated Mirbeau's unusual gifts and understood what Mirbeau meant when he said of one of his characters in *Les Vingt et un jours* that he was not 'un individu, mais une collectivité'.[26] There were critics like Alfred Jarry who spoke of the 'courage' and the 'justice' of these pages and agreed that 'c'est bien, en effet, la société toute entière qui se cristallise dans cette vingtaine de fripouilles, admirable à force d'ignominie'.[27] There were those who, like Jean Grave, welcomed the violent social satire of these portraits and said of them:

> . . . ce sont des dirigeants, des notables, des gens bien posés dans leur monde. C'est comme critique de ce monde qu'ils sont intéressants à noter. Et l'on sait comment Mirbeau excelle à fustiger les laideurs morales.[28]

And there were those, too, who like Roland Dorgelès many years later, actually preferred Mirbeau in this excessively polemical vein, and who would have agreed with Dorgelès when he wrote: 'C'est dans ces pages d'expression directe que Mirbeau m'apparaît le mieux.'[29]

The progression of Mirbeau's novels towards the unveiled expression of his ideas on topics of social interest and concern was continued with the next 'novel', *La 628–E8*. If in *Le Journal d'une femme de chambre* Mirbeau's comments on society were contained within the conventions of a well-conceived plot, and if in *Les Vingt et un jours* he hid behind the faintest of disguises, then in *La 628–E8*, there were no such concessions to the appearance of fiction. In *La 628–E8*, a motor-car trip through northern France, Belgium, Holland and Germany forms the slenderest of pretexts for Mirbeau to bring together in one place a variety of essays on a bewildering multiplicity of subjects. In this volume we hear Mirbeau himself speaking openly on those topics which most occupied his attention during the years 1905–7, when the book was being written; and it is here that we have our clearest picture yet of the kind of man Mirbeau was, what things excited his anger or evoked his sympathy or his admiration, what were his hopes and fears for the future, and why he was so critical of the

France of the *Belle Epoque*. It is Mirbeau himself who speaks to us in these pages and who leads us with disarming frankness through a maze of places and a welter of ideas which spring up as the motor car in which he travels speeds along.[30]

Mirbeau was one of the earliest public figures in France to patronise the motor car and to use it for touring-trips abroad. He bought his first car not long after the turn of the century, and as he did with most things he took a liking for he threw himself enthusiastically into this newest craze: *l'automobilisme*. We have only to read the lengthy preface of *La 628–E8*, dedicated to the maker of his motor-car Fernand Charron, to see how much Mirbeau appreciated the wealth of new experiences Charron had opened to him. Chief amongst these, as always, was the experience Mirbeau prized above all else—freedom: 'Cet hommage, je vous le dois, car je vous dois . . . des mois, des mois entiers de liberté totale . . .'[31] Railways, with their 'voies prisonnières, toujours pareilles', symbolised, in contrast to the go-where-you-will of the motor car, all that Mirbeau sought to shun throughout his adult life, whilst the motor car allowed him to give free rein to his fancies, to stop, start, turn and drive on as he pleased. Just as Mirbeau, in his hatred of the restrictions and barriers thrown up by authority, shrank instinctively from anything even vaguely claustrophobic, so he fastened on enthusiastically to anything which represented freedom and which afforded the super-individualist like himself the opportunity to do as he wished. The motoring diary which arose from this most precious capacity reflects, in their richness and diversity, all the impressions, convictions, suggestions and opinions of a systematically unfettered soul.

The dominant theme of *La 628–E8*, arising not only out of the very nature of Mirbeau's foreign itinerary but also clearly stressed within the text itself (and it was a theme dear to the hearts of the extreme political Left—to none dearer than to the anarchists), was the desire which Mirbeau had for universal brotherhood, for mutual co-operation and understanding between nations. Like all the militants of the extreme Left, Mirbeau was persuaded that such co-operation was the only sure way to peace and harmony. Right up to the outbreak of the First World War the socialists and the anarchists wanted to believe that their fellow-workers in Germany would quickly sabotage any imperialist aggression by refusing to fight; and as Mirbeau looked around the pulsating and impressive industrial towns of Germany, he was deliberately blind to the threat of hostility which a prosperous and expanding Germany could easily pose to her hereditary enemy.

Riding into Germany, Mirbeau interprets the superb road surfaces as favourable ground for the motor car, whose contribution to the life of society is 'de civilisation moins rude, de sociabilité universelle et d'avenir pacificateur'.[32] In his blind idealism too, Mirbeau accepts the assurances of a German acquaintance that the German army is not planning aggression, but that socialism, in its most generic sense, is making great inroads into the German soul and will ultimately bring the blessing of disarmament. It is in sections like this—and *La 628–E8* is littered with them—that Mirbeau openly expresses his extreme left-wing views. With great depth of feeling Mirbeau says, in the words of his German acquaintance: 'Le jour où le socialisme voudra bien répudier cette sort de sentimentalisme nationaliste, qui l'enchaîne encore à de regrettables préjugés, il accomplira de grandes choses . . .'[33] And it was to the anarchists he looked in particular as the most militant party, the ones most likely to succeed in ridding society of these vestigial nationalist organs, for he continues:

> —Alors à quoi bon ces organes inutiles? . . . ce poids mort? . . . A quoi bon ces appendices? . . . La médecine a fait son temps. L'avenir est à la chirurgie . . . L'anarchiste est un chirurgien . . . un chirurgien malgré lui . . .[34]

The First World War was all the more shattering a blow for Mirbeau because of the admiration he had had for the forward-looking zeal of Germany, a zeal which turned to hostility, and which neither the anarchists nor any of the socialists could counteract.

All was by no means sweetness and light in *La 628–E8*, however. If Mirbeau praised Germany in the fond hope that the Prussian aggressiveness was now advancing the progress of humanity towards unity, other countries were not so fortunate. As in *Les Vingt et un jours*, Mirbeau's observations were coloured by his predetermined convictions, with the unlikely result that Dordrecht, with its Boer museum and its reminders of what to Mirbeau was a brave and persecuted minority in South Africa, is described as a charming town, graceful, fresh and bright, while Anvers, hectic, money-mad and conservative in outlook, is systematically taken to pieces stone by stone.[35]

Mirbeau had warned the reader to expect this kind of subjective value judgement. His 'Avis au lecteur' had predicted what was in store and why: '. . . j'ai un estomac, un foie, des nerfs, par conséquent des digestions, des mélancolies, sur lesquels le soleil et la pluie, le plaisir et la peine exercent des influences ennemies.'[36] Yet this 'physiological' explanation of Mirbeau's dislike for so many of the Belgian, and many, though fewer, of the Dutch towns he passes through is partly a front for his polemical temperament, which must have its say however thin the pretext.

To enumerate the moral, intellectual, social and political issues on which Mirbeau expatiates in *La 628–E8* would be to recount *La 628–E8* in all its enormity, diversity and changeability, as the car thunders on its way regardless. The venality of the press, the dangers of religious education, the pettiness and meanness of the police, the iniquity of militarism, the degeneracy of royalty, the horrors of colonial and czarist brutality, the pollution of the environment by the cupidity of an industrialist and capitalist system, the dishonesty of socialist reforms—all these familiar themes, running through Mirbeau's fictional and non-fictional work, and binding him firmly to the political and intellectual Left, figure prominently in *La 628–E8*, and show how much attention Mirbeau gave to the pressing issues of his time. The fact that many of these pieces are newspaper articles able to stand on their own, and which have been drawn only by Mirbeau's amazing persistence into the loose web of a fictional plot, shows yet again how closely, in his later novels as well as in his shorter plays, Mirbeau's art was allied to his polemical preoccupations and to the forms in which they were expressed.

The motor car itself is Mirbeau: a noisy, impatient and hot-running machine with a mind of its own and that likes nothing better than the freedom of the open road. The whole of chapter 6 of *La 628–E8*, 'La Faune des routes', is an allegorical account of Mirbeau's own hectic course through life in nineteenth- and early twentieth-century French society, spreading terror as he moves, ever faster like his motor-car, towards a climax of dizzy speed, himself the personification of progress, leaving his opponents in tattered shreds by the roadside, and crying: '—Place! Place au Progrès! Place au Bonheur!' And including himself in his enormous irony, he adds by way of clarification: 'Et pour bien leur prouver que c'est le Bonheur qui passe, et pour leur laisser du Bonheur une image grandiose et durable, je broie, j'écrase, je tue . . . Je terrifie! Tout fuit, éperdu, devant moi . . .'[37]

La 628–E8, or slaughter on the highway! This is our last view of Mirbeau in full battle-dress—*Le Foyer* was to mark the diminution of his irresistible powers—and the picture that remains as Mirbeau crosses the French frontier and heads for home is of the honesty, tender and ferocious, of the man, the satirist, the disappointed idealist, and the social conscience of the *Belle Epoque*.

Notes

1 *Journal littéraire*, vol. 3 (1965), p. 93.
2 M. Tison-Braun, *La Crise de l'humanisme*, vol. I (Paris: Nizet, 1958), p. 77.
3 The anarchists participated in these new, revolutionary teaching groups, and Mirbeau regularly read parts of his plays there. See Bourdon, *op. cit.*
4 See Chapter VI, note 7.

5 Prompted by the visit of the Czar to Paris, Tailhade wrote a violent article, 'Le Triomphe de la domesticité', *Le Libertaire*, No. 82 (15 September 1901), for which he was jailed for a year, in spite of the efforts of Mirbeau, Zola and Anatole France to save him. It was probably as a result of this affair that the commissioner of the *3e Brigade* of the police in Paris drew up a lengthy report on Mirbeau's activities in 1901 (Dossier BA/1190, item 80. B.A.M.P.P.).
6 Mirbeau and Anatole France were among those who joined forces with Grave, Reclus and Malato in organising protests against the atrocities in Russia. *Cf.* Grave, *Le Mouvement libertaire*, p. 221; also C. Aveline, *Anatole France. Vers les temps meilleurs. Trente ans de vie sociale*, vol. 1 (Paris: Emile-Paul, 1949), pp. 88–9.
7 Mirbeau dossier BA/1190, item 86 (B.A.M.P.P.).
8 *Le Journal d'une femme de chambre* (Paris: Le Livre de Poche, 1964), publisher's preface.
9 *Critiques et romanciers* (Paris: Crès, 1924), pp. 122–3.
10 *Le Journal d'une femme de chambre*, p. 113.
11 *Ibid.*, p. 187.
12 Camille de Sainte-Croix, '*Le Journal d'une femme de chambre*', *La Revue Blanche*, No. 23 (September 1900), p. 75.
13 *Le Journal d'une femme de chambre*, p. 445.
14 Georges Pioch, '*Le Calvaire*', *Le Libertaire*, No. 48 (28 October 1900).
15 '*Le Journal d'une femme de chambre*', *T.N.(S.L.)*, No. 18 (August 1900).
16 '*Les Vingt et un jours d'un neurasthénique*', *Le Mercure de France*, October 1901, p. 197.
17 *Portraits sans retouche* (Paris: Albin Michel, 1952), p. 130.
18 Luchon is specifically mentioned by Mirbeau in a letter to Geffroy, dated 22 July 1897 (F.G.B.A.). See also P. de Gorsse, 'Les Vingt et un jours d'Octave Mirbeau à Luchon', *La Revue de Comminges*, 1966, p. 163–76.
19 Leygues was Ministre de l'Instruction Publique when he promised the committee of the *Revue d'Art Dramatique* (of which Mirbeau was a founder-member) that he would set up a popular theatre. It was a promise he never kept, much to Mirbeau's disgust. *Cf.* Aveline, *op. cit.*, pp. 24–5; also Mirbeau's *Gens de théâtre*, pp. 220–6 and 276–82. The section on Leygues in *Les Vingt et un jours* takes up the whole of chapter 6. The section on Maître Du Buit forms chapter 7. See also note 39 of chapter VII above.
20 *Prétextes* (Paris: Mercure de France, 1947 edition), p. 204.
21 *Portraits sans retouche*, p. 135.
22 Ollivier, Président du Conseil in 1870, fell into disgrace over the secession of Alsace-Lorraine. Ollivier's son Daniel demanded that Mirbeau make reparation for his remarks about his father in *Les Vingt et un jours*; *cf. Débats*, 23 August 1901. Mirbeau refused, and pointed out that his irony about Ollivier had appeared as early as 1896 ('En wagon', *Le Journal*, 20 September 1896). In 1891, Ollivier opposed the award of the Prix de l'Académie Française to Reclus' *Géographie universelle* on the grounds that Reclus was an ex-communard.
23 Louis Archinard (1850–1932) was the French general largely responsible for the conquest of the Sudan. Mirbeau's anti-colonialist satire of the general first appeared in 1896 as 'Maroquinerie', *op. cit.*
24 Gorsse, *op. cit.*
25 G. Geffroy, 'Souvenirs de Mirbeau', *Les Cahiers d'Aujourd'hui*, No. 9 (1922), p. 104.
26 *Les Vingt et un jours*, p. 18.
27 '*Les Vingt et un jours d'un neurasthénique*', *La Revue Blanche*, tom. XXVI (1901), p. 77.

28 'Les Vingt et un jours d'un neurasthénique', T.N.(S.L.), No. 24 (October 1901).
29 Portraits sans retouche, p. 130.
30 La 628–E8 begins: 'Voici donc le Journal de ce voyage en automobile à travers un peu de la France, de la Belgique, de la Hollande, de l'Allemagne, et, surtout, à travers un peu de moi-mème.'
31 Ibid., 'Dédicace'.
32 Ibid., p. 319.
33 Ibid., p. 365.
34 Ibid., p. 367.
35 No doubt Mirbeau also remembered with rancour how, in 1898, Anvers was the first of several Belgian towns to ban Les Mauvais Bergers! Cf. La Volonté, 20 December 1898.
36 La 628–E8, p. 5.
37 Ibid., p. 310.

Chapter IX
Dingo, or 'There's life in the old dog yet!' (1908–13)

C'est ici que se voit le misanthrope vieilli . . .
(Maxime Revon, about *Dingo*)

It was not long after his sixtieth birthday, in 1908, that Mirbeau thought seriously of retiring on a permanent basis to the provinces and of relinquishing the tight grip which he had held for so many years on the journalistic and literary life of the capital. Mirbeau had always exploited the therapeutic effect of a country retreat, and had spent much time out of Paris at his houses in Pont-de-l'Arche, Carrières-sous-Poissy, Veneux-Nadon and Cormeilles-en-Vexin; but when he bought a large plot of land at Cheverchemont-sur-Triel in December 1908, it was with the express purpose of having a house built there to his own specifications and to which he could retire for good.

There were various contributory factors in Mirbeau's decision to retire in his early sixties from the French literary scene. Not the least of his reasons was the sudden deterioration in his health around the time of *Le Foyer* towards the end of 1908.[1] The 'notable habitant' of Paris[2] was also increasingly aware of his difficulties in keeping abreast of the hectic life of the French capital, and the evident resurgence of nationalism and of the spirit of *revanchisme*, coupled with the failure of *La 628–E8* and *Le Foyer* to make much impact on a literary scene which was rapidly changing, caused him to turn away in disgust from political, literary and journalistic life.

Mirbeau's disappearance from the public stage which he had filled for so long coincided with the break-up which was taking place in what one writer calls 'l'Age d'or de la Presse'.[3] For most of the nineteenth century the French reading public had been accustomed to the newspapers being made up largely of chronicles, commentaries and often violent, always extreme, polemical pieces contributed by well-known literary figures, and Mirbeau's position as a journalist-cum-novelist was by no means rare amongst his contemporaries. But the increasing complexity and sophistication of the issues preoccupying French society in those pre-war years, as well as the revision of the attitudes of the French public towards those issues, brought about a marked change in the patterns of journalistic and literary expression.[4] It was now no longer possible for a single man to encompass all the issues of the epoch, as Mirbeau and many of his contemporaries had done.[5] The *grande presse* filled its columns more and more with factual news coverage, and less and less with the semi-literary articles of the writers of Mirbeau's generation. The end of many of those independent left-wing newspapers and literary journals which both during and after the Dreyfus Affair had constituted a healthy counterbalance to the more financially stable reactionary press caused Mirbeau to plan and to carry out the setting-up of his own newspaper to fill the unbridged gap.[6] Yet in spite of the quality of Mirbeau's collaborators, who included Anatole France and Georges Clemenceau, Mirbeau's costly revival of *Paris-Journal* (15 January 1910) was short-lived and was only the token gesture of defiance of a man who knew that time and circumstances were irreversibly against him.

If, from 1910 onwards, Mirbeau was known as the 'hermit of Cheverchemont' and his participation in the political and intellectual life of Paris was reduced to letters of protest or the occasional personal appearance, his influence upon a certain section of French literature and his role as a figurehead in the affairs of many younger left-wing writers and intellectuals was none the less a continuing and valuable one, and Mirbeau's villa on the banks of the Seine became a place of pilgrimage for many whose friendship and admiration for Mirbeau was based on a communion of ideas and of principles.

The most frequent and most welcome visitors to Cheverchemont were the young left-wing writers Francis Jourdain and Léon Werth, both of them associated with the anarchist movement, and both of them forming a reliable communications link between Mirbeau and the important events of the capital.[7] When, for example, Mirbeau wrote a letter of protest in February 1910 at the trial of the antimilitarist Gustave Hervé, it was Jourdain who conveyed the letter to *La Guerre Sociale* for publication; and in August of the same year, it was Werth who took Mirbeau's letter of protest against the repressive policies of Briand's government into Paris for publication in the same newspaper (one of the few which would then publish articles by Mirbeau).[8]

Other visitors included the non-political friends and protégés like the gentle Marguerite Audoux, whose novel *Marie-Claire* Mirbeau championed and prefaced in 1910, the egotistical extrovert Sacha Guitry, whom Mirbeau naïvely regarded as the greatest playwright of the twentieth century, and, of course, the ever faithful Monet, whose friendship for Mirbeau never faltered during the thirty-two years of their acquaintance.

Others were drawn to Cheverchemont because of the principles for which Mirbeau stood, and few, if any, were turned away empty-handed. The left-wing journalist George Besson successfully extracted articles and unpublished parts of *Dingo* and *Un Gentilhomme* from Mirbeau for publication in his *Cahiers d'Aujourd'hui*, and was able to use his position of influence to introduce Mirbeau to young left-wing writers like Vildrac, Crucy and Léautaud, who all visited Cheverchemont during Mirbeau's retirement there.[9] The well-liked Werth and the persistent Egyptian intellectuals Adès and Josipovici succeeded in rousing Mirbeau from his literary apathy enough to write them prefaces for their respective books.[10] They were not the only ones who had cause to be grateful to the 'hermit of Cheverchemont'.

This activity of Mirbeau's within the context of his inactivity, sporadic and limited as it was, and though it was more a question of critical and intellectual witness and reflex than of the exertion of literary and political influence, was none the less a pointer to the surprise which Mirbeau was preparing in the quietness of his country retreat for those enemies and detractors who thought that the voice which had terrorised and scandalised the literary and journalistic scene for so long was now, happily and at long last, silent. This surprise came in the form of *Dingo*, Mirbeau's last completed novel, published in 1913, shortly before the First World War brought a curtain of sadness over Mirbeau's declining years. The quality of *Dingo*, and the subdued vehemence of its allegorical morality, showed quite clearly to Mirbeau's startled contemporaries that there was indeed 'life in the old dog yet'.

To those who thought that illness and old age had brought impotence and sterility to Mirbeau's pen, *Dingo* was sufficient proof that he had lost none of his talents as a novelist and none of his virulence as a critic of society. Many critics have actually maintained that *Dingo* was Mirbeau's best and most readable novel;[11] and there is no doubt that Mirbeau really set out to impress himself upon the French reading public in what proved to be his last offering. It is hard to say whether the original idea for the novel, which is a dog-owner's account of the life and mind of his wild Australian dingo, came to Mirbeau from the tale *Diogène le chien*, written by Mirbeau's lifelong friend Paul Hervieu in 1882, not long before the two were collaborating on *Les Grimaces*, or whether Mirbeau was influenced by the vogue of animal tales which became so popular in the 1900s, and amongst which Tolstoy's horse-tale *Kholstomer* was one of the most successful. The tone of *Dingo* is certainly very close to the ironic nihilism of Hervieu's story.

What is certain is that *Dingo* found the substance of its plot in Mirbeau's own experiences, around the turn of the century, with his inseparable canine companion, which bequeathed its name and its acts, transformed by the imagination of its master, to the world of literature.

It was around 1898 that Dingo—described rather unkindly by an eye-witness as 'une sorte de grand caniche'[12]—made his first public appearances with Mirbeau. Dingo was his master's constant companion at the nocturnal dreyfusard meetings in the offices of *La Revue Blanche*,[13] and their walks all over Paris are faithfully recorded in the eleventh chapter of the novel which arose from their friendship. Where Mirbeau went Dingo followed, and Mirbeau's houses in Paris and Veneux-Nadon were familiar places to Mirbeau's dog. Mirbeau was deeply affected by Dingo's death in 1901, as he wrote to Jules Claretie in October of that year:

> J'avais un chien, une délicieuse bête, que j'aimais comme un tendre ami. Il est mort. Je l'ai enterré dans la forêt. Ç'a été des jours atroces, sa maladie.
> Je ne veux plus rester dans cette maison . . . où mon pauvre Dingo est mort.[14]

Though Mirbeau replaced this first Dingo with another, it was clearly the memory of his first faithful friend which inspired him to write *Dingo* over ten years after the dog's death.

This novel which arose from Mirbeau's affection for an animal revealed, in 1913 when it finally appeared, a mature and more measured Mirbeau, whose irony was tinged with a rather stoical bitterness, but whose talents had gained from experience what they might have lost in ardour. To all intents and purposes Mirbeau had been 'out of the swing', as he always put it, for almost five years when *Dingo* was finished, and there is no doubt that the novel benefited from the calmer state of mind in which Mirbeau was able to write it. As well as having a plot which was as feasible and as continuous as those in Mirbeau's early novels, *Dingo* was a kind of stylistic amalgam of all Mirbeau's talents as a writer. There were the caricatural portraits of the inhabitants of the rural Ponteilles, like those of the mayor, the curé and the village notary—government, religion and the legal system, as always, took quite a pounding from Mirbeau's satire in *Dingo*; some of the anecdotes associated with these satirical figures remind us of the early *Lettres de ma chaumière*, and Mirbeau's vehemence is wisely tempered to avoid descending to the often gratuitous ridicule of *Les Vingt et un jours*. There was the semi-autobiographical tone, the personal involvement of the author–narrator which Mirbeau never abandoned in his novels, and which allowed him, in *Dingo* as in his other works, to express his own opinions on matters of importance within the conventions of the plot. Interpreting the mind of the dog, too, Mirbeau was giving himself twice the licence to speak freely for himself, and Dingo served as a mirror-image of his own soul, as he explained almost apologetically in the novel: 'C'est moi seul, je le confesse, qui, par une sotte et orgueilleuse manie d'anthropomorphisme—non dans une intention d'imposture—me plais à tirer des actes d'un chien ce commentaire humain . . .'[15]

Dingo, who first appears in the novel as a puppy and develops into a fierce and unpredictable hound, faithful to its master and mistress but spreading terror wherever it takes a dislike to man or beast, is undoubtedly an ironic and allegorical representation of Mirbeau's own view of himself, and it is for this reason that the novel takes on added philosophical and biographical importance. The parallelism, implicit or explicit as the case may be, between Mirbeau (the narrator) and Dingo (the eponymous 'hero' of the book) is deliberate and sustained, and confirms the view of Mirbeau's temperament which this study has suggested all along. Looking back on his own life Mirbeau saw that the underlying factor in his existence had been his rebellion, his unruliness, his rejection of authority and tradition, his individualism, and his love of freedom. Allied with this had been his determination not only to defend his own individualism, violently if necessary, but also to make others aware of the tyranny exercised and the abuses perpetrated by authority in its various forms. Mirbeau's dog became the embodiment of all that Mirbeau himself had been.

When Dingo first arrives as a puppy cooped up in a box sent from England, he lets out a yell of protest to the world at the unkind treatment he has received. And remembering no doubt his own rebellion as a child against parental and pedagogical tyranny, Mirbeau is immediately won over to Dingo by the spontaneity of his revolt: 'Je l'avoue, l'idée seule que cet embryon protestât déjà et si spontanement, et sans aucune littérature, contre la stupidité, la malignité, la malpropreté des hommes . . . m'enflamma.'[16] From this moment on Mirbeau makes it clear that the dog has what he calls 'une conception de l'humanité si parfaitement conforme à la mienne'.[17]

Mirbeau's anthropomorphic desire to make the dog a symbolic representation of himself was probably as much a source of the antics of Dingo as the real-life dog on which the story was ostensibly based. The paradox of the fierceness and tenderness in Dingo's character (the same dog could take a piece out of the militaristic sexton's leg and could befriend the village pauper, help an old vagabond to push his cart up a hill, and even allow two poor beggars to burgle his master's house) is too much an aspect of Mirbeau's own temperament and involves too much human judgement for it to be a true reflection of the character of Mirbeau's well-loved dog. The same is true right through the novel. Dingo's preference for the Louis XVI chairs and his dislike of the more austere Empire furniture enables Mirbeau to expatiate on the need for the beautiful to be utilitarian and allows him to agree with his dog that art for art's sake cannot be justified. Dingo's affection for an old man suspected of murder becomes the pretext for Mirbeau to declare, as he had so often declared before:

> J'ai une telle méfiance de l'appareil judiciaire, une telle répugnance pour ces faces indifférentes qu'ont les juges, un tel effroi de ces faces mornes, têtues qu'ont les jurés . . . que je crois toujours, par une sorte de protestation instinctive, à l'innocence des pires criminels.[18]

Chapter 8 of *Dingo* describes the devastation which the now fully grown dog was causing amongst the animals of the surrounding region. The superstitious fear which Mirbeau's friend was evoking in the local inhabitants was a source of financial and personal embarrassment to him, but it was a source of amusement and secret exultation to Dingo's champion, the village pauper Piscot. Piscot was glad that Dingo was thus avenging his poverty by attacking the property of the villagers and filling them with terror and distress! The second Dingo, it seems, was in real life no such source of damage or distress to anyone in the village of Cormeilles-en-Vexin,[19] and there is no evidence to suggest that the original Dingo was any more fierce, save in the literary imagination of his master. Here again Mirbeau was undoubtedly making the fictional dog conform to the allegorical portrait of himself. Dingo's violence was the literary transposition of the disgust and animosity which Mirbeau had felt and expressed about his contemporaries for over thirty years. Mirbeau knew he had a violent side to his temperament, and he gladly used it in his role of social critic. The task which he set himself, as early as *Les Grimaces* in 1882, of 'braving the stupid' and 'unmasking the scoundrels' was made all the more effective by the natural honesty and frankness of his violent outbursts. One critic described Mirbeau as a 'salamandre dans un brasier',[20] while another speaks of 'la généreuse brusquerie qui terrorisait les tièdes et faisait céder les hésitants'.[21] Mirbeau himself insisted that his violence should be seen in terms of his honesty: 'On a dit que j'étais violent', he said in his preface to *Le Livre de Goha le Simple*, 'Pourquoi n'a-t-on jamais voulu comprendre que je suis tout simplement sincère?'[22] And here we come back to the fictional Dingo, for Mirbeau makes it abundantly clear in the novel that Dingo is wild and violent simply because he is being true to his natural feelings and instincts, in spite of the civilised manners which his owner tried, unsuccessfully, to impose upon him:

> ... Dingo, brisant la mince couche de civilisation sous laquelle j'avais tenté de comprimer ses élans, semblait retrouver de jour en jour plus fougueuse, plus déchaînée, cette violence d'indépendance, dont des siècles de liberté, loin de l'homme et de ses lois, en pleine nature sauvage, avaient en quelque sorte pétri sa chair et fait bouillonner son sang.[23]

Mirbeau's contemporaries found him as impossible to tame or even to contain as the narrator of *Dingo* found his fictional dog. Though the critics chose largely to ignore Mirbeau's last completed novel—there were few reviews of *Dingo* in the press—and though the book did not sell after the manner of *Le Journal d'une femme de chambre*, Mirbeau still had his say, and had the satisfaction of saying it in a work which was certainly amongst the best he ever produced.

It has been said, with some justification, that Mirbeau's novels contain very few favourable portraits or likeable characters.[24] In *Dingo* there are only really three figures liked equally by the narrator and his dog. The first, already mentioned, is Piscot the village pauper, whose friendship with the narrator is the pretext for much of the overt social criticism of the novel. Piscot's complaints against the State give Mirbeau the opportunity to attack over-efficient bureaucracy (Piscot's supplementary benefits for his large family are withheld because he has no certificates to prove they are his), the patronising attitude and demoralising effect of public charitable institutions, the economic policies of the government and their effect upon high food prices, and the harshness of provincial justice. Part of chapter 6, adapted from a basic idea which Mirbeau had in an article in *L'Humanité* as early as 1904,[25] was reprinted by the anarchists in the literary supplement of *Les Temps Nouveaux* (No. 42, March 1905), thus indicating how Mirbeau's ideas as late as *Dingo* were still very much in line with anarchist philosophy.

The second character liked by Mirbeau and his dog is the local poacher Victor Flamant, who comes into the story when Mirbeau rents a house near Fontainebleau. Feared by the locals, taciturn, amoral and with a long criminal record, Flamant is interesting as a recurrent type in Mirbeau's novels: the type of the outlaw, rejected by society and in sullen revolt against it. Already in 1891 Mirbeau had written of his instinctive admiration for poachers, and explained how this was part of his universal sympathy for those who refused to buckle beneath the tyranny of the *status quo*.[26] The Abbé Jules, Bolorec and Dingo are the most obvious examples of this type, but there are many more characters, like Jean Roule in *Les Mauvais Bergers*, Germaine Lechat in *Les Affaires sont les affaires* and Arthur Lebeau in *Scrupules*, who fall into this category. The fellow-feeling between the narrator, Flamant and the dog—all three extensions of Mirbeau's own rebellious instinct—is such that the novel closes with an emotional refusal by the poor poacher to accept any money for his part in burying his canine friend. It was not the least of Mirbeau's merits as a human being that he was able to bring out the best qualities of those whom society refused to countenance at all.

The third, and perhaps the most interesting of the characters to whom the narrator felt drawn in *Dingo* was the local school teacher (another of Mirbeau's favourite types), who was being hounded and persecuted for his rather revolutionary ideas and teaching methods. As was so often the case, Mirbeau based this pedagogical rebel on a character from real life—in this instance, the left-wing intellectual Gustave Hervé. Hervé, a socialist militant whose anti-militarism and anarchist tendencies automatically endeared him to Mirbeau, and who tried during the First World War to carry Mirbeau over with him to the opposite extreme of militant nationalism, began his career as a history teacher. His radical ideas and his unusual teaching methods, however, soon lost him his job in 1901, and from then on he dedicated himself to politics and journalism. Hervé's shabby treatment by the authorities deeply affected Mirbeau, and in 1904 he voiced his sympathy for him in an article in *L'Humanité* (31 July 1904), which served, in fact, as the basis for most of chapter 10 of the later *Dingo*. The article, 'Propos de l'instituteur', showed how reasonable were Hervé's pedagogical innovations (variation in teaching speeds, modification of antiquated curricula, relaxation of military discipline, etc.), and how stupid were those who accused him of being 'un anarchiste dangereux . . . et . . . un violenteur de petits garçons'. The teacher in *Dingo* is in danger of receiving the same treatment as Hervé; and Mirbeau, for whom the question of educational reform was a vital one in his desire to bring a little more freedom into the world, reserves all his sympathy and respect for this articulate and dedicated man, a voice in the wilderness of the rural backwater of Ponteilles.

If the power both of the fictional creativity and of the social criticism of *Dingo* came as a shock to Mirbeau's contemporaries, the autobiographical aspect of the work stood as a confirmation that Mirbeau's attitude towards the issues of the age had retained its anarchistic flavour. In *Dingo*, Mirbeau reaffirmed himself not only as a man of the extreme Left who would retain his individualism and independence to the grave but also as a supporter of the specifically anarchist doctrines which he had fought to defend particularly during the

1890s. His comments on the universality of property, on the ineffectiveness of piecemeal social reform (and especially of public charity), on the hypocrisy of organised justice, and on the need to liberalise education, as well as his ubiquitous anti-clerical and anti-militarist sentiments, all stamp *Dingo* as the work of a man whose social and political convictions had changed little from those of the 'journalist of revolt' of the closing decade of the nineteenth century. And if this interpretation should require corroborative evidence, then Mirbeau himself provides it within the text of his last completed novel. For speaking of himself through the character of Dingo, he looks back upon his 'career' as a revolutionary and as an anarchist and remarks:

> N'allez pas croire qu'il fût affilié à un groupement anarchiste, qu'il collât des affiches sur des murs, ou qu'il prît la parole dans les meetings révolutionnaires. Il agissait, voilà tout, et il agissait en solitaire, à sa façon, une façon moins compliquée, plus simpliste et qui 'rendait' davantage . . .[27]

Above all, it is Mirbeau's individualism which pervades these important, autobiographical lines. If in fact Mirbeau did on occasions address revolutionary meetings and did openly participate in anarchist-inspired activities, it was as a free agent that he did so, not as a member of a party nor as an adherent of a movement. It was this individualism, this supreme auto-responsibility—the most essential ingredient of the anarchist temperament—which found him time and again in communion with the anarchists, who were never able to call him entirely their own, but who gratefully accepted his consistent support and greatly respected his systematic and intractable originality. *Dingo* was the last cry of protest of an intellect which for thirty years had remained true to a set of ideals and principles which had advanced, slowly, but which were shortly to be engulfed in a flood of reaction and of human stupidity on a scale never known before. The First World War was to be a blow to Mirbeau's hopes from which he did not live to recover.

Notes

1 Renard, *op. cit.*, p. 820, and Léautaud, *op. cit.*, vol. 2, pp. 300–1 both refer to Mirbeau's poor state of health at this time.
2 The expression is Valéry Larbaud's, in 'Mirbeau l'essayiste', *Les Cahiers d'Aujourd'hui*, No. 9 (1922), p. 133.
3 G. Weill, quoted in Billy, *op. cit.*, pp. 367–8.
4 There is an excellent section on this change in the tone and quality of French intellectual life in *ibid.*, pp. 366–9.
5 Léon Werth explains Mirbeau's success up to 1908 in these terms: '. . . l'époque où

vécut Mirbeau en sa maturité fut moins décomposée que la nôtre. On pouvait tenter de la saisir à bras le corps.' Introduction to *Les Vingt et un jours*, p. 3

6 Between 1903 and 1906 the following literary journals ceased publication: *La Revue Blanche*, *La Revue Bleue*, *La Plume*, *L'Ermitage*, *La Revue d'Art Dramatique*. In December 1909 a police report said: 'Octave Mirbeau est disposé à fonder une feuille de combat politique. Ce pamphlet serait quotidien et combattrait surtout les idées, et encore plus les hommes de l'Action Française.' Mirbeau dossier BA/1190, item 103 (B.A.M.P.P.).
7 Jourdain was a regular contributor to *Le Libertaire*, and was well known for his anarchist sympathies. See his book *Sans remords ni rancune* (Paris: Corrêa, 1953).
8 The comings and goings at Cheverchemont were closely watched by the police, and the information about Jourdain and Werth is contained in Mirbeau's police dossier BA/1190, items 105 and 107 (B.A.M.P.P.).
9 On Léautaud's visit to Cheverchemont, organised by Besson, see Léautaud, *op. cit.*, vol. 3, pp. 80–1 and 162; also *ibid.*, vol. 19 (1966), pp. 144–5.
10 Mirbeau's preface to Werth's novel *La Maison blanche* (Paris: Fasquelle, 1913) suggests that Mirbeau saw in Werth, the enthusiastic, violent and naïve anarchist, a younger version of himself. Adès and Josipovici's novel *Le Livre de Goha le Simple* was not published with Mirbeau's preface until after his death (Paris: Calmann-Lévy, 1919).
11 *E.g.* Léon Daudet, 'Octave Mirbeau. Un aquafortiste du médiocre, du sinistre et du malheur', *Candide*, 29 October 1936. *Cf.* also A. Dinar, *Les Auteurs cruels* (Paris: Mercure de France, 1942), p. 99, and Wilson, *op. cit.*, p. 482.
12 *Cf.* Dorgelès, *op. cit.*, p. 147. It is possible, however, that this was a description of the second Dingo, since the first died in 1901 and never lived at Cormeilles (the Ponteilles of *Dingo*).
13 See Jackson, *op. cit.*, p. 123.
14 Letter of October 1901, quoted in *Gazette des Tribunaux*, 11–12 May 1908.
15 *Dingo* (Paris: Fasquelle, 1913), p. 38.
16 *Ibid.*, p. 7.
17 *Ibid.*
18 *Ibid.*, p. 139.
19 See Dorgelès, *op. cit.*, pp. 146–8.
20 A. Dubeux, 'Le Féroce Mirbeau', *La Revue des Deux Mondes*, 15 March 1968, p. 211.
21 Jourdain, *op. cit.*, p. 198.
22 *Op. cit.*, p. iii.
23 *Dingo*, p. 98.
24 Even Dorgelès, a passionate admirer of Mirbeau, wrote of his works: 'Jamais un beau visage, jamais une belle âme. Ou si rares . . .'. *Portraits sans retouche*, p. 154.
25 'Célébrons le Code', *L'Humanité*, 6 November 1904.
26 'Dans la forêt', *op. cit.*
27 *Dingo*, pp. 328–9.

Chapter X
The pity of war (1914–17)

Tant que durera la guerre . . . je ne veux rien écrire.

(Mirbeau, in 1915)

The First World War, prefaced by the assassination of Jaurès, lamented by friends and opponents alike,[1] was a tragedy for the whole of the western world, and no individual was more heartbroken or more demoralised by it than Octave Mirbeau. In 1914 Mirbeau was sixty-six, but he looked and felt nearer eighty. Enfeebled by ill health, he was already disillusioned by the rising tide of nationalism and by some of the warlike poses of former left-wing colleagues like Clemenceau when the declaration of war came to disturb the hour of relative peace he was enjoying at Chèverchemont after a life of ceaseless activity.

The First World War shattered Mirbeau's most cherished ideals. In the 1880s, even before his blackest period of nervous depression, he had given expression in 'La Guerre et l'Homme'[2] to the pessimistic fears which had haunted him since the horrors of the Franco-Prussian War: that war was an essential and recurrent activity of humanity. By 1907, however, having seen the advances made by socialist and left-wing ideologies, he had convinced himself, somewhat naïvely, that another war between France and Germany was no longer possible. The section of his novel *La 628–E8* which dealt with Germany was impregnated with his pacifistic internationalism, and Mirbeau was able to prove to his own satisfaction at least that Germany's economic and industrial progress represented no threat to the less prosperous French. To Paul Gsell, who interviewed Mirbeau about this time at his château in Cormeilles, he spoke of 'un extraordinaire renforcement de l'individualisme' which was operating in society, and said that people were beginning to realise that society was tending towards a single aim: 'l'individu libre et heureux'.[3] With the revival of so many authoritarian dogmas and a world war just around the corner, Mirbeau could hardly have been further from the truth, and his disillusionment proved all the greater for the suddenness with which his illusions were destroyed. Mirbeau's friend and colleague Thadée Natanson said of the war-time Mirbeau: 'Il n'arrive pas à se consoler de la déroute de toutes les philosophies dont la générosité l'avait conquis. L'insanité qui fait délirer l'univers le met à la torture.'[4]

The war against Germany presented Mirbeau with a dilemma which was common to all the left-wing intellectuals who prior to 1914 had openly expressed pacifist and anti-militarist opinions. Anarchists, syndicalists and socialists of all shades had to decide whether their opposition to war required that they should refuse to condemn and resist the evident aggression of the German Kaiser. Amongst the anarchists, the majority came down grudgingly in support of the allied cause, though there were always the purists like Faure and Armand who refused to countenance the war on any pretext.[5] As for Kropotkin, as early as 1905, when a Franco-German conflict had seemed possible, he had found justification for a defensive war on the grounds that Germany was far more reactionary and authoritarian than France.[6] It was Kropotkin, too, who was the initiator of the *Manifeste des Seize* in 1916, a document which was signed by many leading anarchists, including Jean Grave, and which stressed that peace could only be achieved by the destruction of German imperialism.[7]

Mirbeau, it seems, remained in two minds up to his death in February 1917. He still opposed the principle of war, and like Proudhon and Grave before him criticised it as a means of middle-class exploitation. Only this time, he felt, perhaps it was the German people who were being exploited by their leaders, and perhaps also the French were justified in defending their country and their liberty. Yet the chauvinism and the militarism which was so much a part of the war effort remained abhorrent to him, and his middle-of-the-road indecision filled him with sadness. That sadness, too, would be augmented by the departure for the battle-front of young friends like the anarchist Léon Werth,[8] and by the way in which fervent anti-militarists, like Hervé, Descaves, France and Kropotkin were forced to abandon their now meaningless idealism.[9] If Mirbeau appeared to support the French cause at all during the thirty or so months of the war which he witnessed, it was a rather negative hope which caused him to do so—as Thadée Natanson put it: 'Ce qu'il espère avant tout de la victoire . . . c'est la fin de la violence.'[10]

In the hysterical atmosphere of wartime France, when a man who did not wholeheartedly support the war effort was regarded with suspicion and animosity, Mirbeau judged it his best course to maintain an unhappy silence. His literature, his journalism, and by and large his correspondence, came to an abrupt halt with the outbreak of hostilities, and in the words of a newspaper editorial of 1915, Mirbeau 'se condamnait au silence'.[11]

If Mirbeau thought, however, that the opinions of a man like himself, whose declarations had so often made headline news in the past, would not be sought on an issue which was so deeply affecting the life of the whole nation, then he reckoned without the persistence and ingenuity of both the revolutionary and the reactionary press. Neither the anti-militarists nor the nationalists were prepared to respect Mirbeau's self-imposed silence, nor did either party wish to forgo the opportunity of enlisting Mirbeau's support for their own views. Mirbeau's replies to their respective requests, though naturally more favourable to the Left, only serve to spotlight the helplessness and the angry state of indecision in which Mirbeau found himself.

Before the outbreak of the First World War, Mirbeau had strongly criticised, in a letter to Jean Grave, the French middle class's 'dogme de la patrie guerrière'.[12] And when in the early days of the war Grave wrote to Mirbeau asking for his support in combatting 'le débordement de réaction qui se dessinait',[13] Mirbeau replied, in a letter which makes nonsense of the nationalists' subsequent claim that Mirbeau had renounced his anti-militarist convictions:

> Toute ma sympathie est acquise à toute tentative contre l'esprit réactionnaire, mais je crains bien que toute tentative soit inefficace, jusqu'au jour où la France guerrière, diminuée par sa sottise de quelques provinces, aura reçu la formidable frottée qu'elle mérite.[14]

The phrase to retain here is 'la France guerrière'—it was the French militarists and super-patriots for whom Mirbeau had no sympathy. His replies to the subsequent questions from the reactionary press show how he sympathised deeply with the ordinary French soldiers and how bitterly he opposed the imperialism of the German high command.

It was in reply to the persistent demands of *Le Petit Parisien* that Mirbeau, rather unwisely as it proved, broke his silence in 1915 to express his mixed feelings about the war, and particularly his pity for the soldiers in the trenches. 'A nos soldats' appeared in this right-wing, pro-war paper on 28 July 1915, and it is remarkable for the absence of the heroic vocabulary of so much of the material which appeared in such wartime publications. In simple and personal language Mirbeau spoke directly to the soldiers themselves, expressing his solidarity with them and his concern for their safety: 'Je suis émerveillé de votre endurance et, parfois, songeant aux engins que l'Allemagne invente pour vous accabler, je me demande: «Comment font-ils?»'[15] And after criticising the 'ambition mauvaise' of German imperialism, Mirbeau concluded with the fond hope that France's clear-sighted and intelligent soldiers would return from ultimate victory with that 'habitude de franchise' for which he had always fought himself—the inference being, of course, that he trusted they would be generous and wise enough not to extract the usual great revenge.

While there was little in these few lines to associate Mirbeau with the extreme militarism of the paper in which the article appeared, the editors of the paper, anxious to add publicity to their cause, evidently thought it a good idea to pursue Mirbeau's opinions further, and consequently a young journalist, Jean Lefranc, was sent to interview Mirbeau at his home in Cheverchemont. 'Chez Octave Mirbeau, antimilitariste' was the result of this interview in August 1915.[16] Again, there was only limited joy for the editors, and Mirbeau's carefully chosen replies showed his unwillingness to appear too sympathetic towards those who were known familiarly as *revanchards* or *jusqu'auboutistes*. When asked who was to blame for the war, he replied quite confidently: '. . . le militarisme, le militarisme allemand'. And, having established that he was still an antimilitarist, he again freely admitted his support for the soldiers of the French army: 'Qui sont-ils, ces soldats que j'aime, sinon mes compagnons d'hier, comme moi voulant vivre dans la paix?' And he concluded the interview with the hope, not that France would exact ample revenge, nor that her position in the world would be advanced by her victory, but that humanity itself might learn from this great mistake and that men might improve morally:

> Il faut croire et je crois que l'humanité sortira meilleure . . . Je crois fermement que . . . les hommes seront, la paix reconquise, plus justes et plus sages. Je crois que les idées de liberté et de justice se propageront partout après la guerre.

Mirbeau was evidently in one of his more optimistic moods on this occasion; or perhaps he was already clutching at straws.

Unfortunately for Mirbeau in the fanatical atmosphere of war, his words of sympathy for the French army were easily misconstrued by his political enemies, and his left-wing friends were forced to excuse this falsely-imputed militarism as the machinations of the warmongers exploiting the frequent bouts of prostration and delirium which afflicted Mirbeau increasingly up to his death.[17] Mirbeau cannot have been fully aware of the complicity of his anti-militarist ally Gustave Hervé with the editors of *Le Petit Parisien*, whose rhetorical introductions to Mirbeau's two contributions to their columns expressed the construction which they expected their readers to place on Mirbeau's words. Hervé, whom Mirbeau had come to admire before the First World War for his fanatical anti-militarism,[18] turned completely round on the outbreak of war and became a fervent patriot and a fierce advocate of *la guerre à outrance*.[19] He succeeded, however, in continuing to frequent former left-wing associates, and it was he who was largely responsible behind the scenes for motivating *Le Petit Parisien*'s interest in Mirbeau's 'opinions' on the war. Mirbeau was not the only one to suffer from Hervé's plotting—Anatole France also lived to regret his association with this 'socialiste repenti', for he fell into exactly the same trap as Mirbeau[20]—but Mirbeau was the one whose incapacity and whose weakening hold on life made him the easiest prey for the clever and energetic Hervé.

We have to look no further, however, than the last genuine piece of Mirbeau's writing to understand the true nature of his feelings about the First World War, and to see that there was no room in those feelings for the heroic verbosity or the aggressive vengefulness of extremists like Hervé. Mirbeau's preface to *Le Livre de Goha le Simple* is dated 25 October 1916—less than four months before Mirbeau's death. The style is so obviously Mirbeau's that there has never been any debate about its authenticity, and the young Egyptian authors must have been fortunate to find Mirbeau in one of his now rare clear-thinking moments. Writing of the war—he could never exclude it from his mind—Mirbeau explained his position simply, unequivocally, and without any reference to nationalism, patriotism or any of the other ideologies he was supposed to have espoused:

> Je ne suis pas un de ces spectateurs héroïques, que les deuils de la guerre emplissent d'enthousiasme, qui alignent des phrases et s'en attendrissent. Je ne suis, hélas! qu'un homme et la détresse universelle m'absorbe trop pour que je fasse autre chose que d'y penser et d'en souffrir.[21]

In spite of the pressure of the war years, Mirbeau remained an internationalist and a pacifist to the end. The only patriotism to which he admitted was the kind he had endorsed in 1893 when Jean Grave wrote in *La Société mourante et l'anarchie*:

> Il n'y a pas de patrie pour l'homme vraiment digne . . . ou du moins il n'y en a qu'une: c'est celle où il lutte pour le bon droit, celle où il vit, où il a ses affections, mais elle peut s'étendre à toute la terre. L'humanité ne se divise pas en petits casiers où chacun se parque dans son coin, en regardant les autres comme des ennemis.[22]

These were the feelings with which Mirbeau created the character of Jean Mintié, whose gesture of embracing a dead Prussian officer in *Le Calvaire* was interpreted, even in 1887, as sacrilegious and iconoclastic treason against France. The fact that Mirbeau reprinted the 1887 preface to *Le Calvaire,* in which he explained his own idea of patriotism, and used it in his short anti-reactionary campaign on *Paris-Journal* as late as 1910, shows how little his ideas on the subject, so much in line with anarchist philosophy, had changed in almost twenty-five years. The sadness of his remaining years was not able to break his conviction, in his own understanding of the meaning of patriotism, that 'l'Art et . . . la Philosophie rompent les cercles étroits des frontières et débordent sur toute l'humanité'.[23]

Yet fate, in the person of Gustave Hervé, had one final and unkind trick to play on Mirbeau, and his exit from the world proved to be the flashpoint of the kind of polemics and scandal in which he himself had so long revelled. Mirbeau died on the morning of Friday 16 February 1917—his sixty-ninth birthday—and on the Monday following, the day of his funeral, *Le Petit Parisien* published what purported to be 'Le Testament politique d'Octave Mirbeau'. This document, which Mirbeau had allegedly dictated to his wife only five days before his death, though it by no means constituted the *volte-face* in his attitude to patriotism which his enemies claimed,[24] contained some ideas which immediately appeared as inconsistent with the principles for which Mirbeau had stood for so long during his lifetime, and his friends were either horrified, or were unwilling to accept the document as genuine. One quotation will suffice to illustrate why Mirbeau's left-wing colleagues took such exception to it. With reference to the pre-eminence of France's moral position in the world—an idea which the living Mirbeau would surely never have recognised as his own—the dubious document affirms: 'Ce que nous demandions autrefois à un parti, nous le trouvons dans un pays. Mais pour cela, il faut qu'on découvre, comme je l'ai découvert moi-même, que la Patrie est une réalité.'

Paul Léautaud, at first taken in by the document, was disappointed enough by such an expression of patriotism to write in his diary about Mirbeau: 'Quand un homme a eu, dans toute son oeuvre, une attitude intellectuelle et morale qu'il dément et renie ainsi en cinq minutes, c'est un arlequin littéraire et son oeuvre égale zéro.'[25] George Besson's revelation to Léautaud and to the literary world, however, of the 'abominable cuisine autour du moribond'[26]—the complicity between Mme Mirbeau and Gustave Hervé in this matter of the 'Testament politique'—soon became ample pretext for Léautaud, and many like him, to retract such understandably harsh words.

So many of Mirbeau's closest associates and oldest friends rejected the genuineness of the 'Testament politique'—chief amongst whom were Besson, Montfort and Sébastien Faure—that there now seems little doubt about its apocryphal nature. The verdict of later critics, while not unanimous, leaves serious doubts about Mme Mirbeau's honesty in this affair. One writer speaks confidently of the 'testament politique apocryphe que sa gardienne vigilante va lui attribuer et publier dans un journal avec la complicité d'Hervé!'[27] Another suggests that Mme Mirbeau was actually ashamed of her husband's antipatriotic sentiments, and describes her fabrication of the false 'Testament politique' as 'un sale tour'.[28] As for Besson, as recently as 1967 he continued to witness from personal knowledge to the indecent complicity between Mirbeau's wife and Gustave Hervé, whom he describes as 'pitre entre les pitres, menteur entre les menteurs'.[29]

There is so much contemporary evidence too to indicate that both Hervé and Alice Mirbeau wished to make it appear that Mirbeau had died a patriot that their complicity cannot be in doubt. The very fact that Mirbeau had not written the 'Testament politique' in his own hand—an autograph copy of the document would surely have been Mirbeau's way of proving to the world that he had changed his allegiance—cast doubt on its genuineness from the outset. And if Mirbeau had been too ill to write, would he not also have been too ill to dictate the smooth and flawless prose of the 'Testament politique'? Or if he had been well enough to dictate but not to write, could he not at least have signed his wife's draft of his dying thoughts? All these are questions which Mme Mirbeau preferred to pass over in silence.[30]

It was well known also that Mirbeau wanted no funeral speeches at his graveside.[31] And yet the mourners had to listen to the reactionary ramblings of Gustave Hervé in the Passy cemetery where Mirbeau was laid to rest. The feelings of many in the crowd, half-expressed in the murmurings noted by Paul Léautaud,[32] were openly expressed some hours later in Ernest Gegout's article in *L'Attaque*:

> . . . bien que le mourant eût exigé que là, enfin, on lui flanquât la paix, Hervé, sur le bord de la fosse—pourquoi, ah! pourquoi pas dedans!—se mit à discourir en larmoyant dans son tire-jus tricolore.[33]

Hervé's speech,[34] and the article which he wrote shortly after Mirbeau's death,[35] were almost more concerned with the successful outcome of the First World War than they were with doing justice to the writer and journalist whose passing they were supposed to mark. Small wonder that Mirbeau's admirers considered, like Eugène Montfort, that Mirbeau had been 'mal enterré'.[36] For them at least, the words of Henri Béraud, so critical of the false picture of Mirbeau painted by Hervé, rang out with conviction: 'L'autre Mirbeau seul vit et vivra; nous ne cesserons point d'entendre les éclats de ses belles colères, ni le bruit des gifles qu'il asséna . . .'³⁷

There seems to be no doubt that if Mirbeau had survived the war and had lived, like Anatole France, to refute the construction put by his enemies upon his wartime utterances, he would have picked up the threads of his revolutionary opposition to the middle-class society in which he lived where he had left them in *Dingo* and in the pre-war letters which reaffirmed his anarchistic outlook to his long-standing correspondent Jean Grave. As it was, it remains one of the greatest and most poignant ironies of his existence that just as he had been ushered into the world by the type of rural, lower middle-class conservatives he spent thirty years repudiating and satirising, so he was ushered out by the very right-wing militarist and nationalist patriots he had combatted for the bulk of his journalistic and literary career.

Many of those who, had Mirbeau died earlier, could have given him a send-off worthy of him, were, in 1917, either dead, incapacitated or out of Paris, many of them involved with the war. Only Geffroy, Montfort and Tailhade of all Mirbeau's surviving friends and colleagues were able to give account of Mirbeau's contribution to the intellectual life of France and to do justice to the sincerity of Mirbeau's sustained efforts as a supporter of the most extreme left-wing ideologies and to his dual role of moral satirist and enthusiast of beauty. To Geffroy fell the assessment of Mirbeau's prowess as a critic of the arts.³⁸ Montfort praised the man and the writer, and defended the apparent pessimism of the social philosopher.³⁹ For Tailhade remained the honour of summing up the motivation, the technique and the significance of Mirbeau's unique career.

Rising above the petty squabbles and the reactionary, often hysterical atmosphere of the day, Tailhade penned an epitaph for his late fellow anarchist intellectual, which fully avenged the much-maligned Mirbeau for all the exploitation of his failing mind and dying body which he had suffered so helplessly:

> Passionné dans la haine comme dans l'amour, son esprit . . . savait juger avec une clairvoyante impartialité les ouvrages dignes de retenir son attention ou son estime. Ce révolté qui souffleta l'hypocrisie et les vices bourgeois, ce cruel railleur . . . savait aimer, compatir, s'apitoyer sur la Douleur universelle.
>
> Car, même dans les plus véhémentes détestations, dans les sarcasmes les plus cuisants, son oeuvre tout entière, avec ses cris, ces pleurs, ses grincements et ses colères, son oeuvre, chaotique, fumeuse, ardente, imprécatoire, n'est qu'un appel vers la Justice, un long cri de détresse vers la Pitié, vers la Douceur et vers l'Amour.⁴⁰

Few, if any, critics have ever rendered such adequate tribute as this to the life and work of the violent, passionate, original and inimitable individualist that was Octave Mirbeau.

Notes

1. Even anarchists like Grave, who had often criticised Jaurès, expressed regret at his death. *Cf. Le Mouvement libertaire*, p. 241.
2. *Op. cit. Cf.* chapter I, p. 70.
3. Gsell, *op. cit.*, p. 218.
4. 'Sur des traits d'Octave Mirbeau', *op. cit.*, p.118.
5. See Woodcock, *op. cit.*, pp. 304–5.
6. See *Le Temps*, 31 October 1905, and *T.N.*, No. 27 (4 November 1905).
7. The *Manifeste des Seize* was published in the pro-war paper *La Bataille* on 14 March 1916.
8. To whom André Salmon refers as 'Léon Werth internationaliste faisant de mauvais coeur une guerre approuvée par le prince Kropotkine en personne'. *Souvenirs sans fin*, vol. 3 (1961), p. 202.
9. See P. Kropotkin, 'A Letter on the present War', *Freedom*, October 1914. Also Suffel, *op. cit.*, p. 333.
10. 'Sur des traits d'Octave Mirbeau', *op. cit.*, p. 118.
11. *Le Petit Parisien*, 28 July 1915.
12. This letter, written from Cheverchemont in Mirbeau's failing hand some time after 1912, is in the Institut Français d'Histoire Sociale.
13. Grave, *Le Mouvement libertaire*, p. 247.
14. Quoted from 'Echos', *Quo Vadis*, September 1954.
15. 'A nos soldats', *Le Petit Parisien*, 28 July 1915.
16. *Le Petit Parisien*, 13 August 1915.
17. George Besson, whose testimony must be given much weight since he was a regular and welcome visitor to Cheverchemont until Mirbeau's death, insisted that 'A nos soldats' and Lefranc's interview had been 'arraché purement à la demi-inconscience dans laquelle [Mirbeau] était déjà'. Besson also told Paul Léautaud that for periods of up to three months Mirbeau was unable even to recognise his visitors, and that conversation with him in 1916 was almost impossible. *Cf*. Léautaud, *op. cit.*, vol. 3, p. 235.
18. In the letter to Grave mentioned in note 12 above Mirbeau reproached the authorities for 'l'éternel emprisonnement d'Hervé'. Reference has already been made to Hervé's 'appearance' in *Dingo* as the schoolmaster persecuted for his radical opinions. A letter to Francis Jourdain shows, however, that Mirbeau did have some reservations about Hervé, for he speaks of 'Hervé, qui par quelques côtés, m'est antipathique . . .'. 'Lettres à Francis Jourdain', *Les Cahiers d'Aujourd'hui*, No. 9 (1922), p. 180.
19. On Hervé's dramatic transformation, see M. M. Drachkovitch, *Les Socialismes français et allemand et le problème de la guerre, 1870–1914* (Genève: Droz, 1953), pp. 87–92.
20. Suffel, *op. cit.*, pp. 342–4, gives a fascinating account of the articles squeezed out of Anatole France during the First World War by those like Hervé who were anxious to add prestige to the patriotic cause. What Suffel says of France might apply equally well to Mirbeau: 'En outre, il ne tenait pas à tous un langage identique . . .'. *Ibid*., p. 334. At least France had lived long enough after the war to be able to refute the apparent militaristic patriotism of his wartime writings (*cf. ibid.*, p. 343). Mirbeau was less fortunate.
21. Preface to *Le Livre de Goha le Simple*.
22. *Op. cit.*, pp. 142–3.
23. 1887 preface to *Le Calvaire*, quoted from *Les Ecrivains*, vol. II, p. 268.
24. *La Victoire*, in which the 'Testament politique' was reprinted on 20 February, stressed Mirbeau's hatred for Germany and his 'foi en la victoire définitive'. *L'Action*

Française (18 February 1917) said of the 'Testament' that if Mirbeau had lived it would have been 'le point de départ d'une nouvelle orientation'. Georges Lecomte, who had earlier repudiated his own left-wing ideals, spoke of the 'Testament' as a 'découverte tardive' of Mirbeau's innate patriotism! 'L'Oeuvre d'Octave Mirbeau', *La Grande Revue*, vol. 93, No. 3 (March 1917), p. 20. The text of the 'Testament politique' is given in Schwarz, *Octave Mirbeau*, pp. 160–1.
25 *Journal littéraire*, vol. 3, p. 234.
26 *Ibid.*, p. 235.
27 A. Fournier, 'Parterres et châteaux de Mirbeau', *Europe*, No. 458 (June 1967), p. 210.
28 'Echos', *op. cit.*
29 'Il y a cinquante ans mourait Octave Mirbeau', *Les Lettres Françaises*, 2 March 1967, p. 6.
30 Everyone else closely associated with Mirbeau, with the exception of Hervé and Mme Mirbeau, regarded the 'Testament politique' as apocryphal. Pierre Michel, of Angers, who is himself working on a thesis on Mirbeau, is also satisfied it is a fake.
31 While reproducing Hervé's graveside speech, *La Victoire* admitted as much (20 February 1917).
32 *Journal littéraire*, vol. 3, p. 238.
33 'A l'enterrement de Mirbeau', *L'Attaque*, 19 February 1917.
34 'Sur la tombe de Mirbeau', *La Victoire*, 20 February 1917.
35 'Octave Mirbeau est mort', *ibid.*, 17 February 1917.
36 'Avec Mirbeau', *Le Mercure de France*, 1 June 1917, p. 425.
37 'Notre Mirbeau, en province', *Les Cahiers d'Aujourd'hui*, No. 9 (1922), p. 148.
38 'Octave Mirbeau et les artistes', *op. cit.*
39 'Avec Mirbeau', *op. cit.*, p. 424: 'Il n'était pas décourageant, déprimant, comme beaucoup de pessimistes, comme ceux qui n'ont au coeur que la haine de ce qui existe, il était plutôt rassurant et fortifiant. Anarchiste, mais point nihiliste. Il entreprenait la satire terrible des imbéciles, mais aussi la louange passionnée des autres.'
40 *Les Livres et les hommes* (Paris: Crès, 1917), p. 273.

Appendix
Mirbeau's principal anarchist texts

'La Grève des électeurs' (1888)
'A propos de la Société des Gens de Lettres' (1891)
'Ravachol' (1892)
Preface to *La Société mourante et l'anarchie* (1893)
'Pour Jean Grave' (1894)

'La Grève des électeurs'

Reprinted from *Le Figaro*, 28 November 1888, with Mirbeau's permission, in *La Révolte*, No. 13 (9 December 1888), this article became the most widely-used anarchist abstentionist pamphlet. See Chapter II, note 36; also J. Grave, *Quarante ans de propagande anarchiste*, pp. 560–1. In a letter to Mirbeau, dated 9 July 1893 (J.R.U.L.M.), Grave wrote: 'J'ai 50.000 *Grève des Electeurs* de commandées. Et je crois que ce n'est pas finis[sic]. Il y a 4 ans, il y en a eu plus de 100.000 de distribuées.'

Une chose m'étonne prodigieusement—j'oserai dire qu'elle me stupéfie—c'est qu'à l'heure scientifique où j'écris, après les innombrables expériences, après les scandales journaliers, il puisse exister encore, dans notre chère France (comme ils disent à la Commission du budget) un électeur, un seul électeur, cet animal irrationnel, inorganique, hallucinant, qui consente à se déranger de ses affaires, de ses rêves ou de ses plaisirs, pour voter en faveur de quelqu'un ou de quelque chose. Quand on réfléchit un seul instant, ce surprenant phénomène n'est-il pas fait pour dérouter les philosophies les plus subtiles et confondre la raison? Où est-il le Balzac qui nous donnera la physiologie de l'électeur moderne? Et le Charcot qui nous expliquera l'anatomie et les mentalités de cet incurable dément? Nous l'attendons.

Je comprends qu'un escroc trouve toujours des actionnaires, la Censure des défenseurs, l'Opéra-Comique des dilletanti, le *Constitutionnel* des abonnés, M. Carnot des peintres qui célèbrent sa triomphale et rigide entrée dans une cité languedocienne; je comprends M. Chantavoine s'obstinant à chercher des rimes; je comprends tout. Mais qu'un député, ou un sénateur, ou un président de République, ou n'importe lequel, parmi tous les étranges farceurs qui réclament une fonction élective, quelle qu'elle soit, trouve un électeur, c'est-à-dire l'être irrêvé, le martyr improbable, qui vous nourrit de son pain, vous vêt de sa laine, vous engraisse de sa chair, vous enrichit de son argent, avec la seule perspective de recevoir, en échange de ces prodigalités, des coups de trique sur la nuque, des coups de pied au derrière, quand ce n'est pas des coups de fusil dans la poitrine; en vérité, cela dépasse les notions déjà pas mal pessimistes que je m'était faites jusqu'ici de la sottise humaine, en général, et de la sottise française en particulier, notre chère et immortelle sottise, ô chauvin!

Il est bien entendu que je parle ici de l'électeur averti, convaincu, de l'électeur théoricien, de celui qui s'imagine, le pauvre diable, faire acte de citoyen libre, étaler sa souveraineté, exprimer ses opinions, imposer—ô folie admirable et déconcertante—des programmes politiques et des revendications sociales; et non point de l'électeur « qui la connait » et qui s'en moque, de celui qui ne voit dans « les résultats de sa toute puissance » qu'une rigolade à la charcuterie monarchiste, ou une ribote au vin républicain. Sa souveraineté à celui-là, c'est de se pocharder aux frais du suffrage universel. Il est dans le vrai, car cela seul lui importe, et il n'a cure du reste. Il sait ce qu'il fait. Mais les autres?

Ah! oui, les autres! Les sérieux, les austères, les *peuple souverain*, ceux-là qui sentent une ivresse les gagner lorsqu'ils se regardent et se disent: « Je suis électeur! Rien ne se fait que par moi. Je suis la base de la société moderne. Par ma volonté, Floquet fait des lois auxquelles sont astreints trente-six millions d'hommes, et Baudry d'Asson aussi, et Pierre Alype également. » Comment y en a-t-il encore de cet acabit? Comment, si entêtés, si orgueilleux, si paradoxaux qu'ils soient, n'ont-ils pas été, depuis longtemps, découragés et honteux de leur oeuvre? Comment peut-il arriver qu'il se rencontre quelque part, même dans le fond des landes perdues de la Bretagne, même dans les inaccessibles cavernes des Cévennes et des Pyrénées un bonhomme assez stupide, assez déraisonnable, assez aveugle à ce qui se voit, assez sourd à ce qui se dit, pour voter bleu, blanc ou rouge, sans que rien l'y oblige, sans qu'on le paye ou sans qu'on le soûle?

A quel sentiment baroque, à quelle mystérieuse suggestion peut bien obéïr ce bipède pensant, doué d'une volonté, à ce qu'on prétend, et qui s'en va, fier de son droit, assuré qu'il accomplit un devoir, déposer dans une boîte électorale quelconque un quelconque bulletin, peu importe le nom qu'il ait écrit dessus? . . . Qu'est-ce qu'il doit bien se dire, en dedans de soi, qui justifie ou seulement qui explique cet acte extravagant? Qu'est-ce qu'il espère? Car enfin, pour consentir à se donner des maîtres avides qui le grugent et qui l'assomment, il faut qu'il se dise et qu'il espère quelque chose d'extraordinaire que nous ne soupçonnons pas. Il faut que, par de puissantes déviations cérébrales, les idées de député correspondent en lui à des idées de science, de justice, de dévoûment, de travail et de probité; il faut que dans les noms seuls de Barbe et de Baïhaut, non moins que dans ceux de Rouvier et de Wilson, il découvre une magie spéciale et qu'il voie, au travers d'un mirage, fleurir et s'épanouir dans Vergoin et dans Hubbard des promesses de bonheur futur et de soulagement immédiat. Et c'est cela qui est véritablement effrayant. Rien ne lui sert de leçon, ni les comédies les plus burlesques, ni les plus sinistres tragédies.

Voilà pourtant de longs siècles que le monde dure, que les sociétés se déroulent et se succèdent, pareilles les unes aux autres, qu'un fait unique domine toutes les histoires: la protection aux grands, l'écrasement aux petits. Il ne peut arriver à comprendre qu'il n'a qu'une raison d'être historique, c'est de payer pour un tas de choses dont il ne jouira jamais, et de mourir pour des combinaisons politiques qui ne le regardent point.

Que lui importe que ce soit Pierre ou Jean qui lui demande son argent et qui lui prenne la vie, puisqu'il est obligé de se dépouiller de l'un, et de donner l'autre? Eh bien! non. Entre ses voleurs et ses bourreaux, il a des préférences, et il vote pour les plus rapaces et les plus féroces. Il a voté hier, il votera demain, il votera toujours. Les moutons vont à l'abattoir. Ils ne se disent rien, eux, et ils n'espèrent rien. Mais du moins ils ne votent pas pour le boucher qui les tuera, et pour le bourgeois qui les mangera. Plus bête que les bêtes, plus moutonnier que les moutons, l'électeur nomme son boucher et choisit son bourgeois. Il a fait des Révolutions pour conquérir ce droit.

O bon électeur, inexprimable imbécile, pauvre hère, si, au lieu de te laisser prendre aux rengaînes absurdes que te débitent, chaque matin, pour un sou, les journaux grands ou petits, bleus ou noirs, blancs ou rouges, et qui sont payés pour avoir ta peau; si, au lieu de croire aux chimériques flatteries dont on caresse ta vanité, dont on entoure ta lamentable souveraineté en guenilles, si, au lieu de t'arrêter, éternel badaud, devant les lourdes duperies des programmes; si tu lisais parfois, au coin de ton feu, Schopenhauer et Max Nordau, deux philosophes qui en savent long sur tes maîtres et sur toi, peut-être apprendrais-tu des choses étonnantes et utiles. Peut-être aussi, après les avoir lus, serais-tu moins empressé à revêtir ton air grave et ta belle redingote, à courir ensuite vers les urnes homicides où, quelque nom que tu mettes, tu mets d'avance le nom de ton plus mortel ennemi. Ils te diraient, en connaisseurs d'humanité, que la politique est un abominable mensonge, que tout y est à l'envers du bon sens, de la justice et du droit, et que tu n'as rien à y voir, toi dont le compte est réglé au grand livre des destinées humaines.

Rêve après cela, si tu veux, des paradis de lumières et de parfums, des fraternités impossibles, des bonheurs irréels. C'est bon de rêver, et cela calme la souffrance. Mais ne mêle jamais l'homme à ton rêve, car là où est l'homme, là est la douleur, la haine et le meurtre. Surtout, souviens-toi que l'homme qui sollicite tes suffrages est, de ce fait, un malhonnête homme, parce qu'en échange de la situation et de la fortune où tu le pousses, il te promet un tas de choses merveilleuses qu'il ne te donnera pas et qu'il n'est pas, d'ailleurs, en son pouvoir de te donner. L'homme que tu élèves ne représente ni ta misère, ni tes aspirations, ni rien de toi; il ne représente que ses propres passions et ses propres intérêts, lesquels sont contraires aux tiens. Pour te réconforter et ranimer des espérances qui seraient vite déçues, ne vas pas t'imaginer que le spectacle navrant auquel tu assistes aujourd'hui est particulier à une époque ou à un régime, et que cela passera. Toutes les époques se valent, et aussi tous les régimes, c'est-à-dire qu'ils ne valent rien. Donc, rentre chez toi, bonhomme, et fais la grève du suffrage universel. Tu n'as rien à y perdre, je t'en réponds; et cela pourra t'amuser quelque temps. Sur le seuil de ta porte, fermée aux quémandeurs d'aumônes politiques, tu regarderas défiler la bagarre, en fumant silencieusement ta pipe.

Et s'il existe, en un endroit ignoré, un honnête homme capable de te gouverner et de t'aimer, ne le regrette pas. Il serait trop jaloux de sa dignité pour se mêler à lutte fangeuse des partis, trop fier pour tenir de toi un mandat que tu n'accordes jamais qu'à l'audace cynique, à l'insulte et au mensonge.

Je te l'ai dit, bonhomme, rentre chez toi et fais la grève.

'A propos de la Société des Gens de Lettres' (abridged)

Mirbeau's defence of Jean Grave and the anarchist journal *La Révolte* was first published in *L'Echo de Paris*, 4 August 1891, and was reprinted in the literary supplement of *La Révolte*, No. 49 (22 August 1891). See the text of Chapter III.

Il existe un journal, la *Révolte*, qui est très bien fait, mais très pauvre. Ce journal, qui compte parmi ses collaborateurs les plus assidus des hommes de haute valeur, comme Elisée Reclus, Kropotkine et Malato, ne vit que par la propagande que lui font ses amis, et l'aide matérielle qu'ils lui apportent chaque semaine. Chacun fait ce qu'il peut; l'un donne de l'argent, l'autre son talent, et l'on se débrouille. Il y a, comme bien l'on pense, de rudes moments à passer, mais on les passe, à force de dévouement et de volonté.

La *Révolte* est l'organe le plus indépendant, le plus pur des doctrines anarchistes, un organe d'action, oui; mais aussi un organe d'idées qui ne se perd pas dans le vague des sentimentalités, ni dans l'inconsciente brutalité des provocations inutiles et des coups de main hasardeux. Il sait où il va, il va droit son chemin. Il est très au fait de la philosophie, de la science moderne, et s'inspire de leurs découvertes, de leurs applications « morales » pour préparer la venue d'une société nouvelle, normale, basée non plus sur le mensonge et l'arbitraire, mais sur la raison et la justice. Peut-être, comme le voulait Spinosa, ne tient-il pas assez compte des passions humaines et cruelles à notre nature, et réfractaires à toute évolution! Mais si c'est un rêve, il faut convenir qu'il est beau de rêver ce rêve. Cela vaut mieux que de rêver des impôts inédits, des affamements de pauvres, des lois de plus en plus oppressives. La *Révolte* a ceci de particulier que, s'adressant aux foules, par des qualités de claire éducation et une vulgarisation précise des connaissances supérieures, elle plaît aussi au philosophe, qui y trouve des agréments intellectuels. Enfin, ce journal, que préoccupent exclusivement les importants problèmes de la vie sociale, est évidemment honnête, et très désintéressé. Cela seul suffirait à lui assigner une place à part dans la presse contemporaine.

Par malheur, c'est un dangereux métier que de vouloir battre en brèche les *idées reçues*, attaquer les conventions, les pires routines, les plus lourds préjugés. Les conventions sociales sont sacrées, les préjugés et les routines inviolables, et ils ont, pour les défendre, non seulement toutes les forces gouvernementales, mais toute la lâcheté humaine qu'effare la moindre idée de progrès, que rend féroce la moindre possibilité de changement. Rêver autre chose que ce qui est, travailler à la préparation d'un avenir meilleur, apprendre aux hommes qu'ils ont le droit de n'être pas toujours des machines aveugles et surmenées aux mains des puissants; qu'ils ont le droit de chercher le bonheur, et si on le leur refuse, de le prendre; substituer au principe homicide de la lutte pour la vie, le principe supérieur de la solidarité universelle, cela, de tout temps, a passé pour un abominable crime, et mérite les plus exemplaires châtiments. La *Révolte* vient d'en faire l'expérience; M. Grave, l'un de ses plus actifs, de ses plus intelligents collaborateurs, récemment condamné à six mois de prison, pour avoir exprimé quelques-unes de ces idées, peut, à loisir, aujourd'hui, dans une cellule de Sainte-Pélagie, méditer sur les beautés d'une société qui lui fait un crime de penser autrement que M. Emmanuel Arène, par exemple, lequel résume en lui, si harmonieusement, ce que la pensée humaine a de possible, de permis et de conforme aux lois.

Il pourra ainsi, M. Grave, méditer sur les beautés d'une autre Société, la Société des Gens de Lettres, une société vraiment étrange et superlativement abusive, dont ce n'est pas une des moindres surprises, parmi toutes celles auxquelles elle nous habitue, de voir M. Emile Zola présider sérieusement et sans dégoût à ses petites combinaisons commerciales, et, suprême patron, débiter, en gros et en détail, la littérature des gens de lettres, comme des articles d'épicerie: « Qui en veut? . . . Faites votre choix! . . . Tenez! voilà du Delpit. Ça n'est pas cher, c'est facile à employer, et ça fait de très bon bouillon! » . . .

La *Révolte* publie chaque semaine, un supplément littéraire. De toutes les publications de ce genre, ce supplément est ce que je connais de plus intéressant et de plus instructif . . .

Il va de soi que la *Révolte* est de ces personnes et de ces Idées qui sont, à l'avance, vouées à toutes les rigueurs de la Justice. Mais ni M. Montagne, ni la Justice n'en seront plus riches pour cela, car, comme le disait gaiement M. Grave: « Là où il n'y a rien, le diable perd ses droits ».

'Ravachol'

Mirbeau's article, giving one of the most balanced anarchist views of Ravachol's terrorist activity, was published first in *L'Endehors*, No. 52 (1 May 1892), and was reprinted shortly afterwards in *La Révolte*, No. 32 (7 May 1892). See the text of Chapter IV.

Sa tête échappe au couperet!
Les jurés qui ont osé cela, qui ont osé boucher leurs oreilles aux clameurs de la mort aboyante, ont-ils eu peur? Ont-ils eu peur de tuer un homme dont la mystérieuse vengeance ne meurt pas, toute, avec lui? ou bien, par delà l'acte, dont on leur criait l'épouvantable horreur, n'ont-ils écouté que la voix de l'Idée future, de l'idée dominatrice qui le spécialise, cet acte, qui le grandit? Je ne sais pas. On ne sait jamais ce qui peut se passer dans la conscience d'un juré, ni à quelles injonctions suprêmes il obéit, en distribuant la mort ou la vie.

Les jurés ont moins tremblé que la Presse qui les raille, les insulte et les

Appendix 171

maudit. La Presse voulait du sang. Comme les bourgeois bourrus dont elle résume les instincts aveugles, dont elle défend les privilèges menacés, elle a eu peur. Et la peur est féroce. Pour se donner l'illusion d'un atroce courage, la peur aime à maquiller de rouge sa lividité. Elle croit aussi que le bruit du couteau légal, que le rebondissement, sur la planche infâme, d'une chair, suppliciée, l'empêcheront d'entendre le claquement de ses dents, les galops effarés de son pouls, et ces voix qui, de jour en jour plus audacieuses, plus colères, montent du fond de l'enfer social. Elle se trompe. Il y a des morts qui reviennent; il y a des voix qu'on n'étouffe pas. Et le néant est rempli d'énigmes terribles.

J'ai horreur du sang versé, des ruines, de la mort. J'aime la vie, et toute vie m'est sacrée. C'est pourquoi je vais demander à l'idéal anarchiste ce que nulle forme de gouvernement n'a pu donner: l'amour, la beauté, la paix entre les hommes. Ravachol ne m'effraie pas. Il est transitoire comme la terreur qu'il inspire. C'est le coup de tonnerre auquel succède la joie du soleil et du ciel apaisés. Après la sombre besogne, sourit le rêve d'universelle harmonie, rêvé par l'admirable Kropotkine.

D'ailleurs, la société aurait tort de se plaindre. Elle seule a engendré Ravachol. Elle a semé la misère: elle récolte la révolte. C'est juste.

Et puis, il faudrait compter . . .

Qui donc, durant cette lente, éternelle marche au supplice qu'a été l'histoire de l'humanité, qui donc versa le sang, toujours le même, sans relâche, sans une halte dans la pitié? Les gouvernements, les religions, les industries, ces bagnes du travail, en sont tout rouges. Le meurtre dégoutte de leurs lois, de leurs prières, de leurs progrès. Hier encore, c'étaient les frénétiques boucheries qui, la commune agonisante, transformèrent Paris en charnier; c'étaient ces inutiles massacres où des femmes innocentes, de tous[sic] petits enfants, étrennèrent, à Fourmies, la virtuosité balistique des Lebels. Et ce sont, tous les jours, des mines qui sautent, qui ensevelissent en une minute d'horrible destruction, cinquante, cent, cinq cents pauvres diables dont les corps carbonisés ne remonteront jamais au soleil. Et ce sont encore ces atroces conquêtes aux pays lointains où des races heureuses, des races inconnues et pacifiques râlent sous la botte du négrier occidental, du détrousseur de continents, du violateur impur des terres vierges et des forêts familiales.

Chaque pas que l'on fait dans cette société hérisée de privilèges, est marqué d'une tache de sang; à chaque engrenage du mécanisme gouvernemental, la chair du pauvre, broyée, tournoie et pantèle; et les larmes coulent de partout, dans la nuit de douleur où nul ne pénètre. En face de ces tueries continuelles et de ces continuelles tortures, qu'est donc ce mur qui se lézarde, cet escalier qui s'effondre?

L'heure que nous vivons est hideuse. Jamais le misère ne fut plus grande, parce qu'elle ne fut jamais plus consciente, parce que jamais elle ne côtoya de plus près le spectacle des richesses gaspillées, la terre promise du bien-être d'où on la refoule sans cesse. Jamais la loi qui ne protège que les banques ne pesa plus durement aux épaules meurtries du pauvre. Le capitalisme est insatiable, et le salariat aggrave l'antique esclavage. Les magasins sont bondés de vêtements, et il y en a qui vont tout nus; ils regorgent de nourriture et il y en a qui meurent de faim aux seuils des riches in différents. Aucun cri n'est entendu; quand une plainte plus haute perce la clameur douloureuse, les Lebels s'arment et les troupes s'ébranlent.

Et ce n'est pas tout.

Un peuple ne vit pas seulement de son ventre, il vit aussi de son cerveau. Les joies intellectuelles lui sont aussi nécessaires que les joies physiques. Il a droit à la beauté comme il a droit au pain. Eh bien, ceux qui pourraient lui donner ces joies impérieuses, ceux qui pourraient l'initier à cette beauté vitale, sont traités en ennemis publics, pourchassés comme des criminels, traqués comme des anarchistes, battus comme des pauvres. Ils en sont réduits à vivre en solitaire. Une immense barrière les sépare de la foule à qui sont exclusivement réservés les répugnants spectacles, sur qui s'étend l'énorme, le sordide, l'intraversable voile de la bêtise triomphante. Nous assistons à un fait social inouï: c'est que, à cette époque, si riche en grands savants, jamais le goût public n'est descendu aussi bas, jamais l'ignorance ne se complut à de plus abjectes jouissances.

Eh bien, si l'heure que nous vivons est hideuse, elle est formidable aussi; c'est l'heure du réveil populaire. Et cette heure est pleine d'inconnu. La mansuétude des opprimés, des délaissés a duré assez longtemps. Ils veulent vivre: ils veulent jouir; ils veulent avoir leur part de bonheur, au soleil. Les gouvernants auront beau faire, se livrer aux pires réactions de la peur, ils n'empêcheront rien de ce qui doit arriver. Nous touchons au moment décisif de l'histoire humaine. Le vieux monde croule sous le poids de ses propres crimes. C'est lui-même qui allumera la bombe qui doit l'emporter. Et cette bômbe sera d'autant plus terrible qu'elle ne contiendra ni poudre ni dynamite. Elle contiendra de l'Idée et de la Pitié: ces deux forces contre lesquelles on ne peut rien.

Preface to *La Société mourante et l'anarchie*

This preface, written in 1893, during the intense period of anarchist terrorism (a time when it was unwise to confess anarchist sympathies too loudly), reaffirmed Mirbeau's solidarity with the theories of Kropotkin and the milieu of *La Révolte*, and represented the clearest statement Mirbeau ever made about the nature of his own anarchist views. See the text of Chapter III.

J'ai un ami qui met une bonne volonté, vraiment touchante, à comprendre les choses. Tout naturellement, il aspire à ce qui est simple, grand et beau. Mais son éducation, encrassée de préjugés et de mensonges, inhérents à toute éducation, dite supérieure, l'arrête, presque toujours, dans ses élans vers la délivrance spirituelle. Il voudrait s'affranchir complètement des idées traditionnelles, des séculaires routines où son esprit s'englue, malgré lui, et ne le peut. Souvent, il vient me voir et nous causons longuement. Les doctrines anarchiques, si calomniées des uns, si mal connues des autres, le préoccupent; et son honnêteté est grande, sinon à les accepter toutes, du moins à les concevoir. Il ne croit pas, ainsi que le croient beaucoup de gens de son milieu, qu'elles consistent uniquement à faire sauter des maisons. Il y entrevoit, au contraire, dans un brouillard qui se dissipera, peut-être, des formes harmoniques et des beautés; et il s'y intéresse comme à une chose qu'on aimerait, une chose un peu terrible encore, et qu'on redonbte parce qu'on ne la comprend pas bien.

Mon ami a lu les admirables livres de Kropotkine, les éloquentes, ferventes et savantes protestations d'Elisée Reclus, contre l'impiété des gouvernements et des sociétés basées sur le crime. De Bakounine, il connaît ce que les journaux anarchistes, çà et là, en ont publié. Il a travaillé l'inégal Proudhon et l'aristocratique Spencer. Enfin, récemment, les déclarations d'Etiévant l'ont ému. Tout cela l'emporte, un moment, vers les hauteurs où l'intelligence se purifie. Mais de ces brèves excursions à travers l'idéal, il revient plus troublé que jamais. Mille obstacles, purement subjectifs, l'arrêtent; il se perd en une infinité de si, de cas, de mais, inextricable forêt, dont il me demande, parfois, de le tirer.

Comme hier encore, il me confiait le tourment de son âme, je lui dis:

—Grave, dont vous connaissez le judicieux et mâle esprit, va publier un livre: *La Société mourante et l'anarchie.* Ce livre est un chef-d'oeuvre de logique. Il est plein de lumière. Ce livre n'est point le cri du sectaire aveugle et borné; ce n'est point, non plus, le coup de tam-tam du propagandiste ambitieux; c'est l'oeuvre pesée, pensée, raisonnée, d'un passionné, il est vrai, d'un « qui a la foi », mais qui sait, compare, discute, analyse, et qui, avec une singulière clairvoyance de critique, évolue parmi les faits de l'histoire sociale, les leçons de la science, les problèmes de la philosophie, pour aboutir aux conclusions infrangibles que vous savez et dont vous ne pouvez nier ni la grandeur, ni la justice.

Mon ami m'interrompit vivement:

—Je ne nie rien . . . Je comprends, en effet, que Grave, dont j'ai suivi, à la *Révolte,* les ardentes campagnes, rêve la suppression de l'Etat, par exemple. Moi qui n'ai pas toutes ses hardiesses, je la rêve aussi. L'Etat pèse sur l'individu d'un poids chaque jour plus écrasant, plus intolérable. De l'homme qu'il énerve et qu'il abrutit, il ne fait qu'un paquet de chair à impôts. Sa seule mission est de vivre de lui, comme un pou vit de la bête sur laquelle il a posé ses suçoirs. L'Etat prend à l'homme son argent, misérablement gagné dans ce bagne: le travail; il lui filoute sa liberté à toute minute entravée par les lois; dès sa naissance, il tue ses facultés individuelles, administrativement, ou il les fausse, ce qui revient au même. Assassin et voleur, oui, j'ai cette conviction que l'Etat est bien ce double criminel. Dès que l'homme marche, l'Etat lui casse les jambes; dès qu'il tend les bras, l'Etat les lui rompt; dès qu'il ose penser, l'Etat lui prend le crâne, et il lui dit: « Marche, prends et pense. »

—Eh bien? fis-je.

Mon ami continua:

—L'anarchie, au contraire, est la reconquête de l'individu, c'est la liberté du développement de l'individu, dans un sens normal et harmonique. On peut la définir d'un mot: l'utilisation spontanée de toutes les énergies humaines, criminellement gaspillées par l'Etat! Je sais cela . . . et je comprends pourquoi toute une jeunesse artiste et pensante,—l'élite contem-

poraine—regarde impatiemment se lever cette aube attendue, où elle entrevoit, non seulement, un idéal de justice, mais un idéal de beauté.
—Eh bien? fis-je de nouveau.
—Eh bien, une chose m'inquiète et me trouble; le côté terroriste de l'anarchie. Je répugne aux moyens violents; j'ai horreur du sang et de la mort, et je voudrais que l'anarchie attendît son triomphe de la justice seule de l'avenir.
—Croyez-vous donc, répliquai-je, que les anarchistes soient des buveurs de sang? Ne sentez-vous pas, au contraire, toute l'immense tendresse, tout l'immense amour de la vie, par qui le coeur d'un Kropotkine est gonflé? Hélas! ce sont là des tristesses inséparables de toutes les luttes humaines, et contre lesquelles on ne peut rien . . . Et puis! . . . voulez-vous que je vous fasse une comparaison classique? . . . La terre est desséchée; toutes les petites plantes, toutes les petites fleurs sont brûlées par un ardent, par un persistant soleil de mort; elles s'étiolent, se penchent, elles vont mourir . . . Mais voici qu'un nuage noircit l'horizon, il s'avance et couvre le ciel embrasé. La foudre éclate, et l'eau ruisselle sur la terre ébranlée. Qu'importe que la foudre ait brisé, çà et là, un chêne trop grand, si les petites plantes qui allaient mourir, les petites plantes abreuvées et rafraîchies, redressent leur tige, et remontent leurs fleurs dans l'air redevenu calme? . . . Il ne faut pas trop, voyez-vous, s'émouvoir de la mort des chênes voraces . . . Lisez le livre de Grave . . . Grave a dit, à ce propos, des choses excellentes. Et si, après avoir lu ce livre, où tant d'idées sont remuées et éclaircies, si après l'avoir pensé, comme il convient à une oeuvre de cette envergure intellectuelle, vous ne pouvez parvenir à vous faire une opinion stable et tranquille, mieux vaudra, je vous en avertis, renoncer à devenir l'anarchiste que vous pouvez être, et rester le bon bourgeois, l'impénitent et indécrottable bourgeois, le bourgeois « malgré lui », que vous êtes, peut-être . . .

'Pour Jean Grave'

This article—Mirbeau's first regular contribution to *Le Journal*—was published on 19 February 1894, in the week preceding the trial of Jean Grave, charged with incitement to murder and arson in his book *La Société mourante et l'anarchie*. See the text of Chapter IV.

Un ennemi mortel de l'anarchie n'eût pas mieux agi que cet Emile Henry, lorsqu'il lança son inexplicable bombe, au milieu de tranquilles et anonymes personnes, venues dans un café, pour y boire un bock, avant de s'aller coucher. L'ineptie de cet acte est telle que beaucoup de gens, à imagination romanesque, soupçonnèrent, en lui, au premier moment, une ingérence policière. La police est hardie et elle a de l'invention dans la canaillerie. On lui doit, paraît-il, l'*Indicateur anarchiste*, ou la *Bombe chez soi*, étrange traité de l'explosif, que publia, jadis, un louche journal de Londres. Mais ce n'est pas une raison. Si l'on s'en tenait au fameux précepte criminaliste qui veut que, dans un crime commis, l'on recherche d'abord celui à qui le crime profite, ce soupçon apparaîtrait vraisemblable et motivé. Car le gouvernement triomphe, par cette bombe qui, avec un merveilleux opportunisme, semble justifier, dans l'esprit de ceux qui ne réfléchissent pas, les sanglantes répressions d'hier, les mesures violentes de demain. Une telle explication est bien hasardeuse, encore qu'elle ne manque pas de « séduisances ». Pour une combinaison de ce genre, il faudrait des complicités qui ne sont pas sans danger et qu'on ne trouve point tous les jours. Les choses, même les plus compliquées, arrivent, en général, plus simplement, et la Vie a de ces surprenantes concordances. C'est une grande politique, j'allais dire une grande policière. Elle déjoue les calculs humains ou les sert, on ne sait pas pourquoi, on ne sait pas comment, car son action naît des profondeurs de l'inconnu. J'aime mieux croire que cet Emile Henry ne prit, en cette occasion, conseil que de lui-même, sans obéir à d'autres suggestions que celles de sa propre folie.

Emile Henry dit, affirme, clame qu'il est anarchiste. C'est possible. Mais l'anarchie a bon dos. Comme le papier, elle souffre tout. C'est une mode, aujourd'hui, chez les criminels, de se réclamer d'elle, quand ils ont perpétré un beau coup. Ils espèrent, sans doute, donner à leur crime une expression d'épouvante plus générale, et de désintéressement qui les spécialise ou les grandit. Ce qui m'étonne, c'est que le grand Bandit de Montmartre n'ait point songé à exploiter cet actuel moyen de défense. Peut-être a-t-il d'autres idées. Ce séducteur a des habitudes royales, des façons de gentilhomme qui sentent l'ancien régime . . . On vole, on viole, on tue: « Je suis anarchiste! » C'est bientôt dit. Et la presse est là, ô Brunetière, pour enregistrer ces aveux, les mettre en scène, les dramatiser. Et le bon bourgeois s'horrifie, à ces confessions hurlées par l'un, commentées par l'autre; et le juge conclut gravement: « Vous voyez bien que l'anarchie n'est pas autre chose que le meurtre pour le meurtre, et qu'il est temps enfin de traiter les anarchistes comme des chiens enragés. » Et, par anarchistes, le brave juge entend, cette fois, ceux-là qui pensent que tout n'est pas au mieux dans l'organisation sociale, et qui le disent.

N'a-t-on pas été jusqu'à confondre avec Kropotkine et Elisée Reclus le joyeux fantaisiste qui, pour se venger de la société, voulait tuer le premier homme décoré qui passerait à portée de son surin et s'étant vainement embusqué, tout un jour, dans une rue où il ne passe personne de ce genre, tua, de dépit, un marchand de vins, dont il était l'ami? Vraiment, je voudrais que, pour l'honneur de notre intelligence, on n'eût, dans la critique de ces faits anormaux, je ne dis pas un peu plus de justice,—ce serait trop demander à des gens passionnés,—mais un peu plus de psychologie. Chaque parti a ses criminels et ses fous, puisque chaque parti a ses hommes. Le plus grand danger de la bombe est dans l'explosion de bêtise qu'elle provoque; et la bêtise humaine fait des blessures qui ne guérissent jamais.

Cet événement de l'Hôtel Terminus peut avoir une fâcheuse influence sur l'avenir de beaucoup de gens, que la justice détient, en ce moment, dans ses geôles, et parmi lesquels Jean Grave est la personnalité la plus marquante. Il est à craindre que le jury, lorsque Grave comparaîtra devant lui, ne se souvienne, contre toute justice et toute raison, de cette explosion, et ne veuille lui en faire payer la casse. Le jury a les sursauts de la foule et les nerfs de la femme; il obéit à des sensibilités souvent déconcertantes; il condamne ou absout selon des impressions, la plupart du temps étrangères au cas qu'il est appelé à juger.

Je voudrais lui dire, en quelques mots, quel est l'homme contre qui le ministère public va bientôt lui demander de se montrer inexorable.

Je n'en connais pas de meilleur et de plus digne. Je ne connais pas d'âme plus droite, plus fière et aussi plus douce que la sienne. Et il est la preuve vivante, et, pour ainsi dire, le résultat humain, des doctrines d'amour qu'il precha, et pour lesquelles on le traîne, comme un criminel, devant la cour d'assises, après plus d'un mois de détention préventive.

Grave est né parmi les humbles. Il est d'une famille d'ouvriers. Tout jeune, il apprit le métier de cordonnier, métier ridicule et sur lequel s'exerce, d'ordinaire, on ne sait pourquoi, la verve des gens d'esprit; métier de philosophe aussi, car, étant sédentaire, il est propice à la réflexion. Pendant qu'il était courbé sur son ouvrage, Grave réfléchissait. Il vivait au milieu de la pauvreté; il n'avait jamais sous les yeux que le spectacle des misères et des déchéances humaines. Son coeur s'émut, son cerveau voulut comprendre. Il ne suffit pas de sentir, il faut savoir. Et si Grave sentait profondément, il ignorait tout. Il eut le désir passionné de s'instruire. Tout seul, sans guide, conduit dans le labyrinthe de la science et de l'histoire, par la force de sa volonté, il se fit une éducation complète, et qu'envieraient bien des savants reconnus. Contrairement à ce qui arrive, en pareil cas, Grave, peu à peu, classa, avec méthode, dans son cerveau, toutes ces connaissances acquises, aux moments de loisir, et durant les nuits passées au travail, dans quelle fièvre! C'est qu'il avait le don inné de la critique et de la philosophie. Il a montré ce que peut l'individu soutenu par une idée. En lui, rien de fumeux. Ce n'est pas un demi-savant, un demi-lettré dont la culture trop hâtive, imparfaite et disparate, mêle toutes les sciences dans un chaotique désordre. C'est un des plus clairs cerveaux, et, en même temps, des mieux meublés que je sache. Grave a donné la mesure de sa valeur, la preuve de l'étendue, de la variété de ses connaissances, en faisant, plus tard, le supplément littéraire de la *Révolte*, qui est, certainement, le meilleur recueil de littérature et de philosophie, en ce temps.

On le poursuit, aujourd'hui. Il paraît que la justice voudrait le comprendre dans une association de malfaiteurs, et même, faire de lui, en quelque sorte, le centre de cette association. Je crois qu'elle aura du mal à établir cette conbinaison, mais elle est persévérante, et elle a des lois pour toutes ces fantaisies.

On le poursuit aussi pour délit de presse. Il paraît que la *Société mourante et l'Anarchie*, qui pouvait, il y a un an, au moment où elle parut, s'étaler librement aux devantures des librairies, est devenue, tout à coup, un danger public. On y a, subitement, découvert des provocations au meurtre, au pillage, à la désobéissance des militaires. Or, la *Société mourante* est une oeuvre de critique sociale, un livre de pure philosophie, et non pas un pamphlet. Grave examine, avec sa clairvoyance et sa logique coutumières, tous les vices de notre organisation politique. Il n'y met point de haine, mais du raisonnement, et, comme il est honnête homme, il pousse son raisonnement droit, jusqu'à la dernière limite, sans le faire passer par les dédales tortueux du mensonge et les artifices d'une complaisante métaphysique. Ce qui éclate dans ce livre, c'est l'amour de la vie, c'est-à-dire la justice et la pitié. Même si, de-ci, de-là, il contient des parties de pur rêve, ce rêve est beau, puisqu'il poursuit le bonheur.

Le jury osera-t-il condamner ce travailleur intrépide, ce coeur fidèle, cet

Appendix

esprit puissant et doux? Je ne sais pas. Tout est à craindre, car nous sommes dans un moment de peur où tout est confondu dans une même haine, et la bombe du criminel isolé, et l'idée qui marche, impassible et lente, à travers les siècles.

En attendant, Grave est à Mazas, où il subit une dure et pénible détention: il ne se fait point d'illusions, et il est résigné à tout. Le souci de sa défense n'absorbe point, tout entières, les longues heures de la prison, et il ne se plaint point. La passion du travail, passion qui a dominé sa vie, n'en est pas diminuée. Elle lui fait le coeur fort, et le cerveau libre. Rien ne l'empêchera de continuer son oeuvre. De cette tombe qui est une prison, il reviendra, grandi, parmi les vivants, et mieux armé encore pour la lutte intellectuelle.

Select bibliography

The most complete bibliography of works by and about Mirbeau is in H. Talvart and J. Place, *Bibliographie des auteurs modernes de langue française*, vol. 15 (Paris: La Chronique des Lettres Françaises, 1963), pp. 246–65. J. Maitron, *Le Mouvement anarchiste en France*, vol. 2 (Paris: Maspero, enlarged edition 1975), pp. 207–416, contains the definitive bibliography of French anarchism. Details of items supplementary to both these important publications are given in the author's M.A. thesis. The present bibliography lists only those items which have been found most useful in the preparation of this book. Place of publication is Paris except where otherwise stated.

1. Unpublished material

Archives Nationales, Cartons F7 12506/7 (*c*. 1,500 items on anarchism and anarchist sympathisers).
Carr, R. P., 'Octave Mirbeau and anarchism' (M.A. thesis, University of Manchester, 1971).
Court summons to Mirbeau (Grave trial, 1894) (J.R.U.L.M.).
Five letters, from Jean Grave to Mirbeau (J.R.U.L.M.).
Gribelin, T., 'Octave Mirbeau. Son amitié littéraire et politique avec Emile Zola' (*Diplôme d'éducation supérieure* dissertation, Besançon, June 1965).
Letter from Jean Grave to Camille Pissarro (B.P.U.G.).
Letter from Mirbeau to J.-H. Rosny *aîné* (Collection of M Robert Borel-Rosny).
Letter from Emile de Saint-Auban to Mirbeau (J.R.U.L.M.).
Mirbeau dossier (letters, cards and telegrams from Mirbeau to Gustave Geffroy; letters from Mme Mirbeau to Geffroy) (F.G.B.A.).
Mirbeau dossiers BA/1190 (113 items) and EA/52 (67 items) (B.A.M.P.P.).
Mirbeau and Fénéon dossiers (Bibliothèque de la ville de Fontainebleau: library of the late André Billy).
Patsouras, L., 'Jean Grave, French intellectual and anarchist, 1854–1939' (Ph.D. thesis, Ohio State University, 1966).
Seven letters from Jean Grave to Mirbeau (B.P.U.G.).
Twelve letters from Mirbeau to Grave (I.F.H.S.).
Walker, J. A. 'L'Ironie de la douleur—la vie et la vision d'Octave Mirbeau' (Ph.D. thesis, University of Toronto, 1954).

2. Books by Mirbeau: editions used in this study

Lettres de ma chaumière. Laurent, 1886 (*Achevé d'imprimer* 1885).
Le Calvaire (first edition 1886). Ollendorff, 1900.
L'Abbé Jules (1888). Fayard, 1904.
Sébastien Roch (1890). Fayard, 1913.
Contes de la chaumière (1894). Flammarion, 1924.
Les Mauvais Bergers (1898). In *Théâtre*, II (Flammarion, 1921).
L'Epidémie (1898). In *Farces et moralités* (Fasquelle, 1904).
Le Jardin des supplices (1899). Fasquelle, 1913.
Le Journal d'une femme de chambre (1900). Le Livre de Poche, 1964.
Vieux Ménage (1901). Les Belles Lectures, 1950.
Les Vingt et un jours d'un neurasthénique (1901). Les Belles Lectures, 1954.
Le Portefeuille. Fasquelle, 1902.
La Guerre. Bruxelles: Bibliothèque des Temps Nouveaux, [c. 1903].
Les Affaires sont les affaires (1903). Fayard, 1911.
Les Amants. In *Farces et moralites* (1904).
Interview. Ibid.
Scrupules. Ibid.
La 628–E8 (1907). Fasquelle, 1908.
Le Foyer (1908). Fayard, 1913.
Dingo. Fasquelle, 1913.
La Vache tachetée. Flammarion, 1918.
La Pipe de cidre. Flammarion, 1919.
Un Gentilhomme. Flammarion, 1920.
Des artistes, I and II. Flammarion, 1922 and 1924.
Gens de théâtre. Flammarion, 1924.
Les Ecrivains, I and II. Flammarion, 1925 and 1926.
The Garden of Tortures (trans. by R. Rudorff). London: Tandem, 1969.

3. Mirbeau's articles, prefaces and replies to enquêtes

'Les Abandonnés', *La Révolte (S.L.)*, No. 48 (16 August 1890). Reprinted from *L'Echo de Paris*.
'An Accident', *The Torch of Anarchy*, 1 February 1896. Translation of 'Paysage d'hiver', *Le Figaro*, 23 December 1889.
'A l'Elysée', *Le Journal*, 20 May 1894.
'Amour, amour', *La Révolte (S.L.)*, No. 47 (9 August 1890). Reprinted from *Le Figaro*, 25 July 1890.
'A nos soldats', *Le Petit Parisien*, 28 July 1915.
'Apologie pour vacher', *Le Journal du Peuple*, 3 May 1899.
'A propos de la Société des Gens de Lettres', *La Révolte (S.L.)*, No. 49 (22 August 1891). Reprinted from *L'Echo de Paris*, 4 August 1891.
'A travers la peur', *La Révolte (S.L.)*, No. 17 (6 January 1894). Reprinted from *L'Echo de Paris*, 26 December 1893.
'Au Palais', *Le Journal*, 4 March 1894.
'Autour de la justice', *T.N.(S.L.)*, No. 22 (October 1904). Reprinted from *Le Journal*, 24 June 1894.

'Les Beautés du patriotisme', *Le Figaro*, 18 May 1891.
'Cartouche et Loyola', *Le Journal*, 9 September 1894.
'Célébrons le Code', *T.N.(S.L.)*, No. 42 (March 1905). Reprinted from *L'Humanité*, 6 November 1904.
'Clemenceau', *Le Journal*, 11 March 1895.
'Crescite', *ibid.*, 1 April 1894.
'Dans la forêt', *La Révolte (S.L.)*, No. 31 (11 April 1891). Reprinted from *L'Echo de Paris*.
'Dépopulation', *T.N.(S.L.)*, No. 6 (June 1901). Reprinted from *Le Journal*, 2 December 1900.
'Une Déposition', *ibid.*, 8 April 1894.
'Les Dessous des lois', *ibid.*, 18 March 1894.
'Divagations sur le meurtre', *ibid.*, 31 May 1896.
'Egalité, fraternité . . .', *L'Echo de Paris*, 6 February 1894.
'Emile Zola et le naturalisme', *La France*, 11 March 1885.
'En attendant l'omnibus', *Le Journal*, 27 September 1896.
'L'Envers de la vie', *Le Matin*, 4 December 1885.
'Une Face de Méline', *Le Journal du Peuple*, 1 March 1899.
'Félix Fénéon', *Le Journal*, 29 April 1894.
'La Fin', *Les Grimaces*, 6 October 1883.
'*Germinal*', *La France*, 28 October 1885.
'La Grande Kermesse', *La Révolte (S.L.)*, No. 6 (19 October 1889). Reprinted from *Le Figaro*, 18 July 1889.
'La Grève des électeurs', *La Révolte*, No. 13 (9 December 1888). Reprinted from *Le Figaro*, 28 November 1888.
'La Guerre et l'Homme', *La Révolte (S.L.)*, No. 15 (24 December 1892). Reprinted from *Lettres de ma chaumière*.
'Jean Tartas', *La Révolte (S.L.)*, Nos. 49 and 50 (23 and 31 August 1890). Reprinted from *L'Echo de Paris*.
'Le Legs Caillebotte et l'Etat', *Le Journal*, 24 December 1894.
'Lettre à un prolétaire', *L'Aurore*, 8 August 1898.
'La Loi du meurtre', *L'Echo de Paris*, 24 May 1892.
'*Les Mal-vus*', *Le Journal*, 3 June 1894.
'Maroquinerie', *ibid.*, 12 July 1896.
'Le Mécontentement', *La Révolte (S.L.)*, No. 21 (4 February 1889). Reprinted from *Le Figaro*, 9 January 1889.
'Un Mot personnel', *Le Journal*, 19 December 1897.
'Un Mot personnel', *L'Aurore*, 21 December 1898.
'Nous avons un fusil', *Le Journal*, 2 April 1894.
'L'Oiseau sacré', *La Révolte (S.L.)*, No. 3 (27 September 1890). Reprinted from *L'Echo de Paris*.
'Opinion d'Octave Mirbeau sur le 1er mai', *La Bataille*, 2 May 1891.
'O Rus!', *Le Journal*, 15 April 1894.
'Palinodies', *L'Aurore*, 15 November 1898.
'Le Pauvre Pêcheur', *La Révolte (S.L.)*, No. 2 (20 September 1890). Reprinted from *L'Echo de Paris*.
'Paysage parlementaire', *Le Journal*, 11 November 1896.

'Une Perquisition en 1894', *T.N. (S.L.)*, No. 12 (July 1901). Reprinted from *Le Journal*.
'Le Petit Gardeur de vaches', *ibid.*, 30 September 1895.
'Le Petit Pavillon', *ibid.*, 15 September 1895.
'Les Petit Martyrs', *La Révolte (S.L.)*, No. 35 (28 May 1892). Reprinted from *L'Echo de Paris*, 3 May 1892.
'Pétrisseurs d'âmes', *Le Journal*, 10 February 1901.
'La Police et la presse', *T.N.(S.L.)*, No. 51 (May 1904). Reprinted from *Le Gaulois*, 15 January 1896.
'Potins!', *Le Journal*, 7 May 1894.
'Pour Jean Grave', *Le Journal*, 19 February 1894.
'Pour M. Lépine', *ibid.*, 8 November 1896.
'Préface au 9e édition du *Calvaire*', 1887. Reprinted in *Les Ecrivains*, vol. II.
Preface to: A. Adès and A. Josipovici, *Le Livre de Goha le Simple*. Calmann-Lévy, 1919.
Preface to: J. Grave, *La Société mourante et l'anarchie*. Tresse et Stock, 1893.
'Prélude', *La Révolte*, No. 45 (27 July 1889). Reprinted from *Le Figaro*, 14 July 1889.
'Protégeons-nous les uns les autres', *Le Journal*, 25 February 1894.
'Questions sociales', *ibid.*, 20 December 1896.
'Ravachol', *L'Endehors*, No. 52 (1 May 1892). Reprinted in *La Révolte*, No. 32 (7 May 1892).
'Réponse d'Octave Mirbeau à l'enquête franco-allemande', *Le Mercure de France*, April 1895, p. 21.
'Réponse d'Octave Mirbeau à l'enquête sur l'anarchie', *Le Gaulois*, 25 February 1894.
'Réponse d'Octave Mirbeau à l'enquête sur l'éducation', *La Revue Blanche*, 1 June 1902, p. 175.
'Réponse d'Octave Mirbeau à l'enquête sur les tribunaux militaires', *L'Aurore*, 8 February 1898.
'Réponse d'Octave Mirbeau au référendum sur la contrainte et la liberté', *L'Ermitage*, November 1893, p. 262.
'Rêverie', *La Révolte (S.L.)*, No. 8 (2 November 1889). Reprinted from *Le Figaro*, 21 October 1889.
'Rêverie', *Le Journal*, 11 March 1894.
'Le Rôle de l'Etat', *La Révolte (S.L.)*, No. 28 (25 March 1893).
'Scientismes', *Le Journal*, 30 June 1895.
'Sous le knout', *Le Journal*, 3 March 1895.
'Sur M. Félix Vallotton'. Preface to: *Exposition de peintures de Félix Vallotton . . . 10 au 22 Janvier 1910*. Galerie E. Druet, 1910.
'Sur un député', *La Révolte (S.L.)*, No. 7 (29 October 1892). Reprinted from *L'Echo de Paris*.
'Tous cyclistes', *Le Journal*, 19 August 1894.
'La Vache tachetée', *ibid.*, 20 November 1898.
'Vermine judiciaire', *La France*, 17 June 1885.

4. Printed soirces of reference to Mirbeau, and anarchism

Adam, P., *Critique des moeurs*. Kolb, 1893.
—'Eloge de Ravachol', *Les Entretiens Politiques et Littéraires*, No. 28 (July 1892).
Ajalbert, J., 'Le Flirt rouge', *Le Gil Blas*, 6 June 1893.
—*Les Mystères de l'Académie Goncourt*. Ferenczi, 1929.
Albert, C., 'La Clairière', *T.N.(S.L.)*, No. 51 (April 1900).
—*'L'Epidémie'*, ibid., No. 5 (May 1898).
Arvon, H., *L'Anarchisme*. P.U.F., 1951.
Aubéry, P., *Pour une lecture ouvrière de la littérature*. Les Editions Syndicalistes, 1969.
'Aventures postales', *L'Endehors*, No. 52 (1 May 1892).
Bataille, A., *Causes criminelles et mondaines de 1894*. Dentu, 1895.
Bauër, G., 'Octave Mirbeau, héros de son théâtre', *Les Annales*, No. 106 (August 1959), pp. 5–16.
Bauër, H., *'Les Mauvais Bergers* d'Octave Mirbeau', *L'Echo de Paris*, 15 December 1897.
Beaubourg, M., *'Les Affaires sont les affaires'*, *La Plume*, 15 May 1903, pp. 591–4.
—*'Le Portefeuille'*, *La Plume*, 15 March 1902, pp. 410–11.
Bertaut, J., *L'Opinion et les moeurs*. Editions de France, 1931.
Besson G., 'Il y a cinquante ans mourait Octave Mirbeau', *Les Lettres Françaises*, 2 March 1967, pp. 6–7.
Billy, A., *L'Epoque 1900*. Tallandier, 1951.
Boisson, M., *Les Attentats anarchistes sous la 3e République*. Editions de France, 1931.
Bourdon, G., 'Le Théâtre du Peuple. Opinions', *La Revue Bleue*, 25 January 1902.
'Les Bureaux de placement', *Le Libertaire*, No. 47 (3 October 1896).
Burne, G. S., *Remy de Gourmont. His Ideas and Influence in England and America*. Carbondale: Southern Illinois University Press, 1963.
Burns, W., *'In the Penal Colony*: variations on a theme by Octave Mirbeau', *Accent*, No. 17 (winter 1957), pp. 45–51.
Cachin, F., 'Un Défenseur oublié de l'art moderne', *L'Oeil*, June 1962, pp. 50–5 and 75.
Les Cahiers d'Aujourd'hui, No. 9 (1922) (special number on Mirbeau).
Carassus, E., *Le Snobisme et les lettres françaises de Paul Bourget à Marcel Proust, 1884–1914*. Colin, 1966.
Carrère, J., 'Entretiens sur l'anarchie: chez M. Emile Zola', *Le Figaro*, 25 April 1892.
Carter, L. A., *Zola and the Theater*. P.U.F., 1963.
Catalogue de la vente de la bibliothèque d'Octave Mirbeau. Leclerc, 1919.
Chaughi, R., *'Les Mauvais Bergers'*, *T.N.(S.L.)*, No. 35 (December 1897).
'Chronique des tribunaux', *Le Journal*, 25 February 1894.
Copeau, J., *'Le Foyer'*, *La Grande Revue*, 25 December 1908.
Le Crapouillot, January 1938 (special number on anarchism).
Daudet, L., *Souvenirs*. Volumes 1 and 2. Nouvelle Librairie Nationale, 1920–6.

Descaves, L., *Souvenirs d'un ours*. Les Editions de Paris, 1946.
Dinar, A., *Les Auteurs cruels*. Mercure de France, 1942.
Dorgelès, R., *Portraits sans retouche*. Albin Michel, 1952.
Drachkovitch, M. M., *Les Socialismes français et allemand et le problème de la guerre, 1870–1914*. Genève: Droz, 1953.
Drumont, E., *De l'or, de la boue, du sang: du Panama à l'anarchie*. Flammarion, 1896.
Dubeux, A., 'Le Féroce Mirbeau', *La Revue des Deux Mondes*, 15 March 1968, pp. 211–25.
Dubois, F., *Le Péril anarchiste*. Flammarion, 1894.
'Echos', *Quo Vadis*, September 1954.
Elder, M., *Deux essais: Octave Mirbeau; Romain Rolland*. Crès, 1914.
Faure, S., *Les Anarchistes et l'Affaire Dreyfus*. Au Libertaire, 1898.
—*La Douleur universelle*. Savine, 1895.
—'En passant. *Le Jardin des Supplices*', *Le Journal du Peuple*, 11 September 1899.
—'*Les Mauvais Bergers*', *Le Libertaire*, 25 December 1897.
Fénéon, F., *Oeuvres plus que complètes*. Two volumes. Genève: Droz, 1970.
Le Figaro, Supplément Littéraire, 13 January 1894 (special number on anarchism).
Fournier, A., 'Parterres et châteaux de Mirbeau', *Europe*, No. 458 (June 1967), pp. 191–212.
Gadoffre, G. F. A., 'Mallarmé anarchiste', *Western Canadian Studies in Modern Languages and Literature*, No. 1 (1969), pp. 40–3.
Gaubert, E., 'L'Oeuvre et la morale d'Octave Mirbeau', *Le Mercure de France*, 1 October 1911, pp. 510–32.
Geffroy, G., 'Octave Mirbeau et les artistes', *La Dépêche de Toulouse*, 23 February 1917.
Gegout, E., 'A l'enterrement de Mirbeau', *L'Attaque*, 19 February 1917.
Goncourt, E. and J. de, *Journal*. Twenty-two volumes. Monaco: Les Editions de l'Imprimerie Nationale, 1956–8.
Gourmont, R. de, *Promenades littéraires*, 1ère série. Mercure de France, 1919.
Grave, J., '*Les Affaires sont les affaires*', *T.N.(S.L.)*, No. 2 (May 1903).
—'Bibliothèque anarchiste', *T.N.*, No. 49 (2 April 1898).
—'*Le Jardin des Supplices*', *T.N.(S.L.)*, No. 11 (July 1899).
—'*Le Journal d'une femme de chambre*', *ibid.*, No. 18 (August 1900).
—*Le Mouvement libertaire sous la 3e République*. Les Oeuvres Représentatives, 1930.
—'*Le Portefeuille*', *T.N.(S.L.)*, No. 44 (March 1902).
—*Quarante ans de propagande anarchiste*. Flammarion, 1973 (enlarged edition of *Le Mouvement libertaire*).
—'Si j'avais à parler aux électeurs', *T.N.*, No. 50 (12 April 1902).
—*La Société future*. Stock, 1895.
—*La Société mourante et l'anarchie*. Tresse et Stock, 1893.
—'Soyons logiques', *Le Libertaire*, No. 18 (14 March 1896).
—'*Les Vingt et un jours d'un neurasthénique*', *T.N.(S.L.)*, No. 24 (October 1901).

Gsell, P., 'Octave Mirbeau', *La Revue*, 15 March 1907, pp. 207-21.
Guilbeaux, H., 'Octave Mirbeau und die Gesellschaft', *Das Literarische Echo*, 1913-14, pp. 378-83.
Guilleminault, G., *L'Epopée de la révolte*. Denoël, 1963.
Gustus, 'Exploitation philanthropique', *Le Libertaire*, No. 21 (4 April 1896).
Hamon, A., *Psychologie de l'anarchiste-socialiste*. Stock, 1895.
Herbert, E. W., *the Artist and Social Reform. France and Belgium, 1885-1898*. New Haven: Yale University Press 1961.
Herbert, R. L. and E. W., 'Artists and anarchism', *The Burlington Magazine*, vol. 120, No. 692 (November 1960), pp. 473-82, and No. 693 (December 1960), pp. 517-22.
Hervé, G., 'Octave Mirbeau est mort', *La Victoire*, 17 February 1917.
—'Sur la tombe de Mirbeau', *ibid.*, 20 February 1917.
Huret, J., *Enquête sur l'évolution littéraire*. Charpentier, 1891.
—'Octave Mirbeau', in *La Grande Encyclopédie*, vol 23. Société Anonyme de la Grande Encyclopédie, 1899, pp. 1099-100.
Jackson, A. B., *La Revue Blanche, 1889-1903*. Minard, 1960.
Joll, J., *The Anarchists*. London: Eyre & Spottiswoode, 1964.
Jourdain, F., *Sans remords ni rancune*. Corrèa, 1953.
Juin, H., *Ecrivains de l'avant-siècle*. Seghers, 1972.
Knowles, D., *La Réaction idéaliste au théâtre depuis 1890*. Droz, 1934.
Kropotkin, P., *La Conquête du pain*. Publications de *La Révolte*, 1892.
—'A Letter on the present war', *Freedom*, October 1914.
—*Paroles d'un révolté*. Marpon et Flammarion, 1885.
Lacaze-Duthiers, G. de, 'Les Articles d'Octave Mirbeau', *La Plume*, 15 February 1902.
Lazare, B., '*La Conquête du pain*', *Les Entretiens Politiques et Littéraires*, No. 4 (April 1892).
—*Figures contemporaines*. Perrin, 1895.
Léautaud, P., *Journal littéraire*. Nineteen volumes. Mercure de France, 1955-66.
Leblond, M.-A., 'Un Romancier antibourgeois. Octave Mirbeau', *La Revue Socialiste*, February 1902, pp. 193-7.
Lecomte, G., 'L'Oeuvre d'Octave Mirbeau', *La Grande Revue*, vol. 93, No. 3 (March 1917), pp. 20-35.
Lefranc, J., 'Chez Octave Mirbeau, antimilitariste', *Le Petit Parisien*, 13 August 1915.
'Lettre de protestation de 130 écrivains contre la condamnation de Jean Grave', *L'Echo de Paris*, 26 February and 3 March 1894.
Maitron, J., *Dictionnaire biographique du mouvement ouvrier français, Troisième partie: 1871-1914*. In course of publication. Les Editions Ouvrières, 1973-
—*Histoire du mouvement anarchiste en France, 1880-1914*. Société Universitaire d'Edition et de Librairie, second edition 1955.
—*Le Mouvement anarchiste en France*. Two volumes. Maspero, 1975.
—*Ravachol et les anarchistes*. Julliard, 1964.
'Manifeste de la Coalition Révolutionnaire', *Le Père Peinard*, 23 October 1898.

Mauclair, C., 'L'Esprit révolutionnaire dans les lettres récentes', *La Revue des Revues*, 1 April 1899.
—*Servitude et grandeur littéraires*. Ollendorff, third edition 1922.
Méric, V., *A travers la jungle politique et littéraire*. Two volumes. Librairie Valois, 1930–1.
Monférier, J., 'Symbolisme et anarchie', *Revue d'Histoire Littéraire de la France*, April 1965, pp. 223–8.
Montfort, E., 'Avec Mirbeau', *Le Mercure de France*, 1 June 1917, pp. 414–25.
Muhlfeld, L., '*Le Jardin des Supplices*', *La Revue Bleue*, 5 August 1899, pp. 177–81.
Natanson, T., 'Octave Mirbeau', *Le Figaro*, 29 April 1908.
—*Peints à leur tour*. Albin Michel, 1948.
Nicholson, B., 'The anarchism of Camille Pissarro', *The Arts*, No. 2 (1947), pp. 43–51.
Pilon, E., *Octave Mirbeau*. Bibliothèque Internationale d'Edition, 1903.
Pioch, G., '*Le Calvaire*', *Le Libertaire*, No. 48 (28 October 1900).
Pissarro, C., *Letters to his Son Lucien*. London: Kegan Paul, 1944.
La Plume, 1 May 1893 (special number on anarchism).
Pouget, E. and Pressensé, F. de, *Les Lois scélérates de 1893-4*. Les Editions de La Revue Blanche, 1899.
Reclus, E., *L'Evolution, la révolution et l'idéal anarchique*. Stock, 1914.
'Référendum artistique et social', *L'Ermitage*, July and November 1893.
Renard, J., *Journal*. Gallimard, 1935.
Retté, A., 'Une Année de combat', *La Plume*, 15 December 1893.
—'L'Art et l'anarchie', *ibid.*, 1 February 1893.
—'La Société mourante et l'anarchie', *ibid*, 15 September 1893.
Revon, M., *Octave Mirbeau—son oeuvre*. Editions de la Nouvelle Revue Critique, 1924.
Rodenbach, G., *L'Elite*. Fasquelle, 1899.
Rosny aîné, J.-H., *Mémoires de la vie littéraire: l'Académie Goncourt, les salons, quelques éditeurs*. Crès, 1927.
Rudorff, R., *Belle Epoque: Paris in the Nineties*. London: Hamish Hamilton, 1972.
Saint-Auban, E. de, *L'Histoire sociale au Palais de Justice: plaidoyers philosophiques*. Pedone, 1895.
—*L'Idée sociale au théâtre*. Stock, 1901.
Sainte-Croix, C. de, '*Le Journal d'une femme de chambre*', *La Revue Blanche*, No. 23 (September 1900), pp. 72–6.
Salmon, A., *Souvenirs sans fin*. Three volumes. Gallimard, 1955–61.
—*La Terreur noire*. Pauvert, 1959.
Schwarz, M., 'Une Amitié ignorée: Edmond de Goncourt–Octave Mirbeau', *The French Review*, special issue No. 2 (winter 1971), pp. 97–105.
—'Octave Mirbeau et l'Affaire Dreyfus', *ibid.*, December 1965, pp. 361–72.
—*Octave Mirbeau, vie et oeuvre*. The Hague: Mouton, 1966.
Sergent, A., *Les Anarchistes: scènes et portraits*. Chambriand, 1951.
Serpenoise, 'Chronique parisienne: les sacrilèges', *La Revanche*, 26

November 1886.
Séverine, 'La Parole à l'ennemi', *Le Cri du Peuple*, 29 October 1885.
Shattuck, R., *The Banquet Years*. London: Faber, 1958.
Tailhade, L., *Les 'Commérages' de Tybalt*. Crès, 1914.
—*Les Livres et les hommes*. Crès, 1917.
—'Le Triomphe de la domesticité', *Le Libertaire*, No. 82 (15 September 1901).
Talva, F., 'Octave Mirbeau. Juge sûr, lutteur passionné, ami fidèle',*Europe*, No. 458 (June 1967), pp. 173–82.
Ternois, R., *Zola et son temps*. Les Belles Lettres, 1961.
'Le Testament politique d'Octave Mirbeau', *Le Petit Parisien*, 19 February 1917.
Tison-Braun, M., *La Crise de l'humanisme*. Volume I. Nizet, 1958.
Vandérem, F., *Gens de qualité*. Plon, 1938.
Varennes, H. de, *De Ravachol à Caserio: notes d'audience*. Garnier, 1895.
Veidaux, A., 'De l'évolution de la philosophie et des lettres vers le socialisme', *La Plume*, 1 May 1891.
Vindex, 'Bibliothèque anarchiste', *T.N.(S.L.)*, Nos. 22 and 33 (28 September and 14 December 1895).
Werth, L., 'Octave Mirbeau',*Les Cahiers d'Aujourd'hui*, No. 4 (April 1913), pp. 176–82.
Woodcock, G., *Anarchism: A History of Libertarian Ideas and Movements*. Harmondsworth: Penguin Books, reprinted 1970.
—and Avakumovic, I., *The Anarchist Prince*. London: Boardman, 1950.

Index

This index is selective. Bold type indicates main entries.

Académie Française, 53, 75, 102, 121, 123, 144
Académie Goncourt, 53, 135
Action Française, L', 131, 155, 165
Adam, Juliette, 16
Adam, Paul, 38, 63, 76, 83
Adès, Albert, 35, 148, 160
Ajalbert, Jean, 12, 24, 28, 38, **45**, 81
Albert, Charles, 115, 125
anti-clericalism, 1, **30-2**, 45, 60, 93-4, 106-7, 122, 135, 154
anti-czarist movement, 57, **89**, 135, 143-4
anti-militarism, *see* militarism
anti-semitism, 12, 137
Antoine, André, 102, 111-12, 125, 130, 132
Apollinaire, Guillaume, 130
Archinard, Louis, **93**, 139
Armand, Émile, 157
army, 16, 45, **93**, 101, 104, 113, 138; *see also* militarism
Audoux, Marguerite, xiv, 147
Aurore, L', 100, **103-4**, 107-9
authority, x, 8, 19, 21, 30, 51, **85-6**, 91-3, 100-1, 115, 128, 141, 150, 156
Axa, Zo d', 48, 67

Bakunin, Michael, x, 11, 50, 173
Barbey d'Aurevilly, Jules, x, xiv, 5, 15, 20
Barrès, Maurice, 66, 69-70, 81, 83
Barrucand, Victor, 63, 104
Bauër, Gérard, 111, 130
Bauër, Henry, 112
Beaubourg, Maurice, 131-2
Becque, Henri, 4, 45, **53-4**, 113, 119, 130
Béraud, Henri, 162
Besson, George, 148, 155, **161-2**
Bloy, Léon, xiv
Blum, Léon, 69, 104, 108-9
Boès, Karl, 120
Bonnard, Pierre, xiv, 20
Bonnetain, Paul, 41
Bordeaux, Henry, 120
Boulanger (Affair), 27-8
Bourget, Paul, x, **15-16**, 65-6, 135
Bourses du Travail, 92, 108, 135; *see also* employment
Briand, Aristide, 147
Brunetière, Ferdinand, 119, 175
Büchner, Ludwig, 21
Bulot (Assize court judge), 61, **75-6**, 87
Buñuel, Luis, 136

Cahiers d'Aujourd'hui, Les, xvii, 35, 144, **148**, 154, 164-5

Caillebotte, Gustave, 95
capitalism, xiii-xiv, 29, 42, 60, **112-14**, 119, 128-9, 136, 143, 171
Carnot, Sadi, 60, **67-8**, 86
Caserio, Santo, 56, 60, **68**
Cavaignac, Godefroy, 101
Cézanne, Paul, xiv, 107
charity, **32-3**, 138, 152, 154; *see also* philanthropy
Chaughi, René, 115-16
Christian anarchism, 8, 10, 16
Christie, Stuart, 81
Cladel, Léon, 38
Claretie, Jules, 117, **121-2**, 149
Claudel, Paul, xiv, **37**, 69-70, 83
Clemenceau, Georges, xiv, 1, 35, 81, 84, **90-1**, 103, 147, 156
Club de l'Art social, 28
Coalition révolutionnaire, **108-9**, 135
Cohen, Alexandre, **64-7**, 71, 78-9
colonialism, 51, 62, 72, 85, **93**, 143-4, 171
Comédie-Française, 117, 119, **121-2**
Commune (Paris), x-xi, 1, 15, 62, 69, 90, 171
Conte, Edouard, 89-90
Copeau, Jacques, 120
Coppée, François, 82
Cri du Peuple, Le, 8-9
Crucy, François, 148
Curel, Francis de, 38, 113

Darien, Georges, 132
Darwin, Charles, 21
Daudet, Léon, 1, 84, 101, 103, 109, 155
decadence, 10, 29, 40, **58-9**, 69, 95, 106, 119, 126, 135, 138-9
Descaves, Lucien, **38-9**, 157
Dorgelès, Roland, 138-40, 155
Dreyfus (Affair), 16, 56, 81, 84, 88, 94, **99-110**, 135, 137-9, 147, 149
Dubois, Félix, 73, 82
Du Buit, Maître, 131, 139
Du Camp, Maxime, 123
Dujardin, Edouard, 24
Duval (anarchist), 127

Echo de Paris, L', 29, 34, 43, 48-9, 53-4, 64, 68, 72, 76, 81, **86**, 109, 130, 169
education, 10, 18, 23, **30**, 32, 36, 80, 85, **93-4**, 135, 143, **153-4**, 172

Eekhoud, Georges, 38
electoral abstention, **25-6**, **166-9**
electoral system, 7, 28; *see also* universal suffrage
employment, **89**, 108, 136; *see also* Bourses du Travail

Endehors, L', 48, 54, **59**, **61**, 71, 76, 78, 170
Entretiens Politiques et Littéraires, Les, 41, 81
Ermitage, L', xiii, 38, 41, 155
Etiévant, Georges, **50**, 173

Faguet, Emile, 119
Faure, Félix, 76, 101, 103
Faure, Sébastien, xvi-xvii, 36, 56, 67, 84, 87, 89, **93-4**, 96, 98, 101, 108, 110, 115-16, 135, 157, 161
Fénéon, Félix, 20, **24**, 67, 70, **78-9**, **81**, **86**, **104**
Figaro, Le, x, xii, xiv, 25, 27-9, 49, 53, 71, 73, 95, 102, 109, 114, 166
First International, ix-x
First World War, xiii, 142, 148, 153-4, **156-60**, 162
France, Anatole, 38, **72**, 103, 144, 147, 157, **160**, 163
France, La, xii, **3-6**, 8-9, 12
Franco-Prussian War, xi, xiv, 11, **16-17**, 156

Gallieni, Joseph-Simon, 93
Gauguin, Paul, xiv, 20, 40
Gaulois, Le, x-xii, **3-4**, 13, 71, 76-7, 80, 82, 108, 133
Geffroy, Gustave, 12, **20**, 36, 41, 53, 58, 68, 80-1, 84, 91, 140, 144, 163
Gegout, Ernest, 82, 162
Gide, André, 139
Gohier, Urbain, 103-4
Golberg, Mécislas, 120
Goncourt, Edmond de, xiv, 2-3, 15, **33-4**, 39-40, 54, 56, 102, 119
Gourmont, Remy de, xiv, xvii, **70-1**, 97
government, 8, 27, 50-1, 62, 68, 70, 85, **90-2**, 94-5, 106, 149, 152, 169, 171, 173
Grave, Jean, ix-x, xvi, 12-13, **24-9**, 34, **41-52**, 56-8, **66-7**, **70-7**, 84, 86-7, 90, 93, 96-8, 100-1, 107, 109, 111-13, 115-16, 120, 124, 132, 135, 138, 140, 144, 157-8, 160, 163-4, 166, **169-70**, **172-7**
Grévy, Jules, 59, 68
Grimaces, Les, x, **xii**, 8, 13, 15, 80, 98, **102**, 148, 151
Guerre Sociale, La, 147
Guesde, Jules, 1
Guitry, Sacha, 147
Guyau, Jean-Marie, 21, 41

Hauptmann, Gerhart, 113
Henry, Emile, 56-8, 60, **65-7**, 74-5, 78, **174-5**
Heredia, José-María de, xiv
Hervé, Gustave, 147, **153**, 157, **159-62**
Hervieu, Paul, 148
Hugo, Victor, xiii, 2-4
Humanité, L', 122, **152-3**
Huret, Jules, 18, **40-1**, 59, 71
Huysmans, Joris-Karl, 3

Ibels, Henry Gabriel, 98
Ibsen, Henrik, xiv, **63-4**
Impressionism, xiv, **20**, 53
internationalism, 135, **141**, 156, 160
Intransigeant, L', 121, 123

Jacob, Marius, 127
Jarry, Alfred, 70, 97, 140
Jaurès, Jean, xiv, 156
Jesuits, xi, 9, 22, **29-32**
Josipovici, Albert, 148, 160
Jourdain, Francis, 147, 164
Journal, Le, 12, 73, 76, 78, 81-2, **85-96**, 99-101, 109, 124-6, 128, 130-3, 138-9, 174
Journal du Peuple, Le, **101**, 110
Jullien, Jean, 38
Justice, La, 20, 91

Kafka, Franz, 110
Kropotkin, Peter, ix-x, 1, 8, **10-11**, 21, 26-7, 29, 39, 41, 46, **48**, 50, 52, 57-9, 62, 72, 74, 98, 119, 131, **157**, 164, 169, 171-5

Labori, Fernand, 81
Larbaud, Valéry, xiv, 154
law, **4-6**, 10, 23, 27, 42, 45, 48, 64, 72, 77, 79, 82, **85-90**, 93, 101, 105-7, 127, 138, 149, **151-2**, 170-1, 173, 175
Lazare, Bernard, 76, 79, 83, 85, 96, **100-1**, 103
Léautaud, Paul, 122, 131, 134, 148, 154, **161-2**
Léauthier, Léon-Jules, 63
Lecomte, Georges, 165
Lefranc, Jean, 159
Lemaire, Madeleine, 132
Lemaître, Jules, 114
Lépine, Louis, 92
Leygues, Georges, 139
Leyret, Henri, 103
Libertaire, Le, 35, 97-8, 101, 104, 115, 133, 144, 155
lois scélérates, **64**, 73, 77, 87, 104
Lombroso, Cesare, 128-9
Luce, Maximilien, 53, 69, 98
Lugné-Poë, 111

Maeterlinck, Maurice, xiv, 40
Malato, Charles, 54, 67, 81, 84, 108, 135, 144, 169
Mallarmé, Stéphane, xiv, 2, **22**, 24, 29, 36, 78
Marpeaux (anarchist), 63
Masson, Paul, 71
Matha, Louis, 78
Mathiex, Paul, 108
Mauclair, Camille, 13, 59, 70, 81, 83, 102-3
Maupassant, Guy de, x-xi, 5-6, **14**
May-day, 42
Méline, Jules, **90**, 101
Méric, Victor, 133
Meyer, Arthur, 4, 8, 12
Michel, Louise, x, 27, 56
militarism, **33**, 60, 72, 83, 85, 91, 93, 106-7, 135, 143, 150, 153-4, **157-9**, 163; *see also* army
Mirbeau, Octave, **Novels**: *L'Abbé Jules*,